DOLLY PARTON,

GENDER, *and* COUNTRY MUSIC

DOLLY PARTON,

GENDER, *and* COUNTRY MUSIC

Leigh H. Edwards

INDIANA UNIVERSITY PRESS

This book is a publication of

Indiana University Press
Office of Scholarly Publishing
Herman B Wells Library 350
1320 East 10th Street
Bloomington, Indiana 47405 USA
iupress.indiana.edu

© 2018 by Leigh H. Edwards
All rights reserved

The paper used in this publication meets the minimum requirements of the American National Standard for Information Sciences—Permanence of Paper for Printed Library Materials, ANSI Z39.48–1992.

Manufactured in the United States of America

Library of Congress Cataloging-in-Publication Data

Names: Edwards, Leigh H., author.
Title: Dolly Parton, gender, and country music / Leigh H. Edwards.
Description: Bloomington : Indiana University Press, 2018. |
Includes bibliographical references and index.
Identifiers: LCCN 2017024199 (print) | LCCN 2017025461 (ebook) | ISBN 9780253031563 (e-book) | ISBN 9780253031549 (cloth : alk. paper) | ISBN 9780253031556 (pbk. : alk. paper)
Subjects: LCSH: Parton, Dolly. | Women country musicians—United States.
Classification: LCC ML420.P28 (ebook) | LCC ML420.P28 E39 2018 (print) | DDC 782.421642092—dc23
LC record available at https://lccn.loc.gov/2017024199

1 2 3 4 5   23 22 21 20 19 18

for my family

Contents

Acknowledgments

During the course of writing this book, I have had the good company of fellow travelers who believe, like me, that popular music has something important to tell us. My work on this book started with my earlier one in this field, *Johnny Cash and the Paradox of American Identity* (Indiana University Press, 2009). Many thanks to everyone at Indiana University Press for that book and this one, especially Janice Frisch, Kate Schramm, Raina Polivka, Jane Behnken, and the readers.

On my pilgrimages to Nashville, everyone at the Country Music Foundation archives at the Country Music Hall of Fame and Museum was extremely gracious and helpful, particularly historian John Rumble. Don Cusic, James Akenson, and everyone at the International Country Music Conference (ICMC) provided a wonderful community.

I want to thank especially the intrepid Kris McCusker for her helpful feedback and careful reading of my work. I was honored to have a portion of chapter 1 appear in article form in the edited collection *Country Boys and Redneck Women: New Essays in Gender and Country Music* (University Press of Mississippi, 2016), edited by Diane Pecknold and Kris McCusker. I am grateful to the kind and generous editors, the other essayists, and the fabulous panel of authors at the ICMC for their feedback and lively discussion. That collection is a sequel to their earlier one, *A Boy Named Sue: Gender and Country Music*

(University Press of Mississippi, 2004), which was a trailblazing volume that inspired me and so many others in the field.

A small portion of my work here appeared in my article "Country Music and Class," in *The Oxford Handbook of Country Music* (Oxford University Press, 2017), edited by Travis Stimeling. I want to thank him for his skilled editing and generous community building. A portion appeared in my article in the *Journal of Popular Music Studies*, "Johnny Cash's 'Ain't No Grave' and Digital Folk Culture" (June 2016). My appreciation to the editors and readers there as well. Some of my Parton research appeared previously in my article "Mass Art: Digital Folk Culture and Country Music as Folk Mass Culture," in *Pop Culture Universe: Icons, Idols, Ideas* (ABC-CLIO, 2013). My earlier book on television, *The Triumph of Reality TV: The Revolution in American Television* (Praeger, 2013), has also informed some of this project, and I wish to thank those press editors and readers as well.

My thanks to colleagues at conferences where I have presented this research, including the American Studies Association, the Popular Culture Association, and the International Association for the Study of Popular Music, US branch. I am grateful to colleagues at IASPM-US for their encouragement, particularly the late David Sanjek.

I am very appreciative of the early training I received in American literary and cultural studies from my PhD committee in English at the University of Pennsylvania, Betsy Erkkila (now at Northwestern), Nancy Bentley, Christopher Looby (now at UCLA), and Eric Cheyfitz (now at Cornell), as well as from others at Penn, such as Peter Stallybrass and Herman Beavers. I am also grateful for my undergraduate training in English at Duke University, where I benefited from being an editorial assistant at *American Literature* under Cathy Davidson and from studying with Toril Moi, Annabel Patterson, Tom Ferraro, and Deborah Pope.

I wish to thank my colleagues in the English department at Florida State University (FSU). Special thanks to Andrew Epstein, Darryl Dickson-Carr (now at SMU), and Meegan Kennedy for being exemplary colleagues and friends, and to Meegan for her chapter feedback. A special thank you to Denise Von Glahn and Michael Broyles, musicology colleagues at FSU, who have been extremely supportive of this research from the beginning and who have been very generous in their feedback. Many thanks to the FSU colleagues (past and present) who discussed my research on this topic with me, including Barbara Hamby, David Kirby, Jerrilyn McGregory, Candace Ward, Nancy

Warren, Ned Stuckey-French, Elizabeth Stuckey-French, Jimmy Kimbrell, Robert Olen Butler, Mark Winegardner, Bonnie Braendlin, Paul Outka, Chris Shinn, Anne Rowe, Rip Lhamon, Eric Walker, Elaine Treharne, David Vann, Kathi Yancey, Alisha Gaines, Aaron Jaffe, Christina Parker-Flynn, and many others. My FSU students in my media studies and popular culture classes have been enthusiastic about this case study, which lent me more motivation.

My appreciation to my friend and colleague Katie Conrad, talented both as a scholar and as a mandolin player, for bluegrass discussions, and to my bluegrass guitar teacher, Mickey Abraham. I wish to thank colleagues and friends who have lent their support and happily talked with me about the music or my project, including Vall Richard, Jennifer Proffitt, Bob Batchelor and the popular culture crew, James Mitchell, Gretchen Sunderman, Pam Coats, Giselle Anatol, Michael Todd, Vickie Lake, Maria Fernandez, Monica Hurdal, Diana Rice, Jack Clifford, Bev Bower, Fayanne Farabee, Susan Teel, Charlotte Curtis, Janie Curtis, Ann Duran, Cindy Michaelson, Rosanne Barker, Rita May, Warren May, Lynn Priestley, Margaret Clark, Tom Clark, Ken Johnson, and Jennifer Smith.

Warm thanks to family and friends who went to concerts with me, ranging from Dolly Parton to Rosanne Cash to Kris Kristofferson, including my cousin Allison Carothers and her daughters, Brittney Carothers Harvey and JuliaAnne Carothers Harvey; my cousin Theresa Loper; honorary cousin Karen Campbell Frank; Pam Flynn; Feli Wilhelmy; Tatiana Flores; Lori DiGuglielmo and Karen Barnett for concerts and Dollywood; and the Duke TIP crew for adventures to concerts and to Dollywood: Mary Souther, Mitch Rolnick, Lynn Gieger, Pasha Souvorin, Denise Messer, and David Messer.

I want to thank in particular my dear Chris Goff, Brian Ammons, and Patricia Thomas for their steadfast support; surprise trips to Nashville; adventures to conferences, concerts, and Dollywood; and helpful perspectives and pop culture joyousness.

I dedicate this book to my parents, the late Steve Edwards Jr. and the late Helen Carothers Edwards; they believed in this project and they believed in me, and I can only hope to emulate their integrity, grace, and good cheer. As I am an eighth-generation Floridian from Tallahassee, I had the pleasure of asking my father about his grandfather who was a country fiddler; about southern rural music growing up in Quincy, Florida; and about his brother Ryan Edwards playing piano on an old Jimmy Dean record. My deep thanks and love to my mother; to my sister, Ashley Carothers Edwards; and to my sister-in-law, Kim Hinckley, as well for their support, encouragement, and willingness to listen to still more songs.

I also wish to honor my extended family, including those who have gone before us, from my grandfather Milton Washington Carothers, who passed on a love of education and who makes me, following my father, the third generation of my immediate family to be a professor at FSU, to the youngest ones coming along now. They include Milton Washington Carothers, Julia Stover Carothers, Charles Graham Carothers, NancyAnne Carothers, Charles Graham Carothers Jr., Allison Carothers and her family, Brittney Carothers Harvey, JuliaAnne Carothers Harvey, Melissa Anne Carothers Moon and her family, Milton Stover Carothers, Sarah Jane Carothers, Milton Washington Carothers II, Irene Ryan, Harley Ryan, Theresa Loper, Paul Loper, Jamie Stoneberger Loper, Dawn Loper, James Loper, the Ethel Edwards Loper family, the Pat Edwards family, Kay Edwards, Melanie Joyner, Bradley Joyner, Miller Joyner (who is keeping the music in the family going), Jessica Joyner, my godmother Trudy Williamson, and the Ryan Edwards family. I give thanks for all the roots and branches.

DOLLY PARTON,

GENDER, *and* COUNTRY MUSIC

Introduction
Dolly Mythology

If I hadn't been a woman, I would have been a drag queen.

—Dolly Parton

I kinda patterned my look after Cinderella and
Mother Goose—and the local hooker.

—Dolly Parton

I'm just a backwoods Barbie in a push-up bra and heels. /
I might look artificial, but where it counts I'm real.

—Dolly Parton, "Backwoods Barbie"

Dolly Parton describes her "look" by referring to country Barbies and drag queens, fairy-tale princesses and "hillbilly hookers." The singer has achieved global awareness of her signature "hillbilly Mae West" persona, what she calls her "Dolly image." Parton is instantly recognizable for her big blonde wigs, elaborate makeup that she claims never to remove, five-inch high heels, long fake nails, plastic surgery breast implants, and custom-made campy outfits. She jokes that she once lost a drag queen Parton contest and that she sometimes dresses up as herself on Halloween. Her fans wear massive platinum blonde wigs and stuffed bras in parodic tributes. Not only does Parton's media image depend on a hyperbolic version of femininity, but her presentation of her own autobiography and her lyrical themes in her songwriting underscore her singular performance of gender. How did Parton turn herself into a highly gendered popular music icon? How did such an exaggerated performance of country womanhood become so associated with country music history?

In the song that perhaps most directly explores these issues, "Backwoods Barbie" (2008), which Parton wrote for the 9 *to* 5 musical, she sings, "I might look artificial, but where it counts I'm real." There, Parton portrays a "country girl" with a garish appearance who might come across as "artificial" but is in fact "real" because of her underlying character and genuineness. Parton wrote the "Backwoods Barbie" song for Doralee Rhodes, her character in 9 *to* 5, but she infused it with lyrics about her own life. Throughout her career, Parton has consistently drawn a distinction between her "fake" appearance and her "real" sincerity underneath. She has crafted a visual image of what she calls a "hillbilly tramp," and she presents that look as a knowingly exaggerated performance of gender. At the same time that she embraces a self-aware fakeness or artificiality in terms of appearance, she insists on her underlying realness or "authenticity," based on her well-known autobiographical narratives about how she grew up impoverished in the Smoky Mountains in East Tennessee and made it as a country music superstar in a male-dominated industry. She includes her "fake" look and her "real" life story as important parts of all of her work, from her stage performances to her film roles. Her gendered persona is a multilayered mixture of different elements, ranging from the specific gender tropes from country music performance history that she uses in her look, to tales about her Appalachian childhood. Turning her autobiography into personal mythology, Parton uses it as an "authenticity" narrative to bring all the elements of her persona together and to ground them.

The gendered image Parton has developed is complex and requires parsing. The "Backwoods Barbie" music video is a perfect example of how Parton has consistently combined two opposing gender tropes from country music performance history in her media image: the innocent mountain girl and the scandalous "backwoods Barbie" tramp. The video pictures her as both that mountain girl and the later media star with exaggerated makeup and signature "hillbilly hooker" look. In the video, Parton imagines an innocent, organic childhood source for her later "artificial" media image. She walks down Hollywood Boulevard on the Walk of Fame, clothed in a leopard print mini-dress and a pink negligee robe with impossibly high heels, wearing large amounts of lipstick, eyeliner, mascara, eye shadow, and blush, her blonde wig piled high. She greets struggling street performers and empathizes with them. She gazes sympathetically at scantily clad female mannequins in the Frederick's of Hollywood store window. She sings about wanting to be judged for her substance, not her appearance, and she decries how women can be dismissed as merely sexualized objects. She includes flashback images to her youth, as a child actor plays young Dolly, skipping in the woods outside a mountain cabin, using berries for makeup. Parton sings that she has been ridiculed for how she looks, but she explains that her made-up appearance is merely what she calls "a country girl's idea of glam." Her autobiography likewise identifies an innocent, rural, nostalgic source for her later, consciously scandalous image of what she calls her "white trash hooker" look, which she says she modeled on a "painted lady" prostitute in her Appalachian hometown because Parton thought the woman's look was beautiful.[1]

Ultimately, Parton critiques stereotypical ideas of femininity in country music by combining these two tropes, the innocent mountain girl from her "Tennessee Mountain Home" in her "coat of many colors," and the stereotypical woman of ill repute, the "backwoods Barbie" who wears outlandish clothes and makeup and talks about sex. These gender tropes form a central part of her media image and her formulation of herself as a star and celebrity. They emerge in her lyrical themes, autobiographical narratives, and stage persona and visual imagery. In order to understand what Parton's gender performance is about, it is important to decipher those specific images and their contexts.

This book tells the story of Parton and her gender themes, exploring how she has negotiated and rebelled against gender stereotypes over the course of her career. It is a fitting story to tell because Parton has one of the most distinctive expressions of gender not just in country music history but in popular music more generally. The way she turns her life story into a personal mythology is also noteworthy, given how long running and successful that narrative has been; she has used it to claim credibility throughout her more than sixty-year career. While her autobiography, *Dolly: My Life and Other Unfinished Business* (1994), is familiar in some ways because it fits within a well-known tradition used by other country musicians to emblazon their life story as a religious confessional, it is also highly unusual in other ways.[2] In her book, she explains how she created her persona by combining what she again calls the "fake" versus the "real," balancing her emphasis on the plastic, ironic "look" she embodies with her sincerity, which she underscores in her personality and life story.

Parton's gender performance is important because it illuminates central cultural tensions in country music as a genre and in American popular culture more generally. Her gender subversion shows how there are transgressive strains even in the most seemingly traditional of American popular culture genres. Her complicated navigation of gender ideas has much to tell us about how gender has functioned in country music history and how surprisingly flexible it can be. Critics have previously held that country music has a strict gender binary that is rigid and policed, but more recent academic work shows how gender roles and practices have been more nuanced and unpredictable in the country music industry than scholars once thought.[3] We have more work to do in the field of country music studies to understand how gender has worked historically, and, in particular, how individual performers have grappled with gender role expectations and norms. As Parton's case shows, some of those gender performances can be quite unexpected. It is important to uncover how such performers have wrestled with gender codes in potentially liberating ways, because it shows how people can and have created more fluidity in terms of gender in US culture, even in ostensibly the unlikeliest of places. Parton demonstrates how individual artists can undermine stereotypes and norms, in her case through strategies like exaggeration and playing different gender codes off of each other, making room for one's self in the midst of the contradictions that result.

In this book, I account for the full complexity of Parton's gender performance over the course of her entire career to date. I demonstrate that Parton's implicit model of gender performance is to combine a more traditional version of gender with some subversive elements. Parton does so in a way that is deeply contextual, meaning she takes familiar media images from country music performance history and patches them together. Parton seizes a particular kind of cultural power when she merges her specific image of the "pure" mountain girl, which is a culturally privileged version of femininity, with her subversive image of a "poor white trash hillbilly hooker." In so doing, Parton claims the power of dominant cultural narratives of feminine purity and innocence. But she also challenges how the stereotypical "poor white trash" "fallen woman" has been put down or stigmatized. Parton incorporates elements of the oversexed female hillbilly in an exaggerated way that draws attention to how it is a problematic stereotype; her parody of the tramp creates ironic distance from that stereotype. By bringing the two gendered images together, she critiques the stereotypical ideal of feminine "purity" by combining it with its opposite, the "fallen" woman. She shows both to be mere stereotypes, and she condemns the way those images have been limiting for women.

Crucially, Parton also makes a class critique with her gender performance. Her media image places her "poor white trash" femininity in resistant opposition to middle-class domesticity, criticizing a stereotype of rural, white, working-class womanhood and reclaiming Parton's own version of a female "hillbilly." She thus uses a subordinated white, working-class femininity to critique a dominant white, middle-class definition of femininity, slamming middle-class norms. By questioning how the "pure" mountain girl is idealized and the "fallen woman" is stigmatized, Parton in effect interrogates the idea that some versions of femininity should be culturally valued while others should be stigmatized.

In the following chapters, I examine the longer cultural histories of both kinds of images in order to demonstrate precisely how Parton uses her hillbilly image to make a working-class critique of middle-class domesticity. I also link that critique to gender and country music as a genre. In country music history, the "pure" mountain girl persona has been familiar in country performances since the 1930s. While no other female country star explicitly references a prostitute in her stage look, something Parton has done with what she calls her "town tramp," the oversexed female hillbilly image has been familiar to audiences since the early twentieth century. It has notably appeared in the cartoon *Li'l Abner*, in the character of Daisy Mae Yokum, whom Parton has explicitly posed as.

In another example of how she explains her look, Parton points to a shocking mashup of a "pure" image and a promiscuous one: "I kinda patterned my look after Cinderella and Mother Goose—and the local hooker."[4] Although her comment is obviously designed for maximum shock value, what Parton implicitly references is the broader, long-running stereotype of women being seen as either virgins or whores in Western culture. For country music performance history specifically, what Parton's look does is reveal how unstable the dominant ideas of femininity are in the genre. Parton can explode those ideas by exaggerating them, doing ironic send-ups of them and turning them into critical parodies, as if her appearance is always in ironic quotation marks.

As I demonstrate, her gender politics are truly transgressive in the sense that she critiques gender stereotypes rather than being trapped by them; her critique is not recontained or placed back into traditional images of femininity. She expressly politicizes her performance in ways that allow her to resist its commodification by others. For example, as I quoted in one of my epigraphs, one of Parton's most repeated lines is, "If I hadn't been a woman, I would have been a drag queen."[5] Her engagement with drag and camp and her related deployment of country authenticity in the service of lesbian, gay, bisexual, and transgender (LGBT, or more broadly LGBT+) rights advocacy is politicized.

More broadly, I want to show why her work matters and what Parton has to tell us about gender and popular culture. Because her enactment of excessive femininity is exaggerated to the point of critical parody, Parton emphasizes the idea that gender roles are artificial in the sense that they are socially constructed, made up of each society's changing ideas and stereotypes about gender rather than some inherent, supposedly natural gender role. Parton's work also implicitly registers how these gender tropes intersect with class and race stereotypes. In terms of country music history, her oeuvre helps shift the context for the genre's cultural politics. For example, I argue that Parton's advocacy for progressive causes such as LGBT rights could be seen as part of an important progressive strain in country music history. While country music has traditionally been seen as a conservative genre in American popular culture, more recent scholarly work has found more multifaceted political affiliations, including some progressive elements. For example, some white, working-class audiences supported progressive alliances for working-class advocacy and LGBT rights historically, and they also engaged in instances of cross-racial class alliances.[6] In the context of a multilayered reading of country music's cultural politics, I argue that Parton's "hillbilly hooker" image does the cultural work of critiquing how the hillbilly has been framed as the "low Other" in country music history, a put-down of the white working-class, just as her mountain girl image critiques how the Appalachian girl has been idealized and has created a limiting stereotype of the white working-class in country music history. Parton's own complicated, long-running gender imagery itself creates a fuller range of gender expression and possibilities in country music.

Authenticity Debates and Folk Culture

In combining the so-called pure and fallen, Parton's gender model also crucially illuminates country music's familiar authenticity debates. The genre is intensely obsessed with what is supposedly true, pure, and genuine versus what is a "sell-out" or a base, manufactured, fake version of country. Insistently, the genre includes in its foundational rhetoric the idea of a pure, untainted, rural folk culture basis for the music versus a commercialized, tainted, and fallen mass culture. This ongoing tension between the pure versus the manufactured keeps reappearing in the genre and in the country music industry's rhetoric.[7] Part of that tension involves a nostalgia for an earlier way of life, specifically a rural, agricultural mode. It also involves nostalgia for a supposedly purer past, looking back wistfully on a purportedly "simpler time" and comparing it to modernity, that is, the conditions of social life after the rise of capitalism and industrialization. That dynamic is in keeping with a more general nostalgia that modern mass culture often expresses for earlier folk culture it has marginalized or commodified.[8]

The country music binary between purity and the market is a false one, a fantasy not based on historical fact, because country music had commercial elements from the beginning, when it began to be distributed on a mass scale in the 1920s, but also in the folk and old-time music of earlier eras. The larger notion of a conflict between the market and some kind of traditional American folk culture is, of course, fabricated. Even in early American folk culture, the popular was always mixed with the folk; there was no noncommercial "purity" or split with the market, since early folk music was always simultaneously folk and popular. It was during a period of interest in folk music at the turn of the twentieth century that academics and song collectors imported this idea of a tension between purity versus the market. But that tension was not part of the folk practice itself. Instead, these academics imposed their own conception of a somehow "pure" folk music in opposition to commercial music.[9] Yet even though this opposition is not accurate, country music still hews to it as a central concept in the genre.

I argue that Parton's oeuvre and image offer a fresh take on the folk culture–mass culture split, and on country music authenticity narratives, because she heals that tension by saying both things are true at once: her work is both folk and mass, real and fake. In effect, she questions the distinctions between such categories. In so doing, she illuminates the history of folk culture and mass culture in country music as a genre and offers a new perspective on the genre's authenticity debates.

Furthermore, Parton's gender image of the pure versus fallen woman relates to country music's story about pure versus fallen popular music on a broader level involving the gender politics of popular culture. As one of its recurring authenticity narratives, country music has long had a tension between the so-called authentic, masculinized "hard country" music that is closer to the genre's idealized folk roots versus the feminized, sell-out "soft" country-pop music that is seen as corrupted by mass culture.[10] As I discuss more fully in chapter 1, this gendered idea in country music of a corrupting mass culture as feminized and fallen fits in with a much broader trend in cultural history that likewise sees mass culture as a feminized, "fallen," corrupting, commercialized force in US culture.[11] Of course, these gender stereotypes are problematic and impossible to maintain, since they are subjective social beliefs rather than essential truths, just as the distinctions between folk culture and mass culture are arbitrary and impossible to uphold. Thus, Parton's gender performance not only critiques gender stereotypes and social hierarchies based on them. It also implicitly critiques some of these foundational genre assumptions, specifically country music's attempt to maintain a distinction between folk and mass culture.

As I demonstrate in the chapters that follow, Parton's media image resolves these larger cultural tensions involving both gender and genre stereotypes. Just as her implicit solution to gender tensions is to claim both sides of a binary opposition at once, so too does she bridge the folk versus mass culture split. She is both the pure and the fallen woman, the high and the low. She brings the two kinds of stereotypes together and embodies them both, thereby critiquing them as stereotypes. Gaining cultural power through her careful navigation of those stereotypes, she plays the two off of each other. Meanwhile, she also implicitly offers a solution to the country music genre tension of folk versus mass culture, because she inhabits both sides of that binary opposition. She claims both folk culture and mass culture, the vernacular roots of country music and the highly commercialized mass culture version of it. She is the most pure and the most fake. She is both things at once.

For example, Parton is identified with folk elements in her music on some of her most critically lauded albums, but she has also recorded some of the most successful country pop albums in history, gaining wider fame in a crossover genre associated with mass culture. She is well-known for incorporating features of old-time Appalachian ballads in her songwriting as well as other elements of earlier folk music, and her work has often been broadly described publicly in press coverage as folk-inflected country songwriting. Parton uses her own term, "blue mountain," to refer to her mixture of Appalachian folk and traditional music as well as bluegrass. Musicologist Kate Heidemann helpfully describes Parton's music as a use of "old-time musical elements within a modernized country context"; she observes that Parton's song "Jolene," an exemplary case in point, uses metaphorical lyrics similar to Appalachian ballads while at the same time incorporating modernizations of old-time elements such as an instrumental mix of keening fiddles and modern honky-tonk pedal steel guitar.[12] In contrast, Parton's crossover country pop recordings have made her well-known for music strongly identified with mass culture, as some of her crossover albums and songs have achieved notably high levels of commercial success, from her *Here You Come Again* (1977) to her Kenny Rogers duet "Islands in the Stream" (1983).

Taken together, her gender performance in the context of country music history offers an image of freedom. Her oeuvre lifts stereotypes for women as well as for the genre itself, suggesting that neither women nor the country music genre needs to conform to limiting notions of purity or corruption. Instead, Parton provides a model of identity that questions purity and embraces contradictory, opposed ideas and identities at the same time.

Trajectories and Contexts

In what follows, I analyze these gender themes in her media image, stage persona, and autobiographical narratives. I place these ideas in the context of country music history by addressing her songwriting and her career trajectory, particularly how she has often been read as an icon of popular feminism for her pro-women songs and for seizing control of her own career in a still male-dominated music industry.[13] In chapter 1, I make my case for why Parton is transgressive. I provide an overview of her gender model over time, detailing how Parton, by taking a stigmatized or stereotyped version of femininity and combining it with a culturally acceptable version, uplifts the "low Other" gender image and critiques how it has been stigmatized. At the same time, she also insists on the humanity and dignity of "hillbilly" women who have been negatively stereotyped. I demonstrate how she both embodies and questions the exaggerated version of femininity she uses in her stage persona. In that chapter, I also elaborate on how Parton's work helps illuminate the long-running country music narrative about authenticity and offers her both/and solution to the folk-mass culture tension. I elaborate on the academic context for this book, and I explain how my work contributes to the scholarship in the field.

Chapters 2–5 draw out the story of Parton's gender performance through different stages of her career, since her performance has evolved and become more nuanced over time, and the cultural politics of her image have changed depending on context. Chapter 2 focuses on Parton's class critiques of the hillbilly stereotype in her early career. I discuss the period from 1956 to 1977, from her professional beginnings as a child singer at age ten, to her "girl singer" years on *The Porter Wagoner Show* and break with him, up through her preparation for her pop crossover efforts and her first self-produced album, *New Harvest . . . First Gathering* (1977). In this epoch, Parton took on popular images of the hillbilly but also challenged them as she criticized working-class stereotypes. I demonstrate how Parton, by critiquing gendered stereotypes of hillbilly women, intervened in country music's long history of using the hillbilly to depict the southern, white working class. The hillbilly has often been used to represent the low, working-class "Other" who is upheld as an image of a simpler time in the past but disparaged and disavowed in the present.[14] When the country music industry was professionalizing midcentury, it targeted an upwardly mobile working-class audience trying to enter the middle class, precisely moving away from a hillbilly stereotype.[15] I argue that if the hillbilly stereotype is the reminder of a working-class identity that some tried to jettison, Parton's insistence on her hillbilly tramp is a recuperation of that image and a rejection of the belittling rhetoric about it. I also establish how even during this early era of her career, Parton played off culturally validated versions of femininity against marginalized ones, questioned idealizations of the mountain girl image, and used her references to her folk culture to justify her gender critiques.

Chapter 3 examines how Parton's crossover period complicated her gender performance by adding a gendered rhetoric of film stardom to her media image and by taking Parton outside country music genre boundaries, beyond a primary address to a country music audience to a broader, mass culture, middle-class audience. Considering the period from 1977 through the early 1990s, I trace her career developments from the time she did her country-pop crossover album *Here You Come Again*, up through her 1980s and early 1990s movie career, including *9 to 5* (1980), *The Best Little Whorehouse in Texas* (1982), and *Steel Magnolias* (1989), as well as Dollywood's opening (1986) and her albums up until the release of *Heartsongs* (1994).

I provide two particular case studies, one of her "Real Love" tour with Kenny Rogers (1985) as it exemplifies her musical evolution and one of *The Best Little Whorehouse in Texas* (1982) to trace how her media image was impacted by her work in film and television. In that chapter, I examine the cultural work Parton's star persona does and how it sheds light on the evolution of star discourse, or ideas of stardom in US popular culture. While star discourse has always involved balancing the ordinary with the extraordinary and encouraging audiences to search for moments of authenticity, glimpsing the supposedly "true" person beneath the star image, more recent versions of stardom involve even more complex layers of authenticity and fragmented performances of the self as a character.[16]

Parton's model of artificial self as entrée to a genuine self includes elements of the older stardom model but is adaptable to the digital era of stardom, as I discuss in more detail in chapter 5.

In chapter 4, I explore how Parton has used her autobiography to justify her relationship to folk and traditional music, and how she has fashioned her own authenticity story wherein she tries to claim her place in country music history. Because Parton's autobiography creates such a complex model for authenticity, both real and fake, folk and mass, Parton actually ends up trying to reshape country music history and authenticity into her own image. In this chapter, I look at the time period of her so-called return to country music and her three critically acclaimed albums of bluegrass and folk music during the 1990s through the early 2000s, honing in on how she deployed her authenticity narrative in new ways during that period as she reframed her connection to country music. I look specifically at the period between 1994 and 2002, marked by her *Heartsongs* album and her autobiography, which she published as part of her album promotion, through her third album containing traditional folk as well as bluegrass, *Halos & Horns* (2002). I assess how Parton adapted her oeuvre to fit into the context of the Americana roots music revival beginning in the 1990s, and I analyze her gender performance in relevant albums and films from that era, including *Blue Valley Songbird* (1999). I discuss her autobiography and how it explores gender socialization and gender themes in her childhood, specifically a mid-twentieth century Appalachian mountain context.

In chapter 5, I detail how Parton fits into an updated version of stardom and authenticity in the digital era, which prizes emotional realism in the midst of obvious fakery as well as performance of the self as multiple.[17] I establish how her increasingly campy gender performance—as knowingly "trashy"—as well as her social media presence and active fandom contribute to her developing version of star authenticity. This recent epoch, from the early 2000s to the present, has been characterized by a higher degree of camp and fluidity in her image and a more multifaceted approach to her music, beginning with her album of patriotic and spiritual songs, *For God and Country* (2003), up through *Blue Smoke* (2014) and her most recent studio album, *Pure & Simple* (2016). During this period, after her three bluegrass and folk albums, Parton embraced an eclectic array of genres, including, patriotic, folk covers, and mainstream country albums, as she tried on different approaches. I also address her highly publicized NBC television films based on her life, beginning with *Dolly Parton's Coat of Many Colors* (2015) and its sequel, *Dolly Parton's Christmas of Many Colors* (2016), with two more slated, including one based on "Jolene." I assess how she has once again adapted her combination of mountain girl and country tramp to new contexts, incorporating flexible markers of camp that she can amplify or diminish in different settings.

As I explore in that chapter, Parton has also taken her image more fully into cyberspace, where it engages knotty questions of gendered embodiment and identity. I show that Parton's camp dynamic is amplified in a new media setting, and I address the wealth of digital media Parton is now generating, alongside the digital fandom practices she encourages from her fans. Her fans have generated a high degree of digital participatory fan culture. For example, for one crowd-sourced Parton music video, fans took campy pictures of a "Travelin' Dolly" cutout in sites from around the world, then sent their pictures to her website to be edited into a music video. Focusing particular attention on an analysis of Parton's fandom, I assess key fan documentaries, Parton's websites and social media presence, including her smart phone app and her Twitter joke feed of Dollyisms, as well as her online merchandizing. Exploring recent models of stardom in the age of reality television, I analyze her 2008 appearance on *American Idol* for "Dolly Parton Songs" week and her attempts to launch *9 to 5: The Musical* (2008), as well as her appearance on other reality TV shows such as *The Bachelorette* (2012) and *The Voice* (2015 and 2016). Reality TV is one of the best media spaces to analyze in order to unravel complicated performances of identity, because the genre asks people to perform the role of themselves, that is, to play themselves as a character.[18] I demonstrate how Parton is staging her persona as a highly successful commodity in an ever-increasing array of contexts.

My conclusion looks at Dollywood as a synthesizing case study for how Parton has adapted her image over time to balance the folk and mass culture elements, and for Parton to claim a complicated "authentic hillbilly" status for herself. Dollywood epitomizes how Parton has herself commodified her media persona. I discuss the park's history, evolution, and impact on the region as well as how it frames Parton and sells her as a brand. Some aspects of her brand are perhaps enacted most powerfully at her theme park, including the simulation of Appalachian folk culture, her claims about "authentic hillbillies" working there, and how Dollywood uses the model of transmedia storytelling—telling a story in a coordinated way across multiple media platforms—which currently dominates the media industry.

This book is an academic work, not a popular biography, and I focus on analysis of Parton's media image. My methodology, drawn from the discipline of English and the multidisciplinary field of media studies, involves literary studies techniques of textual analysis combined with sociohistorical and cultural context, alongside discussions of relevant cultural theory. In order to analyze a multilayered star image, I am careful to evaluate a range of media texts, including her song lyrics, music, album covers, film and TV roles, interviews, music videos, and autobiographical stories, because that kind of interwoven media combination is often how audiences and fans experience such artists as texts.[19] I address primarily issues of text and context, although where possible I also note some issues of production and consumption.[20] I analyze her gender performance alongside issues of class and race, such as Parton's gendered references to the hillbilly tramp as white, working-class abjection. I am not making an argument about Parton as auteur or about authorial intention but rather about the multiple significations of her work and image as texts. This book is a work of media studies and cultural theory, not ethnomusicology or musicology. (Articles or book chapters with musicological discussions of Parton include, most notably, Mitchell Morris's book chapter on Parton in the 1970s, Nadine Hubbs's article on Parton's "Jolene," and Heidemann's article comparing Parton's "Jolene" and Loretta Lynn's "Fist City."[21]) While I recount relevant biographical contexts, again, this book also does not claim to be a biography (for that, one can consult Alanna Nash's classic early biography and Nancy Cardwell's recent book of journalism).[22] Instead, I look at Parton's media image, specifically her gender performance and how she uses it to create a space for herself in the country music industry by crafting a new version of authenticity. This case study sheds light on gender tropes in country music and larger popular music, since Parton's performance of gender is so intricate, and she negotiates different gender norms, stereotypes, codes, and ideals in a very elaborate way. While she is obviously not the only singer to engage in a complex gender performance, and other musicians routinely use contradictions in their media image, she does do distinctive cultural work with hers.[23]

Life Narratives

While I provide a brief overview of the basic outlines of her familiar biographical account here, individual chapters offer a much more in-depth discussion of each historical period and her specific career developments. There are several common theoretical issues in country music that I see framing her biography. First and foremost, Parton's emergence as a country star followed a highly gendered script in some ways but departed significantly from gender role conventions in others. Meanwhile, in terms of genre, although some accounts describe her as leaving country and returning to it after her pop crossover, it is more accurate to say that she created a careful balance of both pop and country throughout, fashioning a different mix in different market contexts at various moments of her career. Another related issue is how Parton's work focuses on genre crossings and resulting controversies. While a recurring rhetoric in country music expresses fears about the blurring of genre boundaries, about whether certain music is "real country," the genre has always mixed different stylistic influences, and Parton's oeuvre illuminates that dynamic as a particularly strong case in point. While the country genre has sometimes been oversimplified as a stand-in for traditional virtues, Parton's multifaceted persona likewise demonstrates how complicated the genre is, as are its "authenticity" claims, with authenticity being a constructed set of ideas and values that reflect particular sociohistorical contexts of produc-tion and reception, as well as changing beliefs about taste, values, identity, and models of artistic creation.[24] Likewise, the concept of "genre" itself is arbitrary and subjective, infamously permeable, and changes across time and context. By exploring what musical "authenticity" means for each artist and genre context, one can show what such ideas reflect about US culture.[25] Finally, one particularly vital media context for Parton is how her career evolved alongside the mediums of television and film over the course of her career, with her appearances on TV since the 1950s and in film since the 1980s.[26]

In a typical formulation of her life story, Mary A. Bufwack and Robert K. Oer-mann posit Parton as a role model for artists and working women. They insist that "hers is a true Horatio Alger, up-by-your-bootstraps success story—Daisy Mae Yokum of Dogpatch who turned into Mae West of Hollywood, a mountain butterfly who soared with eagles."[27] Their cheerfully hyperbolic comment speaks to the careful positioning that has gone into Parton's legend.

Spanning over six decades, Parton's career has established her as a country superstar as well as a crossover success, with her prominent appearances in film and on television adding to her fame. While in the late 1970s and the 1980s, at the time of her crossover efforts, Parton was criticized for moving from country into pop music, she has subsequently been seen as a forerunner in popularizing country music for a wider audience and in developing some country-pop styles. Parton has also been seen as a pioneer in terms of women's roles in the country music industry, from her long span of hit-making successes to her determination to control her own career, including establishing song publishing companies, such as Velvet Apple Music (BMI), and owning the publishing and copyrights for her songs, as well as having her own record labels.

Musically, Parton is known as a masterful songwriter and for her pitch-perfect soprano voice, her use of vibrato, her engagement with musical traditions in her Appalachian mountain home region, and her ability to work in a variety of genres, including country, pop, folk, old-time, bluegrass, rockabilly, rock, R&B, soul, and gospel. Also well known as a multi-instrumentalist, Parton's repertoire includes guitar, banjo, fiddle, dulcimer, autoharp, piano, drums, and harmonica, and she often showcases her musicianship during a segment of her concerts. Her level of music industry success is notable, as she is one of the bestselling country artists in history with industry recognitions as a member of the Country Music Hall of Fame, the Songwriters Hall of Fame, and the Gospel Music Association Hall of Fame. Parton says she has written over 3,000 songs and recorded over 300 of them. She has sold over 100 million records, has had a top-five country hit in each of five decades, and has over 40 Top Ten country albums and over 110 charting singles. In addition to her frequent Grammy, Country Music Association, and Academy of Country Music awards, she has had two Oscar-nominated songs ("9 to 5" [1980] and "Travelin' Thru," for the film *Transamerica* [2006]). Her song "I Will Always Love You" is in the Grammy Hall of Fame.[28]

In terms of cultural reception, her high record sales give some sense of the degree to which Parton has secured audience awareness and a pop culture icon status. Her broader cultural recognition is also apparent from her numerous national cultural awards (most notably a Kennedy Center Honor and National Medal of Arts) and other designations that register the degree to which her image has circulated, such as a star on the Hollywood Walk of Fame and numerous audience-voted awards, like the People's Choice Awards. In terms of the cultural politics of her reception, Parton has been validated by a range of organizations with different political bents, with honors as varied as the *Ms.* Magazine Woman of the Year award (1986) and an invitation to serve as the keynote speaker for the National PTA Convention (2003). One layer of Parton's cultural reception involves a formulation of her as "hip" or "cool," such as her ironic embrace as a camp icon for some in the New York art scene. She was painted by Andy Warhol, who also featured her in his *Interview* magazine. Meanwhile, one of the more unusual markers of her fame speaks to how decidedly her image is gendered. In 1996, scientists at the University of Edinburgh cloned a sheep, the first of a mammal from an adult cell, dubbed the "most famous sheep in the world." They named her "Dolly" after Parton, because the sheep was cloned from mammary glands. One of the scientists, Sir Ian Wilmut, explained his rationale: "Dolly is derived from a mammary gland cell and we couldn't think of a more impressive pair of glands than Dolly Parton's."[29] His comment is one of the more unusual "boob jokes" in a long line directed at Parton. Meanwhile, Parton herself often repeats such jokes and turns them into ironic comments.

Parton's background context is not just southern, white working class but more specifically Appalachian and Pentecostal. Her geographical positioning and socioeconomic class and religious upbringing are key elements. Parton was born in 1946 to sharecropper Robert Lee Parton and his wife, Avie Lee Parton, the fourth of twelve children, in Sevier County, Tennessee. Struggling for them to survive on the farm, Parton's father also did construction work and was a moonshiner. Growing up in the foothills of the Great Smoky Mountain National Park, Parton and her family were impoverished, without running water or electricity. Parton frequently jokes that she appeared as a singer on television before her family even owned a television. The remark is typical of the one-liners that pepper her humor, but her comment speaks to how little access she and her family had to some modern conveniences in her childhood.[30]

Parton describes herself as singing almost before she could talk, crediting influences such as her musical and creative family as well as her Pentecostal religious upbringing in the Church of God, which urged a freedom of singing. She often says her first song composition was "Little Tiny Tasseltop" around age three, in honor of her corncob doll (a song Parton will still sing on cue and which she composed before she herself could read or write). She composed another song, in the vein of a melancholy, Appalachian-style ballad, "Life Doesn't Mean That Much to Me," at age five. She began singing in her maternal grandfather Jake Owens's church at age six, and she started playing guitar at age seven, when she made her first guitar from an old mandolin and two bass guitar strings. Her uncle Bill Owens, himself trying to launch his own career in music, gave Parton her first real guitar, a Martin, when she was eight. He took her to meet her first boss, Cas Walker, when she was ten, and he continued to pursue music industry dreams with her.[31] Owens played and co-wrote with Dolly, made industry contacts, and was one of the adults in her family who helped transport and house her at various times as she established a career as a teenager.

Parton began her oeuvre in the persona of a "child star," a young Appalachian girl dressed in her "Sunday best." Her earliest recordings exhibit a mixture of traditional folk and country and crossover genres such as rockabilly. The first professional portion of her career involved her youthful success in local markets and her initial entry into recording. She first sang on the Sevierville, Tennessee, radio station WSEV at age nine, and within a year she was performing on TV and radio in Knoxville, on the Cas Walker *Farm and Home Hour* broadcasts, earning twenty dollars a week in salary.[32] Parton has commemorated her experiences as a regular on his radio and TV shows with a Walker-themed 1950s section of her Dollywood theme park.

Parton recorded her first single at Gold Band Records in Lake Charles, Louisiana, "Puppy Love," which she co-wrote with Owens, as well as "Girl Left Alone," in 1959. She spent her subsequent teen years performing on the Cas Walker show until age eighteen, while at the same time trying to break into songwriting and performing in Nashville with her uncle. Parton did have some initial success. She and Owens garnered a songwriting deal with Buddy Killen at Tree Publishing when Parton was fourteen, and Killen got her a recording contract with Mercury Records, which released her single "It's Sure Gonna Hurt" (1962), a song she co-wrote with Owens in a pop style like that of Connie Francis, and "The Love You Gave" (1962). She sang on the Grand Ole Opry for the first time in 1959, where she recalled with relish being introduced by Johnny Cash.[33] Her songwriting and recording gained some circulation but not enough traction to launch a full-time career in Nashville, so she decided to return home to finish high school. After graduating in 1964, the first in her family to do so, she left home the next day to move to Nashville permanently. There she toiled trying to gain circulation and exposure for her songwriting and singing, as she lobbied record companies, performed, and appeared on morning television shows. She famously met her future husband Carl Dean at the Wishy Washy laundromat on her first day in town; they were married in 1966.

During the next, mature phase of her career, Parton began gaining significant recognition for her songwriting skills. Parton herself notably claims to identify first as a songwriter, and it was that facet of her work that provided the engine for her career success. Parton continued to do both pop and country recordings, although she has insisted that her driving artistic motivation was to write and record "her version" of country music.[34]

Producer Fred Foster, owner of Monument Records and Combine Publishing, signed Parton and Owens to a deal in 1964. Foster invested in and promoted her, initially trying to market Parton as bubblegum pop on singles like her cover of "Happy, Happy Birthday Baby" (1965), with the B-side recording "Old Enough to Know Better (Too Young to Resist)," which Parton co-wrote with Owens. "Happy, Happy Birthday Baby" was her first single to chart (at 108, just out of the *Billboard* Hot 100, listed at number 8 on the *Billboard* Bubbling under Hot 100 Singles). Parton even sang it on national television on Dick Clark's *American*

Bandstand. Recurring to her authenticity narratives, Parton describes those re-leases as uncomfortable departures from her "natural" affinity with country mu-sic. Because she wanted to sing country, she was frustrated when Foster had Ray Stevens produce her as a pop star for several years at Monument. Foster wanted her to incorporate more youthful, rockabilly elements, which she thought meant he wanted to promote her as a "female Elvis." He suggested that it was because of her thin, youthful voice that he was targeting a pop market for her, encourag-ing her to record pop songs with Stevens as her producer. Citing one example of what she identified as sexism in the music industry, Parton later claimed that Stevens stole her version of "Everything Is Beautiful" because he produced her recording of it and then later did a version himself.[35]

Parton argues that she convinced Foster to let her record country singles after a song she and Owens co-wrote, "Put It Off until Tomorrow" (1966) was recorded by singer Bill Phillips; it became a top-ten country hit and BMI Song of the Year. Parton sang backup harmony on the single and garnered radio interest and in-dustry attention as a result, with both listeners and insiders eagerly asking about the uncredited backup singer. In Parton's characterization, she claims Foster realized his mistake and dropped the bubblegum pop efforts, instead letting her sing the country music she insists she was "born to sing."[36] Foster later argued that he let her record country because she wanted to do so, not because he was responding to the market, but he also maintained that he always envisioned her crossing over into pop and even larger platforms like Hollywood films.[37] At Monument, Parton's "Dumb Blonde" (1967), penned by Curly Putman, became a top-ten country hit, and "Something Fishy" (1967), written by Parton, reached the top twenty on the country chart. Her debut country album, *Hello, I'm Dolly*, was released in 1967.

Parton then entered a new phase of her career when Porter Wagoner hired her to join his popular syndicated television and touring show in 1967, when she was just twenty-one years old. Her hiring and positioning on his show reflected highly gendered dynamics. Wagoner had heard her on the radio and wanted her to replace his "girl singer," Norma Jean. Norma Jean publicly said she was leaving Wagoner's show to marry and move to Oklahoma, but Wagoner much later claimed she left because of fallout from an affair between them. Parton famously had to work to get the audience to accept her as the new "girl singer," since they kept calling for Norma Jean during Parton's first year on the show. Rumors of Wagoner's involvement with other "girl singers" would affect how audiences viewed and received Parton as well. Wagoner's show, which ran from

1960 to 1981, was a dominant one in the country genre. It reached almost 100 markets, garnered over 3 million viewers, and his road show played 260 dates a year. Wagoner hired Parton at a salary of sixty thousand dollars.[38]

Parton's affiliation with Wagoner not only formed the context for her entrance onto a bigger stage of country music television and touring but also impacted the framework for her recording career. Wagoner secured Parton a recording contract at RCA, which Parton claims he had to guarantee for any losses.[39] He convinced her to sign with them instead of staying with Monument when her contract was up for renewal. Fred Foster later claimed that Parton had intended to re-sign with him but that Wagoner misled her into believing that RCA head Chet Atkins would not record Wagoner and Parton duets unless Parton was under contract with RCA. Atkins later insisted he never made such a stipulation, just as Atkins has denied Wagoner's famous claim that Atkins initially disliked Parton's voice.[40] After the success of Wagoner's and Parton's first duet, "Holding on to Nothin'" (1968), RCA released Parton's solo single "Just Because I'm a Woman" (1968), which reached number seventeen on the country charts. Parton was able to feature many of her original songs on Wagoner's show. Wagoner and Parton had a number of hit duet albums, with fourteen of their duets reaching the top ten on the country charts, and they gained duet recognition, such as the Country Music Association's Vocal Group of the Year (1968) and Vocal Duo of the Year (1970, 1971). Parton's first solo album on RCA was *Just Because I'm a Woman* (1968), and RCA went on to release one or more Parton albums a year into the 1980s, with most charting, until Parton left RCA for Columbia in 1987.

She spent an important period of her career largely associated with Wagoner as her established male duet partner to her "girl singer" during her time on his highly successful show from 1967 to 1974, a common trope in country music performance history. However, much less common was how she broke from Wagoner to establish her artistic and economic independence from him. As Parton branched out from her Wagoner duets, she began to gain more solo recognition. She joined the Grand Ole Opry (1969) and wrote solo hits such as "Joshua" (1971), "Jolene" (1973), "Coat of Many Colors" (1971), and "Love Is Like a Butterfly" (1974). In a highly publicized and controversial move that bucked gender role norms at the time, Parton decided to break from the controlling producer Wagoner and go solo. He responded by filing a $3 million lawsuit against her, which Parton settled for $1 million, a difficult sum for her to pay at the time. Parton famously wrote "I Will Always Love You" (written in 1973, released in 1974) for Wagoner when she left his show, and she noted at the time that she had only intended to stay for five years and had remained seven. That song has gone on to earn Parton some of her highest levels of circulation; it became a number one country hit that year and again when it was later released on the soundtrack for *The Best Little Whorehouse in Texas* (1982) (reaching the top slot on *Billboard*'s Hot Country Songs chart). Parton later released it as a duet with Vince Gill in 1995, when it charted in the top twenty. It reached blockbuster status when Whitney Houston recorded it for *The Bodyguard* soundtrack (1992), which sold over 4 million records.

Parton's and Wagoner's feud and much later reconciliation formed an ongoing backdrop for Parton's career, as I discuss more fully in later chapters. Wagoner technically continued as a producer on Parton's records until 1976, with the parties disagreeing about their contractual obligations. After Wagoner tried to hold her to the very broad terms of an informal contract, he leveled the lawsuit against her, and they began legal proceedings, including Parton's lengthy depositions defending her authorship of her own work and image. The disagreement resulted in their estrangement for a decade. Her first onstage reunion with him was when she invited him to appear on her *Dolly* variety television show on ABC in 1988, her second eponymous TV variety show. After Parton's and Wagoner's reconciliation in the late 1980s, Parton helped Wagoner pay off a tax debt by buying his songwriting catalogue and returning it to him for free, and they made some subsequent joint appearances and performances. Parton famously later inducted Wagoner into the County Music Hall of Fame (2002). At the end of his life, she visited him when he fell ill, and she was with his family at his bedside when he died of lung cancer in 2007.

In Parton's solo career, a notable feature is how she served as one of the pioneers of country-pop crossovers; while she was not the first to do country pop (she was preceded by others such as Crystal Gayle), she was one of the first established female country stars to take her country pop to a mass market. After breaking away from Wagoner, Parton pursued her pop crossover ambitions while retaining her country output, seeking a larger mass audience. She signed with Hollywood manager Sandy Gallin, which prompted a gendered backlash against her in Nashville, with industry and audience members objecting to one of "their women" leaving country.[41] She coproduced her more contemporary country sound with some pop crossover on *New Harvest . . . First Gathering*, then embarked more fully on crossover pop albums with *Here You Come Again* (1977), with the title song a hit on both country and pop charts, and *Heartbreaker* (1978). With her Oscar-nominated debut acting role in the film *9 to 5* (1980), Parton's title song and women's labor concept album, *9 to 5 and Other Odd Jobs* (1980), brought her bigger audiences and critical recognition.

During this important stage of her career, Parton was achieving film stardom and a greater television presence, thus elaborating on her own star persona. The movie *9 to 5* made Parton a film star, building on her earlier television success on *The Porter Wagoner Show* as she continued to grow into a multimedia star. Parton expanded on her early accolades with several major films over the years, including *The Best Little Whorehouse in Texas, Rhinestone, Steel Magnolias, Straight Talk*, and *Joyful Noise*. Her television work has included two short-lived variety shows of her own, the syndicated country market *Dolly!* (1976–1977) and later the ABC national market *Dolly* (1987–1988). As a marker of her status as a media mogul, it is significant that her multimedia ventures have included her own production company. *Straight Talk* was produced by the film and television production company Parton started with Sandy Gallin, Sandollar Productions, which produced other films and television series (including the cult TV series *Buffy the Vampire Slayer*, the *Father of the Bride* movies, and the Academy Award–winning AIDS quilt documentary *Common Threads: Stories from the Quilt*).

While Parton continued to have hit records in the 1980s and into the 1990s, her highest profile musical successes in that era were collaborations. In the late 1990s, she eventually relaunched her solo efforts with a focus on folk and traditional music. Some of Parton's most notable collaborations during this period included the Bee Gees–penned duet with Kenny Rogers "Islands in the Stream" (1983); *Trio* (1987) and *Trio II* (1999), her critically acclaimed albums with Linda Ronstadt and Emmylou Harris; her "Rockin' Years" duet with Ricky Van Shelton (1991); and *Honky Tonk Angels*, with Loretta Lynn and Tammy Wynette (1993). Parton had waning solo sales in the late 1990s, a situation many of her peers shared, caused by narrowing demographic programming models in the industry, as I discuss in chapter 4. In response to her slowing success, Parton turned to the Americana roots music movement with three critically celebrated bluegrass and folk albums, *The Grass Is Blue* (1999), *Little Sparrow* (2001), and *Halos & Horns*. All were released on the Sugar Hill Records label, a bluegrass and Americana label, in conjunction with her own label, Blue Eye Records. Parton refers to these albums as part of what she calls her "blue mountain" music, again, her term for her mixture of Appalachian folk and traditional music as well as bluegrass.

The extensiveness and reach of Parton's business ventures are highlighted by her own theme park. Her version of expansive transmedia storytelling, Dollywood makes her somewhat like a country version of Walt Disney. Parton opened

Dollywood in 1986 in partnership with an existing theme park. Dollywood now draws over 3 million annual visitors and is billed as a cultural heritage theme park for the Great Smoky Mountains National Park area; it provides cultural preservation of mountain folk crafts and helps support the region economically. Some estimates put Parton's own net worth at over $450 million.[42] Her Dollywood Foundation (1988) supports the Dolly Parton Imagination Library, which gives each preschool child a book a month from birth to kindergarten. The program distributes more than 5 million books a year in over forty states, Canada, and Europe, and it has been studied for how effective it is in aiding literacy.[43] Parton's philanthropic aid to the area around Dollywood reached national news in December 2016 when she pledged to help families displaced by the devastating wildfires around Gatlinburg and Pigeon Forge by giving them a thousand dollars a month for up to six months; she also held a benefit concert and started the My People Fund, which raised over $9.3 million and served around 900 families.[44] As I discuss in my conclusion, Dollywood stages mountain folk culture as a tourist product, but it also aims to preserve those folk practices, with artisans from leather smiths to dulcimer makers teaching tourists their crafts.

Parton has continued to try to control the power and economics of her musical output. She took another independent stance when she started her own record labels and publicly castigated the country music industry for ageism, given their radio programming–driven business model that depends on a youth demographic. She used her first label, Blue Eye Records, from 1994 to 2006. Frustrated that major labels did not want to release her records because they thought she was too old for their youth-oriented markets, Parton started her second record label, Dolly Records, in 2007.

In the most recent period of her career, from the 2000s to the present, Parton has exhibited an even higher degree of fluidity in terms of musical genres, just as she has been embracing more fluidity in branding her digital identity online and in her heightened campiness. She has moved back and forth among several genres, including traditional country; a mainstream, more pop-inflected country; and rock covers. Her albums in this period include a patriotic tribute *For God and Country*; an album of covers of 1960s and 1970s pop and folk music called *Those Were the Days* (2005); a song for film, her pro-transgender Oscar-nominated song "Travelin' Thru," for the *Transamerica* soundtrack (2006); and her efforts to expand her music into musical theater with her score for *9 to 5: The Musical*, which helped launch her concurrent studio album *Backwoods Barbie* (2008). Her output also includes country studio album *Better Day* (2011) and

Sha-Kon-O-Hey! Land of Blue Smoke (2009), a Dollywood exclusive concept album keyed to her musical show there, featuring her version of the history of the Smoky Mountains. Her most recent studio albums are country albums, *Blue Smoke* (2014) and *Pure & Simple* (2016). She describes *Pure & Simple* as an album of love songs of various kinds in honor of her fiftieth wedding anniversary. Her promotional publicity for that album includes her interviews about renewing her wedding vows with Dean for their anniversary, which demonstrates how much she continues to incorporate her life story into her stage persona and marketing.

Parton's life story, polished for over six decades, has continued to be a rich commodity as source material for entertainment properties. The way she has fashioned her autobiographical narrative as mythology has made it especially well-suited to a television storytelling environment. In 2015, she signed a deal with NBC for four television films to be made of her life over the subsequent two years. The first two have been marketed as holiday season, family-friendly films with religious messages. The first, *Dolly Parton's Coat of Many Colors*, aired on December 10, 2015, to record ratings; it was the most-watched broadcast television movie in over six years with more than 15.5 million viewers and a particularly strong showing in a targeted younger demographic of viewers aged eighteen to forty-nine.[45] It features the song Parton wrote for the film, "Angel Hill." Based on her autobiographical "Coat of Many Colors" song but with amplified religious themes, the film follows Parton's impoverished family as her younger brother Larry died as a newborn, her father questioned his own religious faith, and a young Parton survived the bullying she experienced from other children at school when she wore the patchwork coat her mother made her. The film starred Jennifer Nettles, Gerald McRaney, and Ricky Shroeder, as well as child actor Alyvia Alyn Lind in the role of a nine-year-old Parton. Parton built audience interest in the film with an online viral video that captured her surprising the young actor Lind with the news that Lind had won the part. The second film, a Christmas-themed sequel to the first with the same cast, titled *Dolly Parton's Christmas of Many Colors: Circle of Love*, originally aired on November 30, 2016. It garnered 11.8 million viewers and featured a tie-in children's book authored by Parton.[46] The film follows the Parton family in Locust Ridge, Tennessee, during the 1955 Christmas season when her father and the children sacrifice so that he can buy their mother a wedding ring that he had not been able to buy her before. In it, Parton herself comes full circle and plays the role of the "painted lady" local prostitute who was the model for her own stage "look," exaggerating her own makeup and costuming even more in order to suggest the woman's appearance. It features the title song "Circle of Love," penned by Parton. Other proposed NBC films based on Parton's life and work include an adaptation of her song "Jolene" and a film based on her religious song "The Seeker."

In the analysis that follows, I explore all of these Parton elements in her oeuvre, the biography and the mythology, the musical output and the stage persona, the fact and the fiction. All have combined to shape her cultural image and generate multilayered connotations for her audiences.[47] In my next chapter, I elaborate on precisely how Parton is transgressive and what the origin and cultural history of her gendered media image is.

Notes

1. Bufwack and Oermann, *Finding Her Voice*, 363.
2. On the standard country music confessional autobiography, see Malone, *Singing Cowboys*.
3. McCusker and Pecknold, *A Boy Named Sue*; Pecknold and McCusker, *Country Boys*; McCusker, *Lonesome Cowgirls*; Ching, *Wrong's What I Do Best*; Fox, *Natural Acts*; Hubbs, *Rednecks, Queers, and Country Music*; Stimeling, *Cosmic Cowboys*, 26; Stimeling, "Narrative"; Jensen, "Patsy Cline's Crossovers"; Sanjek, Foreword. My previous work provides a larger context for my arguments: Edwards, *Johnny Cash and the Paradox of American Identity*; "Johnny Cash's 'Ain't No Grave'"; "'Backwoods Barbie'"; and Edwards, "Mass Art." See also the broader move in cultural history to show that the gendered public/private sphere was more fluid in practice than critics once thought. Davidson and Hatcher, *No More Separate Spheres!*
4. Bufwack and Oermann, *Finding Her Voice*, 363.
5. Parton, *Dream More*, 104.
6. Hubbs, *Rednecks, Queers, and Country Music*; Pecknold and McCusker, *Country Boys*; Bertrand, *Race, Rock and Elvis*; Stimeling, *Cosmic Cowboys*; Dent, *River of Tears*; Samuels, *Putting a Song*. See also my earlier arguments for how Johnny Cash used the country genre to make social justice critiques involving gender, class, region, and race. Edwards, *Johnny Cash and the Paradox of American Identity*.
7. Ching, *Wrong's What I Do Best*; Peterson, *Creating Country Music*; Jensen, *Nashville Sound*; Fox, "Jukebox of History"; Pecknold, *Selling Sound*; McCusker and Pecknold, *A Boy Named Sue*.
8. See George Lipsitz on mass culture's nostalgia for folk culture. Lipsitz, *Time Passages*, 22, 3.
9. Malone, *Singing Cowboys*, 68; Fox, *Real Country*.
10. Peterson, *Creating Country Music*.
11. Huyssen, *After the Great Divide*.
12. In Kate Heidemann's careful musicological analysis of "Jolene," she catalogues other old-time elements in Parton's song, such as the use of the Dorian mode typical of older styles, improvisatory phrasing similar to 1930s music and the ballads and hymns recorded by the Carter Family, and guitar fingerpicking remi-

niscent of picking and banjo roll patterns as in the song's opening riff. Heidemann, "Remarkable Women."

13. Neal, *Jimmie Rodgers*; Bufwack and Oermann, *Finding Her Voice*; Fillingim, *Redneck Liberation*.

14. Fox, *Natural Acts*.

15. Pecknold, *Selling Sound*.

16. Dyer, *Stars*; Dyer, *Heavenly Bodies*; Holmes, "'All You've Got.'"

17. Holmes, "'All You've Got.'"

18. I argue that in reality TV's reversal of traditional narrative, instead of trying to make fictional characters seem real, it turns real people into fictional characters. Edwards, *The Triumph of Reality TV*.

19. Brackett, *Interpreting Popular Music*, 76.

20. For media circuit theory models that analyze multiple interrelated sites to see how meaning is created, see D'Acci, "Gender." In country music studies, I agree with Joli Jensen's claim that an artist's popular image stems from the interplay of such forces as production (the media), consumption (the audience), and the aesthetic (the work itself). Jensen, "Patsy Cline's Crossovers."

21. Morris, *Persistence of Sentiment*, 173–208; Hubbs, "'Jolene'"; Heidemann, "Remarkable Women."

22. Nash, *Dolly*; Cardwell, *Words and Music*; Miller, *Smart Blonde*.

23. As Barry Shank notes, each artist is specific in how they engage with American contradictions in distinct sociohistorical contexts, yielding insights particular to their work. Shank, "'That Wild.'"

24. Barbara Ching has called for more attention to complexity in the genre, noting the problems with reifying country music's construction of simplicity and the dangers of trying to make the genre transparently stand in for traditional virtues or a "simpler" life. Ching, *Wrong's What I Do Best*, 5. See also Jensen, *Nashville Sound*, 15.

25. Ching, *Wrong's What I Do Best*; Jensen, *Nashville Sound*; Peterson, *Creating Country Music*; Bertrand, *Race, Rock and Elvis*.

26. As Mary A. Bufwack and Robert K. Oermann have noted, Parton was one of the first to achieve country stardom on television. Bufwack and Oermann, *Finding Her Voice*, 366.

27. Ibid., 360. Bufwack and Oermann reference the character from Al Capp's *Li'l Abner* comic strip and the "buxom babe" stereotype later appearing on *Hee Haw* as "*Hee Haw* honeys."

28. Dolly Parton Productions, "Dolly Parton Life and Career."

29. "1997: Dolly the Sheep."

30. Bufwack and Oermann, *Finding Her Voice*, 364.

31. Parton, *Dolly*, 77–85.

32. Ibid., 96–101.

33. Ibid., 113–114.

34. Ibid., 311.

35. Ibid., 145, 155.

36. Liss, "Blond Ambition."

37. Nash, *Dolly*, 70.

38. Miller, *Smart Blonde*, 90, 104–105.

39. Cardwell, *Words and Music*, 16.

40. Ibid.

41. Nash, *Dolly*, 229–245.

42. Gordon, "Frequently Asked Questions."

43. Hall and Jones, "Making Sense."

44. Whitaker, "Dolly Parton."

45. Maglio, "Dolly."

46. Whitaker, "Dolly Parton."

47. Joli Jensen (discussing Patsy Cline) and David Brackett (assessing Hank Williams) both observe how star figures are made up of mythology as much as biographical details; there is no "real" or "true" version of the artist, only complex layers of representation that produce meaningful connotations for listeners. Jensen, "Patsy Cline's Crossovers"; Brackett, *Interpreting Popular Music*, 76.

"Backwoods Barbie"
Dolly Parton's Gender Performance

When Parton makes her trademark jokes, such as, "It takes a lot of money to look this cheap," she frames her own gender performance as being highly staged.[1] To elaborate more fully on the evolution of Parton's gender performance, it is important to outline the precise ways in which Parton plays on both aspects of her gender performance in her media image, her mixture of the artificial, "fake," exaggerated appearance and the genuine, "real," sincere personality. She continues to expose the artificiality of gender through her charismatic excessiveness. While she is, of course, not the only performer to turn herself into a parody of a sex object in a way that both banks on gender stereotypes and critiques them, her folksy country "town tramp" persona is distinctive, constructed with a knowing wink, and we are all in on the joke with her. Ranging from the "girl singer" on *The Porter Wagoner Show* (1967–1974) to her "Backwoods Barbie" persona (2008) and more recent variations, Parton has navigated gender role expectations in country music in ways that reflect on gender in the genre's history and in southern regional culture and American popular culture more generally.[2]

In this chapter, I examine in greater depth Parton's specific gender performance, how it fits into country music history, and why it is transgressive.[3] In particular, I explain how camp, or an exaggerated style of knowingly "trashy" performance, is central to what Parton is doing. After first discussing the origins of Parton's gender images and dynamics, I go on to explore a particular camp case study and place Parton in the context of gender and country music performance history more broadly. The case study is Parton's appearance on *The Graham Norton Show* (BBC) in 2001, where Norton, an out gay male icon who reveres Parton, engaged her in over-the-top play: he had her don fake costume "Dolly breasts," challenge a Dolly impersonator, and speak to fans through a "Dolly bear" stuffed animal phone. Dressed in a dominatrix-style leather mini-dress, Parton joked with Norton about her being in drag. She performed her folk ballad "Marry Me" in her "blue mountain" style, mixing traditional folk, Appalachian, and bluegrass music. From the outlandish fake breasts to the arch banter, that appearance encapsulates Parton's camp performance. As I discuss more fully in the final section of the chapter, that performance also speaks to the way she navigates the folk versus mass culture tension, since she was bringing her own folk music onto the mass culture stage there. I conclude the chapter with a fuller case study of the "Backwoods Barbie" song and video, as one of Parton's most direct treatments of that folk culture–mass culture theme.

As I begin elaborating on my argument here, allow me to place my work in its academic context. Although this book builds on important recent work in the subfield of gender and country music studies, it seeks to fill several gaps in the scholarship on Parton. Parton is often mentioned in academic studies as a relevant example of larger trends in country music, but she has received scant academic attention in greater detail. There is no other academic monograph on her at this time. Her oeuvre, I argue, warrants more sustained scholarly attention and in-depth study. We need to account for the evolution of her entire career. There are popular biographies, of course, and Nancy Cardwell's quite helpful book of journalism.[4] But the few examples of scholarly work solely about Parton are in the form of articles or book chapters, shorter pieces that necessarily must have a tighter focus or cannot fully address the detail of her six decades in the music industry.[5] Most often, she appears as a brief case study among many others in writings that focus not on her but on other genre issues or artists. While the scholarship notes how vital she is to the genre, particularly in broader accounts of the history of country music, critics have tended to cite her as an example in passing. In some cases, she even functions as a shorthand reference, given a quick "read," with the perhaps unintended implication that her exaggerated gender performance is too surface-level to warrant further discussion—as if to say she is putting on an obvious show and we all know what it is. I instead argue for complexity in her gender performance and that it would be a mistake to sell short the intricacy and importance of what she is doing. While at first glance her exaggeration of gender stereotypes might seem obvious, it nevertheless involves quite convoluted roots and references that require much more substantive analysis and contextualization.

Let me be precise about what my book contributes to the scholarship: I demonstrate in her oeuvre as a whole that Parton is truly transgressive in the sense that her gender performance makes a substantive critique of gender norms that is not coopted or contained, thus I establish a more subversive dynamic that is present in Parton's gender performance and can be traced through her entire career. I show that she has a specific model of gender performance where she plays dominant and marginalized versions of femininity off of each other in a way that can change based on context. She achieves her gender performance precisely through her critical authenticity narrative, which depends on her distinctive bridging of the folk culture–mass culture tension in country music. Moreover, my work brings in new critical contexts when I link Parton's persona to the evolution of star discourse in US film and television, including more recent developments like reality TV. Likewise, I show how she incorporates recent media techniques, particularly new media interactivity and participatory fan culture, and I provide an in-depth study of her fandom.

In this chapter, as part of my case for how Parton is transgressive, I elaborate on her use of camp. Here, I differ from earlier key readings of Parton because while several critics have noted that her exaggerated gender parody shows gender to be arbitrary and performative, they have concluded that she is ultimately trapped by her own sexual objectification. In her important early article on Parton, media studies scholar Pamela Wilson assesses how Parton mediates conflicting social identities related to gender, class, and region. She argues that Parton's gender parody does rise to the level of a gender critique, but that the critique is undermined because Parton is constrained by her own sexual objectification.[6] In cultural studies scholar Pamela Fox's key book on rusticity, in which she traces gender as a vehicle for race and class identities in country music, Fox addresses Parton in a chapter on gender instability in female country star memoirs, including those of Loretta Lynn, Tammy Wynette, Sarah Colley Cannon (Minnie Pearl), Naomi Judd, Reba McEntire, and Parton. Fox avers that in her autobiography, Parton successfully uses her gender performance to critique class-based objectification, but that she is ultimately confined by gender objectification, thus she does not achieve a critical gender parody.[7] Meanwhile, in her brief discussion of Parton in a study of gender in popular music, musicologist Sheila Whiteley maintains that Parton's gender parody does not achieve the level of critique because of the exaggerated, stereotypical femininity content that Whiteley believes fails to challenge dominant gender codes.[8] Differing from such arguments, I read transgressiveness in Parton's gender parody and trace it in detail throughout her entire oeuvre and career; I show it to be a gender critique that is not recontained, and one that she makes through elements such as her use of feminist camp. I tell the full story of what I see as a more subversive strain in Parton's gender performance.

It is only fitting that the function and meaning of Parton's gender parody would be a matter for more debate. It is common in popular music for female singers, from Madonna to Beyoncé to Lady Gaga, to play with sexual objectification and criticize it while also trying to use it, and scholars tend to disagree widely on how successfully female singers can use sexual objectification without being imprisoned by it.[9] Thus Parton is an important model of gender performance within country music but also in popular music more broadly, because she does offer paradigms of critique. While other performers have used parody and exaggeration for critique, what Parton is doing is distinctive within country music performance history.[10] Her distinctiveness comes not only in the features of her specific gender performance, which I have been detailing, such as how she combines different gender images from country music performance history and is the only country performer who has explicitly modeled her look on a prostitute. She has also had the unusual longevity of over sixty years in the music industry and a high level of stardom. As a result, she has become her own singular icon of gender performance.

Camp Contexts

Parton makes her gender critique by uplifting a negative image and linking it to a positive one, mixing the country music trope of the innocent and virtuous "mountain girl" with her "hillbilly tramp" persona. In juxtaposing the two, she reveals both to be artificial images and uplifts the demeaned, "fallen woman" image, in effect critiquing how the "hillbilly tramp" stereotype has been used to reinforce gender and class hierarchies. She reclaims a rural, southern, white, working-class stereotype in order to critique white middle-class norms of domesticity. More generally, in different ways at specific moments in her career, Parton also mashes up a privileged version of femininity with a marginalized one, criticizing the very stereotypes of emphasized femininity that she is performing. As she combines the two, she uses the privileged version of femininity to question how the marginalized one has been stigmatized.

Parton's media image uses elements of camp, burlesque, satire, parody, and irony to critique gender. Her "Dolly Parton" character is a flexible symbol that she adapts to different audiences and sociohistorical contexts, generating multiple meanings. While she markets a version of herself as a sexualized object, playing into dominant gender stereotypes, she at the same time embraces subordinated, campy versions of femininity. Many of her signature lines speak to her sense of camp gender performance in her own look, such as her references to being like a drag queen.[11] Parton inhabits both dominant and marginalized gender roles at the same time. Through such complex negotiations of gender expectations, she gains cultural currency.

Because her gender performance is complex and depends on context, it is not always subversive; some of her enactments could sometimes reinforce stereotypes. Nevertheless, I do see substantial transgressive elements in some uses of her persona. Her star image does not simply profit from the gender codes she parodies; it also destabilizes them, particularly because her camp and artificial elements have only increased over her career. Her multilayered engagement with feminist camp and gay camp speaks to how camp can have complicated cultural politics, sometimes used in service of political critiques of the status quo and sometimes appropriated by mainstream culture.[12]

Camp can be defined as a style and performance mode in which a performer presents exaggerated, over-the-top, ostentatious, theatrical artifice meant to be amusing to a sophisticated, in-the-know audience precisely because it is framed as tacky, trashy, or outlandish. Camp historically grew out of twentieth-century gay subculture, with elements such as a knowing address to a gay audience, often a performer's purposefully failed aesthetic presentation of the self, and knowingly "bad taste" content.[13] It has since the 1980s in some instances been appropriated by mainstream culture in a way that commodifies it and empties it out of critical political content. Examples of the more general camp mode include drag queens and female-female impersonators whose excessive performances of femininity are parodies. There are also key expressions of gay camp and feminist camp that do make political critiques of power hierarchies involving gender and sexuality. Indeed, even though camp is cheesy and can be consumed ironically, that does not mean camp performers and audiences are not serious about and deeply invested in the styles, behaviors, and subcultures they reference in the performance. When Parton presents herself as a country drag queen, she is an instance of what Susan Sontag termed "deliberate camp," because Parton know-ingly performs a tongue-in-cheek, exaggerated femininity, one that she describes as tacky or trashy.[14]

However, just because Parton is doing a send-up of what she calls "poor white hillbilly trash" does not mean she is delivering ridicule via outlandish stereo-types. Rather, she is making a marginalized image of femininity visible, because she parodies the stereotype but is nonetheless engaging seriously with it. Ad-ditionally, her approach to gender politics is always tied to her autobiographical authenticity narratives. For example, she often calls her approach working-class "Appalachian feminism" rather than aligning herself with the middle-class lib-eral feminist movement, particularly in the 1970s when she and many of her peers, like Loretta Lynn, refused to identify with that movement. She thus frames her feminism as popular rather than elite.[15]

Gender Image

In order to account for Parton's gender image, it is important to address how she developed her image and how it relates to that of other country stars, as well as how Parton has become well known for some gender dynamics in her career. Parton has regularly engaged recurring gender tropes in country music. Some of her songs, such as "Jolene" (1973), in which the speaker begs the "other woman" not to take "her man," have famously been interpreted as affirming gen-der stereotypes (although I discuss some counter readings of that song in chapter 5).[16] However, some Parton songs also explicitly critique stereotypes, including "Dumb Blonde" (written by Curly Putman; 1967), "Just Because I'm a Woman" (1968), "The Bargain Store" (1975), "Eagle When She Flies" (1991), and "Travelin' Thru" (the pro-transgender song she wrote for the film *Transamerica*; 2005).

Some of Parton's musical performances have helped blaze the trail for greater access and agency for female singers. As Jocelyn Neal has demonstrated in her book on Jimmie Rodgers, Parton's cover of Rodgers's "Mule Skinner Blues" (1970) signaled a new and somewhat higher degree of agency for women in country music at that time, in the context of second-wave feminism.[17] One key example of her engagement with the history of female singers in country music is her album of country standards with Loretta Lynn and Tammy Wynette, *Honky Tonk Angels* (1993), which features songs often sung by female country singers, with an emphasis on music that questions double standards. In the lyrics to one female lament, "Silver Threads and Golden Needles" (a song originally recorded

by Wanda Jackson in 1956), a wife rejects her husband's attempts to get her to accept his cheating by bribing her with money and mansions. That album includes
their cover of the most famous country "answer song" in the battle of the sexes,
"It Wasn't God Who Made Honky Tonk Angels," originally popularized by
Kitty Wells in 1952, whose voice also appears on this Parton recording. The song
argues against scapegoating fallen women, insisting that cheating men should
be held accountable because their actions created unfaithful women. Wells's
signature hit was an answer song to Hank Thompson's earlier "The Wild Side of
Life" (1952), which blamed dance-hall women for straying men. While the Wells
song's message was incendiary in the 1950s, a threat to middle-class domesticity,
by the 1990s Parton version, it would signify as a popular feminism truism.

Gendered power dynamics are likewise evident in some crucial moments in
Parton's music career in which she has used a careful negotiation of gender role
expectations in order to gain greater economic agency. Obviously, a key example
is her break from Wagoner and her abandonment of the "male chaperone" and
"girl singer" model in order to pursue her solo crossover career. But other instances include how she has insisted on retaining ownership of her songs against
those who tried to take them from her, as when Colonel Tom Parker unsuccessfully tried to buy her rights to "I Will Always Love You" (1974) as a prerequisite
for Elvis performing a cover of it. When she remade an existing amusement park
into Dollywood, she revitalized the economy of her impoverished, rural Smoky
Mountain home region. When she started her own record label in response to
indifference from major labels, Parton asserted her independence from them:
"I put it on my own label because many of the majors really didn't want me
because of my age, thinking I was over. But I feel different about that. I figured
the major labels are pretty much a thing of the past anyway, kind of like they
thought I was."[18] Parton observed that in the new popular music economy, which
depends on active online fans, the major labels are the ones who are becoming
irrelevant, not her.

Parton shares some broad similarities with other female country stars across
time, including Loretta Lynn's popular feminism and Appalachian working-
class songs and Tammy Wynette's early "girl singer" image in her appearances
on *The Porter Wagoner Show*. Parton also has some affinities with Tanya Tucker's
and Dottie West's sexualized images, Barbara Mandrell's and Crystal Gayle's
crossover careers, Reba McEntire's multimedia superstar "show queen" image,
Emmylou Harris's affiliation with traditional music, and Gretchen Wilson's
references to "trash" in her "redneck woman" trope. Others have also obviously

combined country's gender performance tropes such as the "girl singer" accompanied by the male "stage chaperone" (figured as family member or band leader), the mountain girl and sentimental mountain mother, the country sweetheart, the western cowgirl, the female comic rube, and the crossover glamor queen.[19] However, none have, like Parton, mashed them up with a highly elaborate "hillbilly Mae West" burlesque version of the "town tramp." Parton is unique in the way she deconstructs competing gender tropes by juxtaposing them in her persona.

The cultural history of Parton's two main specific gender performance tropes—the chaste mountain girl and the town tramp—is important. Parton began toying with aspects of the "trollop" look onstage during high school. She used elements of it during her Wagoner show years, then amplified it as a sexualized image during her crossover period starting in the late 1970s. That mixture has continued to evolve over time. Parton came back to it in a more subdued way during her 1990s so-called return to country music, while again, in her eclectic musical period since the 2000s, she has accentuated camp and parody in her gender image to an even greater degree.

The mountain girl singer aspect of Parton's performance contains elements of the longer-running tropes of the mountain girl and mountain mother, gendered country performance modes that emerged during barn dance radio in the 1930s, based on idealized portraits of Appalachia by local color writers like Emma Bell Miles at the turn of the century.[20] Kristine McCusker has shown how barn dance radio executives fashioned the chaste mountain girl as a variation on the earlier musical trope of the sentimental mother; here, the mountain girl could signify as a future mountain mother.[21] Appalachian mountain culture was idealized as premodern and pure, somehow free from the corruptions of modernity. The mountain female figure was framed as the keeper of the folk tradition, and she also served as moral guardian to legitimate both radio's entrance into the private home and women being on the stage or on radio, a counter to the long-running association of women on the stage or in the theater audience with prostitution and indecency.

Parton links to this trope in a variety of ways in her mountain music, her lyrics, and her life story. She stresses how her mother preserved and passed on to her folk tunes and ballads. She includes some celebrations of pastoral nostalgia, such as "My Tennessee Mountain Home" (1973), "Tennessee Homesick Blues" (1984), and "Back Home" (1973), among many others. Likewise, she has songs about mountain men who migrated to cities and were nostalgic for home, including "Appalachian Memories" (1983) and its later reimagining, "Smoky

Mountain Memories" (1994), which Parton advertises as based on her father's sojourn working in a Detroit factory before returning home to them. However, she also critiques that pastoral nostalgia, such as with "In the Good Old Days [When Times Were Bad]" (1968). In her press interviews, she insists she did not leave the mountains behind but rather took them with her around the world. She claims that she still sees herself as that young mountain farm girl, impoverished and hard-working but happy in family, home, and nature.[22] She is also often framed in the press as a metonymy for the entire Smoky Mountain National Park and region, even more so since she was named park ambassador in 2008, her life story becoming linked to pastoral nostalgia for the area. One measure of how much of a symbol of the area she has become is that when Parton undertook her aid efforts for wildfires there in December 2016, she herself appeared in televised public service announcements with Smoky the Bear, urging families to follow the directions of emergency personnel to evacuate. Her appearance with Smoky the Bear, the national park mascot, implies that both are vitally symbolically associated with the Smoky Mountain National Park.

Parton has elaborated on the source of her overtly sexualized town tramp imagery when discussing her explicit use of prostitute imagery in her stage persona. She has widely circulated in press interviews the story of how she came to model her look on a prostitute in her hometown. Describing how she was inspired by the makeup and clothing style of a woman her mother called a "trollop," Parton explains: "I often tell the story of how I thought the most beautiful woman in the county was the woman most people called trash. In my eyes—with her big dyed hair, her bright red nails, her feet squeezed tight into her high heel shoes, and all her paint and perfume—she was just perfect. I wanted to look just like her."[23] Parton does domesticate that sexualized image and make it less threatening because she cloaks it in the innocent impressions of a girl growing up in the mountains. Nevertheless, because she tackles the "fallen woman" trope directly by using prostitute imagery, Parton's work actually questions gender categories in a substantive way rather than simply playing with them for cultural capital or profit. For example, in Parton's Christmas of Many Colors (2016) NBC movie, she presents the female prostitute as a sympathetic character, with Parton playing the character called "The Painted Lady." The woman dresses flashily (with Parton making her regular makeup even more overdone), drives her own stylish car, and responds to approbation by telling disapproving townspeople to question the straying men's behavior as well. What is striking is that for a film overtly about Christian principles, one that asks viewers to believe in Christian miracles and that is marketed for family viewing at the Christmas holiday, Parton presents the prostitute character as sympathetic in a more substantive way. In the film, she is not simply the fallen woman who is the object of Christian charity and forgiveness, with Mary Magdalene analogies. Rather, she is a character who supports young Dolly's musical ambitions, who encourages her to think of a larger world of opportunity, and who represents mobility, at least to young Dolly. She also, as Parton is careful to observe in her voiceover narration, provides her with a "look" that young Dolly finds beautiful and vows to emulate.

As in her oeuvre as a whole, Parton undermines the virgin-whore stereotype by embodying both at once. She gives voice to the ostracized fallen woman, letting her speak and be represented just as much as the pure woman. Likewise, she insists on the humanity and dignity of "hillbilly" women who have been negatively stereotyped, while showing how limiting both stereotypes are.

As I discuss more fully in chapter 2, Parton fits into a longer history of the hillbilly trope in country music. However, her use of irony and camp makes her depiction of the trope distinctive. More specifically, when she takes the common Appalachian mountain girl trope, in which women are idealized as representing premodern purity and as the keepers of a folk culture tradition, and combines it with her "white trash hillbilly tramp" image, which she plays as feminist camp, she creates an ironic distance from both stereotypes. She recuperates the hillbilly from negative connotations in a distinctive fashion because it comes through her ironic, campy gender performance. She dramatizes that idea as a recurring theme in her many songs decrying double standards, the demonization of female promiscuity, and the vilification of prostitutes, from "Just Because I'm a Woman" (1968) to "Blue Ridge Mountain Boy" (1969). Throughout, she critiques the way fallen women and the working class are stigmatized.

Her use of camp aspects in that performance also moves beyond mere gender parody to subversiveness. For example, the mountain girl trope in literature and popular culture led to a folk image of "contemporary ancestors," in which mountain people were imagined as part of an older, simpler time, even though they were still living; Appalachia stood in for a lost, idealized past, with the living representatives positioned as quaint throwbacks.[24] In addition to critiquing that pastoral nostalgia in some of her songs, Parton brings the "contemporary ancestor" fully into the present by merging it with all the contemporary references in her image, such as glamorized, mass media elements. Thus, her mountain girl is also a modern star. In a camp recycling of images from the past, she does not allow the mountain girl to remain "past," nor the hillbilly tramp to remain "low."

Parton even turns her own past into parodic camp as critique. She defends her ridiculed "trash" image in the present by saying she dresses like that because she is staying true to her roots when she was a young mountain girl who dreamed of looking pretty and thinking the "town tramp" was an ideal of beauty. By repeating that image in her own star persona, Parton suggests she is upholding that original childhood dream. When Parton tells those girlhood tales, she repeats her own authenticity narrative in which she associates her "trash" look with childhood innocence and the pure mountain girl trope; she thus uses her own autobiographical stories to defuse putdowns of her image that position her in terms of negative, rural, southern, white, working-class stereotypes.

Her use of her life story to defend her image also reflects camp dynamics. In her autobiography and press interviews, she says she first teased her hair up high during high school in the early 1960s in order to get attention by following popular styles.[25] When the teased hair went out of style within a couple of years, she retained that outmoded style as her gimmick to get attention, because it made her look different from everyone else. She later purposefully wore shoes and clothes that she says were ostentatiously marked as being from earlier decades. As camp performers often do, Parton knowingly recycles an earlier style to draw attention to the artifice of it as a style. In the 2010s, Parton retains the mountain girl mixed with the "hillbilly hooker," and she does so in a much more campy way than she did five decades ago.

Parton clearly could choose to change her look at any time, but she does not do so. Her consistency is part of what Jimmie N. Rogers terms country music's "sincerity contract," which entails the idea of 'staying true' to one's roots and not 'selling out.'[26] In a famous 1977 interview with Barbara Walters, when Walters asked how Parton reacts to people thinking her look is a joke, Parton replied that the joke was "on the public," because she knew exactly what she was doing in constructing the image, and she could change it at any time.[27] Thus, she continues to recycle elements of her own past style as part of an artificial camp image.

It is important to attend to how Parton developed her town tramp image as a knowing gimmick. As part of Parton's nuanced, layered star image, she uses her "trash" elements as a rhetorical tool and style, melding them with other gender performance codes to develop a flexible repertoire. Parton developed her image with a cognizance of other options, from the movie stars she admired for their Hollywood feminine glamor to the other country stars she watched. She was aware of female stage personae such as the demure, gingham-clad country sweetheart Kitty Wells. Likewise, she observed the rockabilly of Brenda Lee, a model of teen star success who took the masculine rebellion and overt sexuality of rockabilly in the 1950s and 1960s and recontained it with a cutesy little girl image—witness Dolly's first record, "Puppy Love" (1959), a novelty rockabilly youth number she wrote with uncle Bill Owens. The point is that Parton's image articulation is figurative, rhetorical, and knowing, and suggests a complex engagement with irony and parody. My reading here is in line with Barbara Ching's calls to address country music's complexity and use of figurative language, not to consign it to simple transparency or literal realism.[28]

The mountain girl–town tramp image is of course not the only one Parton has deployed, and her other personae display their own gender and genre tensions. When Parton broke from Porter Wagoner as a producer and moved to have a solo career at RCA in 1976, her *New Harvest . . . First Gathering* (1977) album not only marked a transition point as she worked toward the pop crossover of such hit albums as *Here You Come Again* (1977) and *Heartbreaker* (1978); she also used it to change her imagery.[29] She replaced her Travelin' Family Band with the rock-oriented Gypsy Fever Band and for a short time used gypsy imagery, including head scarves over her wigs and hoop earrings. As part of her crossover effort, she highlighted in press coverage that her wigs and look were a promotional tactic, so that no one would mistake it for ignorance. An interview from *Time* magazine about her 1977 tour for *New Harvest . . . First Gathering* quotes Parton: "'It's a gimmick,' she says, pointing to her huge wig. 'It takes pure gall to go around under this. I always had a big hairdo. When the style went out, I still loved it. Wigs are great. I can get ready in 15 minutes, faster than any woman I know.'"[30] Her experimentation with this different look (still evident in footage from her first variety show, *Dolly!* in 1976–1977) marked her changing performance personae during this period. Meanwhile, responding to harsh criticism for "abandoning country" and having "gone Hollywood" when she hired Los Angeles manager Sandy Gallin, Parton insisted that rather than leaving country behind, she was taking it with her into new contexts.[31] Parton later pointed to her close relationship with Gallin as one motivation for her gay rights advocacy; an out gay man, the late Gallin often framed Parton's kitsch in terms of its appeal to a gay male subculture.[32]

Camp and Gender Politics

Parton's use of feminist and gay camp introduces a particularly subversive element into her gendered imagery. She does not simply turn gay camp into a commodity to sell nor does she depoliticize it. Rather, Parton links it to her gay rights advocacy. Her media image bucks heteronormativity. In her autobiographical narratives, she implies that she has had extramarital affairs with other men in what is in effect an open marriage (although Parton does not claim that term). Asked by reporters about rumors of an affair between her and Judy Ogle, her longtime best friend and assistant, Parton has denied the rumors and critiqued homophobia. Parton has said that she has talked with Oprah Winfrey about how Winfrey's close friendship with Gayle King is similarly misread in the press, with both stating that if they were gay, they would say so.[33] Parton has publicly supported gay marriage, and she has a planned dance album and a song, entitled "Just a Wee Bit Gay," with content supporting LGBT rights. Parton can be seen as a version of feminist camp, and her performance includes some aspects of a female-female impersonator trope (a woman playing an exaggerated drag version of a woman).[34] She references not only drag queens but also exaggerated parodies of femininity, such as her explicit nods to Mae West, whom she cites as an influence, as I discuss in chapter 3.

Parton is explicitly transgressive in some contexts, as when she wrote and performed the Oscar-nominated song "Travelin' Thru," a pro-transgender song for the soundtrack of the movie *Transamerica*. Nodding to her mountain girl authenticity trope, Parton references "I Am a Pilgrim" and the folk ballad "The Wayfaring Stranger," using a folk ballad style for that stanza, which includes the lines, "Like the poor wayfaring stranger that they speak about in song / I'm just a weary pilgrim trying to find my own way home." She thus accentuates her own song's links to folk tradition. She sings from the point of view of the film's transgender protagonist, and the music video draws analogies between her made-up appearance and the character's by intercutting images of her singing with film footage of the character. In the song's lyrics and performance, Parton merges her own authenticity narratives with advocacy for transgender rights and acceptance for people "as they are." Her advocacy of human rights here is not simply due to a profit motive.

Parton uses an ostentatious trash parody that signifies within a country music performance context as parody. In her study of feminist camp, Pamela Robertson argues that camp can be both critique and containment and can take past taste and recode it in new contexts, rehistoricizing it as a form of what she calls "productive anachronism" and "recycling."[35] Parton references her own past ("a country girl's idea of glam") and authenticity narrative to ground a parody that was always about recycling out-of-date styles as camp and artifice as an attention-grabbing style, such as her knowing use of out-of-date teased hair, dresses, and shoes. I read that movement as liberatory, emphasizing the denaturalization of gender codes through excessive repetition and undermining them through hyperbolic style.

The cultural politics of Parton's use of camp depend on the context, just as the political effects of camp more generally, as David Bergman asserts, vary by context.[36] For example, Parton's camp in moments of knowing cornpone humor can signify in a country music context as a burlesque of the rube, a comic figure meant to poke fun at rural stereotypes.[37] The rube functions as an excessive "other" who assuages class anxieties in working- and middle-class audiences trying to access a middle-class norm. Parton does a send-up of the rube character with her knowingness similar to Mae West's burlesque of the 1930s, critiquing the put-down or othering of the rube. Other moments of Parton's camp could also link to an older vaudeville tradition of bodily exaggeration (which was imported into barn dance radio), in which very tall or very large performers as visual departures from norms parodied the norm and critiqued it through the "freakish," as a way to comment on those norms. Parton repeatedly invokes the term "freakish" to refer to her exaggerated bodily appearance, but her knowing camp performance rescues the "freakish" other from elitist scorn. She dramatizes this dynamic, for example, in her mountain carnival sideshow setting for her "Better Get to Livin'" (2007) music video and in her joining the ranks of street performers and some "circus freaks" on Hollywood Boulevard in the "Backwoods Barbie" video.

Parton's use of feminist and gay camp is in keeping with her frequent efforts to speak out for social justice, as when she advocates gender or racial understanding or tolerance. Again, I read the politics of Parton's use of feminist and gay camp as transgressive and part of a vital progressive strain in country music history. In Nadine Hubbs's important critique of how country music and a white working-class have both been stereotypically associated with homophobia and intolerance, she reads in some iterations of country music working-class practices that are progressive, such as antihomophobic and cross-racial alliances that have not been recognized by the dominant middle class.[38]

Camp Case Study: "Graham Goes to Dollywood"

Parton's own gay camp significations are perhaps best exemplified by her appearance on *The Graham Norton Show* (2001). Norton has long professed his Dolly fandom, as evidenced by the fact that the Duchess of York once presented him with a lock of Parton's hair on a velvet pillow. He and other out gay male media stars have claimed her as an icon. In the United States, Bravo TV talk show host Andy Cohen refers to Dollywood as the "mothership" for a gay male subculture.[39]

In one segment on Norton's explicitly gay camp subculture British talk show, Parton emerges from a wedding cake structure dressed in a dominatrix-style leather mini-dress and tie, with Parton telling Norton she is wearing "a boy-tie" for him. There to promote her bluegrass album *Little Sparrow* (2001), Parton sings her song "Marry Me," a combination of bluegrass and mountain folk. She mixes camp, her "blue mountain" music, and her white trash hillbilly tramp parody all together. Norton cheerfully plays up the camp aspect, square-dancing with her while she sings. In the interview segment, he uses exaggerated style to enact camp and parody. He gives her a large pillow shaped like breasts that he specially had set with rhinestones for her; she plays along with the joke, and they both wear pillow breasts, campily exaggerating how Parton's body is fetishized. The moment reads as the kind of critique Robertson ascribes to feminist camp, exaggerating stereotypical femininity in order to create ironic distance from it.[40]

The segment also focuses attention on Dolly impersonators, toying with the idea that the original and the copy are indistinguishable and equally artificial. Parton says she is honored that both "boys and girls" dress up as her. Again, she delivers a version of her frequent one-liner, saying because if she "hadn't been a girl," she "would have been a drag queen for sure." Norton replies that she would have made a "really good one." He pokes fun at Dolly impersonators as kitsch, testing whether Parton can recognize herself versus impersonators on a website. Going to outlandish hyperbole, Norton holds up a Dolly phone that is a stuffed bear designed to look like her, with a phone embedded in the stomach. He playfully calls a Dolly impersonator and asks her to critique unknowingly the actual Parton's own voice, and the woman judges what she hears (Parton herself) as a bad impression. Norton then calls a Kenny Rogers impersonator, on a Kenny bear phone of course, and has the two impersonators sing "Islands in the Stream" (1983) together over the phones. Parton herself finally breaks in to sing the song for the two struggling impersonators, yet they still cannot believe it is her. Norton has to convince them. In the rest of the interview, Parton combines campy jocularity with some often-repeated life stories.

Parton here performs both irony and sincerity, with the substantiveness of her music thrown into greater relief by the stylized artificiality of her appearance and the interview's camp elements. The staging implicitly critiques laws prohibiting gay marriage, with Parton singing "Marry Me" to Norton. Norton references the

Parton drag queen rhetoric. She says she dressed up "like a boy" just for him, laughing: "You said you were looking for a blond boy." In reply, Norton points to her chest and says she cannot pass as a boy, saying, "I appreciate the effort" but "do you know, I don't think you're still fooling anyone, Dolly."

Likewise, another episode, "Graham Goes to Dollywood" (2001), depicts Norton's Dollywood visit. He stages his visit with maximum kitsch. He notes a drive-through wedding chapel in Pigeon Forge, rides a rollercoaster with fifty Dolly impersonators, and sings the duet "Islands in the Stream" with Parton while floating down a river with her on a Dollywood inner-tube ride. In one sequence, he gets a faux wedding picture made with her. He has her don a southern belle dress, while he wears a Confederate soldier's uniform. After their wedding picture is taken, he rhapsodizes that he has "died and gone to heaven." The "wedding" photograph contains multiple layers of camp, including an implicit subcultural tourist amusement at southern stereotypes and the costumes as "poor taste," which reinforces dominant stereotypes of the South. Meanwhile, the sequence foregrounds the idea that the two are already in drag even before donning the period costumes, a camp dynamic that critiques normative gender codes. Norton layers in more drag performance when he switches their hats in one picture, with him in the bonnet and Parton in the soldier's hat. These references signify alongside Parton's familiar image of the parodic tramp. Norton references the familiar Parton tropes of astute entrepreneur and advocate for her region, as he describes what Parton has done for her "home region" with Dollywood. The layers of gay camp here are strikingly complex.

Parton's camp in the Norton setting plays differently than her camp in other contexts, which is not always subversive. For example, Parton did not signify transgressively when she wore a garish train conductor outfit to open a train-themed rollercoaster at Dollywood, or when she donned a gingham Mother Hubbard bonnet and dress for an event for her Imagination Library child literacy program. Likewise, her costumed gaudy red-white-and-blue 1940s style dress and hat in the video for her patriotic song "Welcome Home" (2003) is not a critical parody; rather, it references a history of earlier military efforts and civilian support, reaffirming that imagery. Consistently, her exaggerated style draws attention to itself as artificial and parodic, yet she deploys sincerity by combining her camp image with her authenticity narratives. Her performances are at once cheesy and hip, ridiculous and satirical, ironic and sincere. She continually combines both dominant and marginal gender codes into a flexible rhetoric through which she appeals to multiple audiences at once, such as Norton's core gay camp audience alongside traditional bluegrass fans, many of whom would have multiple identifications and wide-ranging tastes of their own and could not necessarily be "typed" by group in their fandom.

Of course, not all audiences recognize Parton's multifaceted camp. On a *Larry King Live* interview (2010), King asks if she worries she might have been a bad role model for goddaughter Miley Cyrus, who at the time was receiving bad press for her own risqué performances as a teenage singer. Parton replies that she hoped not, since that was not "her message," and she hopes singers did not think they had to look "trashy" to get ahead. Parton distances her own camp performance from the kind of objectified image that reinforces stereotypes, the implication being that Cyrus misunderstood her star text if she missed the parody (although Cyrus's subsequent use of camp and gender fluidity in her own media image would suggest that she gets the parody). However, of course, Parton herself cannot control the multiple meanings audiences take from her, especially since Parton can signify differently in different contexts.

Historical Contexts: The Cultural Politics of Gender in Country Music

Since the most crucial context for Parton's gender performance is country music, it is important to establish what the relevant gender performance history is within the genre. The context in which Parton was starting out in country music reflects mid-twentieth century gender dynamics in the country music industry. It is worth tracing out the evolution of gender and country music contexts relevant to her career, from that period to the present.

In terms of that gendered dynamic in which Parton first became famous, she and Wagoner in the late 1960s were performing in an era when country music had gone from honky-tonk and the threat of rockabilly in the previous decade to the Nashville Sound in the 1960s, all of which had specific gender, race, and class dynamics. The late 1940s and early 1950s honky-tonk music of Ernest Tubb or Hank Williams was disruptive to postwar domesticity, a masculine retreat from the pressures of home, with a louder style, strong dance beats, and lyrics about the working-class bars and dance clubs that generated and showcased this style. Williams and others were also expressing southern poor and working-class resistance to new 1950s postwar baby boom, middle-class norms of modern nuclear family unit domesticity, consumerism, and the rise of the suburbs.[41] Richard Leppert and George Lipsitz argue convincingly that Williams undermined an emergent masculinity of middle-class domesticity because he represented the troubled drifter (in his "Luke the Drifter" persona) who resisted the modern nuclear family; rather than embracing a return to patriarchy, Williams's themes featured an effort to get closer to women, not to dominate them, often as working-class partners, perhaps a residual reference to the Depression-era South where women frequently presided over extended families in which the men had to roam to look for work.[42] Williams's identification with a southern white working class was expressed through musical elements that have been typed feminine, such as a high pitch, seen here with the "high lonesome" voice and the "twang" of southern white folk culture.

Likewise, in my book on Johnny Cash, I have argued that Cash uses rockabilly rather than Williams's "high lonesome" mode of address, but that in his work, Cash articulates similar themes that trouble the modern nuclear family, although his characters are more clearly torn between rambling and home.[43] Meanwhile, Kitty Wells could sing in a honky-tonk style that, as a genre, threatened middle-class domesticity, but she domesticated it with her gendered demure self-presentation, gingham dresses, and family orientation.[44] Thus, Wells could sing "It Wasn't God Who Made Honky Tonk Angels" (1952) as push back against dance hall women being vilified for men who cheat, all while signifying in a nonthreatening, domesticated way.

In the mid- to late 1950s, rockabilly merged country (honky-tonk) and rhythm and blues (jump blues) styles into a high-energy performance with themes of youth rebellion, as early rock 'n' roll. Artists like Elvis and Cash were seen as a threat to suburban, middle-class society and signaled the potential of cross-racial class bonding. A young Brenda Lee sang in this style but was positioned as a nonthreatening teenybopper. Meanwhile, the smooth Nashville Sound of the late 1950s through the 1960s, with lush string and horn sections, background choruses, and a more pop sound, with singers like Patsy Cline, Jim Reeves, and Eddy Arnold, was country music's effort to fight back against an encroaching, disruptive rock 'n' roll that was stealing listeners. In contrast to rock 'n' roll's rebelliousness, the Nashville Sound tried to embrace a modern nuclear family ideal.

Porter Wagoner utilized some aspects of the Nashville Sound but was primarily associated with more traditional country music, and he has often been categorized as "hard" country. Parton engaged with those country influences but was also associated with folk and traditional music influences in her songwriting, which would have placed her in a more working-class context. Parton's and

Wagoner's duets included traditional and contemporary country, but also some of Parton's folk and blues influences, in duets that ranged from tragic ballads to Wagoner's story songs to jokey battle-of-the-sexes songs. While many of their duets restored a projected vision of domestic tranquility, some focused on the threats to a happy marriage and home.

As a duet team, they signified in terms of the domesticated "girl singer" and her "male chaperone" on stage. That model would be recognizable to the kind of "respectable working-class" and aspirational audience they were targeting as a demographic at that time. Fans often thought of them as a couple, even though both denied rumors of any romantic involvement.

Wagoner and Parton together fit into larger paradigms of country music style in interesting ways, particularly since some of those larger paradigms are gendered. Related to the familiar market versus purity binary, for example, other key country metanarratives involve identifying a binary of stylistic differences that often take on gendered stereotypes. As I noted in my introduction and detail more here, in sociologist Richard Peterson's "hard-core" versus "soft-shell" country dialectic, the "pure" roots of traditional country (Hank Williams) oppose the more "pop" or market-oriented form such as the Nashville Sound and its descendants (Jim Reeves).[45] Likewise, historians have noted how the "founding moment" of commercial country music, the 1927 Bristol sessions, generated two different paradigms of "authenticity," one linked to the band the Carter Family, the other to singer Jimmie Rodgers. The Carter Family was seen as representing home, family, and domesticity-focused traditional music (which they advertised as "morally good") versus Jimmie Rodgers's rambler, genre-crossing music.[46] That Carter ideal of domestic harmony was carefully created and hid familial strife, yet it managed to establish an ongoing paradigm of domestic purity for the country genre.[47] Since the Bristol sessions, where Ralph Peer recorded "hillbilly" acts in Bristol, Virginia, for the Victor recording label (to be marketed to poor southern whites), marked the beginning of mass distribution of this music, the way the two different models of performance from Bristol have been seen as gendered is significant to the genre's history. Parton's many nostalgic songs about home fit the Carter Family paradigm, but again, she has her own careful constructions of authenticity as well.

While Peterson identifies Wagoner within the "hard-core" style and notes that Parton's appearance would fit a "hard-core" style of gaudiness, Parton has also obviously engaged with the other side of the binary in terms of her country-pop crossover efforts. For Peterson, "soft-shell" involves mainstream country's standard American English, smooth singing style, lack of pronounced accents, and broader emotional themes with wide appeal, versus "hard" country's nasal twang, nonstandard English, and strong southern or southwestern accents, focusing on personal stories of suffering and hardship. Using Peterson's model, musicologist Mitchell Morris reads Parton as moving between the "hard-core" and "soft-shell" styles at different moments in her career.[48]

These gendered stylistic models have broader applicability. For example, some scholars have critiqued Peterson's influential account of authenticity in commercial country music, arguing that the distinction between "hard country" authenticity and "soft" country-pop inauthenticity imports some unexamined gender assumptions. That is, the masculine-associated "hard" styles enjoy greater credibility, while the feminized "soft" styles are seen as "sell-outs."[49]

In my thinking, such a discussion calls to mind Andreas Huyssen's examinations of a masculinized modernist celebration of a "pure" or "high" art in danger of being diminished by a feminized mass culture.[50] In some sense, for country music, the idea of a purer "hard" country is masculinized and associated with working-class roots and folk culture, while the idea of "soft" country represents a feminized and potentially middle-class-dominated mass culture watering down the folk culture roots. Those larger cultural issues would have had currency in the 1950s as Parton was breaking into the country music industry. Of course, country music is a particularly interesting case here because the masculinized pure art would be the residual, supposedly premodern folk culture sounds like the "high lonesome" pitch and "twang" in the voice (sounds that can also be stereotyped as feminine). Indeed, since the intricate staging of authenticity in country music has been a topic of much critical debate, gender becomes an important site for this discussion because gender paradigms are strongly linked to authenticity issues.

To trace Parton's stylistic and gender significations through the rest of her career in broad terms, in the 1970s, with her solo output, Parton was also important in the context of popular feminism. While she distanced herself from middle-class liberal feminism and the women's liberation movement of the 1970s, often saying she did not know what "women's lib" was when asked by reporters, Parton's strong pro-women songs did signify in a popular, rather than middle-class, feminism context, alongside singers like Loretta Lynn. Her underground fans, drawn to her folk influences beginning in the 1960s, would signify differently, part of an urban folk culture revival that later filtered into the 1960s counterculture and sexual revolution.

Her later pop crossover efforts in the late 1970s into the 1980s placed her in a much broader, mainstream, middle-class-dominated popular culture context in addition to a "countrypolitan" trend within country music. As I discuss in chapter 3, in her starring roles in Hollywood films in the 1980s and early 1990s, she was framed in terms of the women's movement and women's power films like 9 to 5. In her music, as Parton incorporated more R&B and pop songs into her oeuvre, lyrically, she would continue to signify in the same "strong woman" vein.

The style she was already adopting fit in with the countrypolitan style that became popular in the early 1980s, with its use of disco and pop elements. Jocelyn Neal has argued that both Parton and Willie Nelson negotiated their musical identities through the countrypolitan period of mainstream country in the 1970s and 1980s because they maintained their identities as decidedly country singers but also achieved larger crossover appeal as mainstream entertainers. She cites some of Parton's specific songs that reflect her pop-crossover sound in this context, such as "Single Women" (1981), with its saxophone solo; her disco jam "Baby I'm Burning" (1978); and her recording of the Donna Summers disco song "Starting over Again" (1980).[51] While country music had other stylistic developments during this era, such as a 1980s neo-traditionalism reaction against countrypolitan, the pop influences contributed to the 1990s' broadening of country's appeal, a trend Parton helped generate with her pop crossover success.

With the industry's changed political economy of the 1990s and the narrowing of playlists, Parton's turn to bluegrass and folk signified in terms of the more progressive gender politics of the Americana roots music movement. Since the 1990s and 2000s, Parton has maintained her ability to perform in more pop crossover as well as traditional styles, with output ranging from country pop to folk to bluegrass. Parton's wide array of multimedia output targets both niche and general mainstream audiences in country music and beyond, thus the cultural politics of her gender performance more recently are quite varied in different settings.

However, more generally, her "strong woman" popular feminism symbolism can be seen as a counterpoint to an opposing gendered trend in country music since the 1990s, one in which strains of commercial country music express masculine anger and frustration, part of a broader cultural backlash against feminism. Country radio's current "bro country" trend reflects this dynamic ("bro country" is a term used by journalists to refer to the wealth of male country artists singing about masculinity and repeated themes like women, trucks, and beer). This trend might not have masculine anger, but it does have masculinity and male bonding as its focus, with women appearing as passive, idealized sexual objects. Stemming from the development of country radio targeting a female audience demographic in the 1990s, and narrowing playlists, today female singers are fighting to get very sparse country radio airplay, and women country artists have become extremely marginalized on country radio, as I detail in chapter 5.

In an account that speaks to how this dynamic in country music reflects larger cultural trends, sociologist Michael Kimmel turns to country music as a popular culture space in which he sees a profound expression of a "new masculine anger." Along with the hypermasculinity he perceives in heavy metal and hip-hop, Kimmel identifies the surging popularity of what he calls "rockified country and western" music as a symptom of the rage of "NASCAR dads" who are turning to nostalgic songs that include fantasy resolutions to their identity crises alongside a more aggressive rock attitude; song topics include lost love and turning to simpler pleasures like cars and beer to cope with economic troubles. Kimmel distinguishes this new trend from traditional country music, which, as what he calls the "music of America's rural working class," is a form able to explore the realities of working-class life and gender, including trepidations about its challenges. He argues that unlike a slightly earlier superstar like Garth Brooks in the 1990s, who combined bravado with compassion as a "sensitive S.O.B.," a new generation of stars in the 1990s and 2000s like Toby Keith focus on white, lower middle-class resentments with unbridled masculine aggression, lauding the Everyman father, husband, and soldier who does not get the respect he deserves and threatens male violence in response (witness any of Keith's post-9/11 anthems to the "American way" of macho violent retaliation or the reaction to the Dixie Chicks).[52]

In the country genre's multilayered formulations of gender, this kind of gendered trend illustrates how convoluted constructions of masculinities can be. Likewise, the kind of popular feminism Parton articulates can be equally complex. These gender ideologies become especially complicated in a southern, white, working-class context.

It is important to note that even though country music has always had a broader audience demographic, it is still symbolically associated with a southern, white, working-class audience and milieu. Linking the two because of the regional folk culture roots, historian Bill C. Malone observes that other groups still consume their fantasy of a southern, rural, white working class through the music.[53] One 1970s study found that core country music listeners are largely "urban living, white adults with rural roots who are established in home, family, and job, and yet who are content with none of these," just as there remains a large working class component nationally, with a high percentage in urban areas.[54] The symbolic association with a southern, white, working-class culture continues to matter to the music, as it can express what Raymond Williams calls a "structure of feeling," or a particular group's shared perceptions and values at a particular time, their lived experience, here conveyed through a musical form that is at once folk poetry and mass media.[55] One key context country music could speak to that is relevant to Parton's career is how it illuminates the post–World War II southern, rural, working-class migration to cities in large numbers and the 1950s suburban middle-class explosion with all the resulting tensions. Likewise, the gender role expectations Parton comments on and parodies have particular resonance in a southern, white, working-class, especially Appalachian, setting.

Finally, within a larger cultural context, Parton's more recent gender performance speaks to debates about postfeminism, a cultural discourse since the late 1980s that involves a backlash against feminism by suggesting that all the aims of the feminist movement have been reached, therefore we are "beyond" gender and there is no need to address ongoing structural inequities. Postfeminist discourse, as theorists Tania Modleksi and Angela McRobbie have detailed, is characterized by an emphasis on women as sexualized objects and the idea that they are expressing female agency; these critics would argue that women are instead being trapped as objects and commodities, with the illusion of freedom of choice.[56] McRobbie describes postfeminism as a development in popular feminism that repudiates feminism as something in the past, already achieved, therefore no longer necessary; she finds the source of it in the ongoing backlash against feminism as well as a self-critique within feminism. Postfeminism presents young women with a rhetoric of choice and individualization to choose to be objectified and to express postfeminist irony about it, as a backlash against so-called political correctness.

I contend that Parton is not postfeminist. Instead, she uses camp in her image to do a critical parody of gender stereotypes, such that she breaks up that postfeminist dynamic where women are conscripted into being only the sexualized object. The politics of her plastic surgery are an object of considerable cultural debate.[57] There were already rumors about her plastic surgery in the 1970s. Johnny Carson asked her about the subject on her famous *Tonight Show* appearances with him (1977), but she did not confirm the rumors until later in the 1980s.[58] Some critics might argue that her plastic surgery is a reactionary cultural construction, a capitulation to Western patriarchal standards of female beauty, which prompt some women to want larger breasts in order to meet that

sexualized ideal in a way that makes the women objects and commodities offered up for consumption. However, her exaggeration and camp context creates
ironic distance, commenting on that embodiment and drawing attention to it
as artificial, claiming self-expression rather than capitulation to norms. Thus,
today, her signature look might be interpreted in terms of third-wave feminism
and a new emphasis on gender fluidity, valuing her individual expression of selfhood and viewing her performance of excessive femininity as just one of many
possible gender expressions. A positive reading of Parton in that cultural context
would also argue that her plastic surgery, while it falls into traditional patriarchal
gender ideals of beauty that have historically been quite harmful and limiting to
women, nevertheless can be seen as gender self-expression, meaning that body
modification becomes a means for self-expression rather than simple compliance
with gender role ideologies. Again, her camp and ironic components, which
draw attention to her look as artifice and performance, would support that kind
of sympathetic reading. As I discuss in chapter 5, Parton fits into paradigms of
gender fluidity and a range of self-expression in today's culture.[59]

Authenticity Narratives

Parton's own self-expression vitally depends on her projection of genuineness.
Since she makes her gender imagery cohere by using her life story, that strategy
brings us back to the larger issue of authenticity narratives in country music and
the cultural values and taste hierarchies they illuminate. In Parton's case, her
rhetoric often downplays her potentially incendiary messages by contextualizing
them in terms of her autobiography as an authenticity narrative. When asked
to discuss feminist messages in her music, Parton often frames them merely as
"country girl" wisdom in response to her life experiences with the gender role expectations of southern, white, working-class femininity. In her autobiography, she
jokes that her response to male chauvinism in the East Tennessee mountain culture she experienced growing up involved her own "early Appalachian feminist"
tactics.[60] As Parton often advocates for social justice, including women's rights,
racial equity, and gay rights, her statements are striking for how she anchors them
in her own discourses of authenticity, perhaps making them seem more genuine
to some audiences by framing them in terms of her sincerity as well as her rural,
working-class background. Likewise, she calls her business acumen "good ol'
horse sense," downplaying her economic power by framing it in domesticated
rhetoric, the common sense of mountain folk.[61]

Parton continually uses her autobiography to justify elements of her media image, pointing to an indigenous folk culture origin even for manufactured mass culture components of her performance. As Parton engages in this kind of intricate retrieval of her own past, and as she becomes emblematic of an idealized Appalachian folk past, she merges it with mass media images and the trappings of modernity. Thus, her star image speaks to how popular culture responds to modernity. Although mass media turns music into a commodity, popular music is not wholly determined by its commodity status. It can also be a site of generative historical meaning for artists and audiences. As George Lipsitz has demonstrated, popular culture uses historical discourse to generate a sense of memory and continuity in response to modernity's break with the past, as when postwar twentieth-century mass culture fixated on the very loss of folk culture that it was accelerating. Indeed, Lipsitz believes that popular music can serve as "a repository of collective memory" and profoundly expose "the tension between music as a commodity and music as an expression of lived experience."[62]

At times, Parton and some of her audiences could be seen to engage in this kind of generative process, using mass media to ponder the loss that mass culture furthers. Her song "Applejack" (1977), and her use of older country icons such as Kitty Wells, Chet Atkins, and Minnie Pearl to sing backup on it, enacts this kind of meditation. Her lyrics express nostalgia for the figure of an apple-picking, banjo-playing mountain man who is now gone: "All I have are memories, old Applejack is gone." However, she uses her music as mass media to recreate and remember this symbolic figure and his folk culture. Tellingly, she grounds her lyrics in her own life story as an authenticity claim. She explains in her autobiography that Applejack was based on a neighbor she describes as a "mountain man" whom she knew growing up and would visit, as she sang while he played banjo.[63]

Another specific example of how Parton links her "authentic" autobiography to those parts of her performance aligned more closely with the genre's folk culture roots is her release of her autobiography, *Dolly: My Life and Other Unfinished Business* (1994), as part of her promotion for her folk music album *Heartsongs: Live from Home* (1994). In that book, Parton exclaims that she had always wanted to do an acoustic album of the songs she grew up "lovin' and singin'," and describes the album's contents as songs from England, Ireland, Scotland, and Wales, as well as from the Smoky Mountains and some that she herself had written that were influenced by "all these places." Parton here gives her version of country music's origins as influenced by European folk music merged with American immigrant folk cultures. She highlights the album for its connection to her memoir, saying it pairs perfectly with her life story and that this album is the one she wants to be remembered for the most.[64] Parton thus once again links her folk music and her life story in her claims for authenticity.

Likewise, for her 1990s albums that met Americana's folk revival (as each generation seems to seek out its own folk revival), Parton heavily referenced her autobiography as the roots of her "blue mountain" style in order to claim authenticity. She engaged in genre mixing on those three albums—the bluegrass album, *The Grass Is Blue* (1999); *Little Sparrow* (2001), which included bluegrass as well as traditional Appalachian folk; and the folk and bluegrass album *Halos & Horns* (2002). She included bluegrass covers of Led Zeppelin's "Stairway to Heaven" rock song on *Halos & Horns* and a cover of Collective Soul's "Shine" alternative rock song on *Little Sparrow*.

Again, instead of Parton being a case of the folk being corrupted by the mass, her oeuvre demonstrates that the mass has the folk in it, both real and fake, both authentic and manufactured, just as Parton's work, in effect, questions the distinctions between those categories. Cultural critics Stuart Hall and Paddy Whannel have famously argued that popular music, particularly youth culture, is both art and commodity, writing that "teenage culture is a contradictory mixture of the authentic and manufactured: it is an area of self-expression for the young and a lush grazing pasture for the commercial providers."[65] That complex mixture means we must analyze the interplay between those dynamics in each case, just as we must analyze the interplay between the mass and the folk. Even though a piece of cultural expression has been commodified or commercialized, communities and listeners still make meaning out of it in unpredictable ways that are not entirely controlled by the culture industry. There is no strict dichotomy between mass and folk but instead a far more complicated interaction between the two. Other popular musicians have used their star image to enact a tension between artifice and authenticity.[66] But again, the way each artist does so is distinct and engages in its own cultural work. Each case study can be revelatory in terms of how these forces work, how the two categories intersect, and how each artist struggles with them, which tells us a far more nuanced and interesting story about country music and popular culture.

Because Parton's work and media image combine both mass and folk culture elements, she has in effect found new ways to reconcile country music's tension between the two, by bringing them together. It is important to flesh out the cultural history and context for Parton's star image as it tries to heal the tension between fake and real, the market and purity, manufactured and authentic, mass culture and folk culture by joining them.[67] Her image makes both things true at once. The most artificial persona is also the most genuine. As I noted in my introduction and explore more here, the way Parton balances her rhetoric of "real" and "fake" in her gendered persona references the long-running country genre tension between the genuine and the manufactured, a tension historians have verified in country music's authenticity narratives.[68] One of the genre's central contradictions is that country music has always been commercial, yet the nostalgia for the supposedly "pure" or non-manufactured persists, a yearning for an agricultural, premodern past even as the genre takes its place as part of mass culture.[69] Within the country genre, the rhetoric of what is "good" and "pure" is often cast in terms of artistic purity versus the market: a seemingly organic rawness versus commercial sheen, an antimodern nostalgia for rural agrarianism versus modernity and the commercialization of mass media.[70] It expresses a nostalgia for its folk culture roots, for a pastoral, premodern purity, even as it traffics in mass communication technology and is composed of the commodities and products of the mass culture industry. Country music is of course not unique in linking folk and mass cultures, as it developed from vernacular culture passed from person to person and evolved into mass culture produced and mediated via mass communication technology, but it does have its own distinctive variation on that folk-mass mixture. We see highly commercialized singers producing mass-marketed country songs while wearing cowboy hats as props to establish "authenticity" and singing about their nostalgia for a "simpler" agrarian way of life down on the farm. The genre scripts that narrative of purity onto idealizations of a rural, pastoral, agricultural way of life. Yet it stages that nostalgic fantasy via mass media, the very form that helps perpetuate the conditions of modernity that the country genre expresses alienation from in its search for the folk and the pure.[71]

We can see this contradictory dynamic recurring at key moments in country music history. That trend is not surprising, given that the rhetorical distinction between folk purity and mass culture commercialism was an imposed idea and not historically accurate.[72] Scholar Benjamin Filene has demonstrated how folklorists and music industry executives in the late nineteenth and early twentieth centuries created a "folk" distinction that was subjective and reflected their cultural values at the time.[73] Thus, from the start, the distinctions between the categories of folk and mass culture have been arbitrary and can blur quite easily.

In relevant examples of this folk-mass blurring in country music, Diane Pecknold has shown convincingly how the country music industry in the 1960s used commercialism to advance itself, often by creating images of professional musicians and respectable, "affluent" working-class fans (even though the genre started out with broader audience appeals), which it used to counterbalance negative stereotypes of "hillbillies" or backwoods country bumpkins. Meanwhile, the fans used what they understood to be self-consciously theatrical representations of a rural past in order to create an identity for themselves (since many of these fans were rural-to-urban migrants from the South in the 1920s through the 1960s). While traditional histories suggest that country fans were resistant to commercialism in their embrace of traditional, even past-obsessed culture, Pecknold demonstrates that it would be more accurate to say that fans were aware of commercialism and often embraced it because the mass media, especially radio, is precisely what allowed them to engage with a national imagined community formed through appreciation of this music. That paradoxical merger of tradition with modernity is what defines the genre.[74]

Likewise, I offer here an especially apt case study of how country music has evolved as an intricate mixture of folk and mass culture: Johnny Cash and the figure of the singing cowboy. In twentieth-century country music, Western music and singing cowboys became popular in part through 1930s Hollywood films (with Hollywood's singing cowboys including stars like Roy Rogers and Gene Autry). Country music's Western images and influences came from a combination of earlier nineteenth-century folk culture along with these movies, another example of folk culture mixing with twentieth-century mass media fantasies. Received as part of the 1960s folk revival movement, Johnny Cash's Western concept album, *Johnny Cash Sings the Ballads of the True West* (1965), illustrates how the tension between folk culture and mass culture is foundational to the Western genre. In his liner notes, Cash writes that he was trying to return to original folk sources rather than simply using the Hollywood film fantasies in order to recover the "true West." He wants his album to tell "the cowboy's story" through "legends, songs and stories," to get "a glimpse *beyond* the movies and television, back to when a few tales could show us THE TRUE WEST." Cash is interested in dispelling myths and getting beyond the mass media's spin on the cowboy. Yet when he tries to find "pure" folk sources, he can actually only locate sources that reflect the folk culture–mass culture mix. He searched for folk culture sources by reading John Lomax, Carl Sandburg, and every issue of *True West* magazine, but he also consulted Tex Ritter, who was a Hollywood singing cowboy as well as a folk music preservationist and stylist. In both the album's liner notes and a spoken word recording entitled "Reflections," Cash describes his research as what is essentially a folk-mass culture mix. He explains that he updated the sounds in the songs to a twentieth-century mass media context, because the songs were "meant to be heard" via radio and sound recordings. Detailing how he updated Western classics, Cash describes himself as adapting the spirit of "the true West" to a twentieth-century mass media context.[75]

Cash was using mass media to be nostalgic for an earlier folk culture that was pushed to the margins by that mass media. Cash's description of the appropriateness of using modern media to deliver his incarnation of the structure of feeling of the Old West speaks to one of the central contradictions in country music. Despite its investment in rural origins, it was originated in the 1920s by the decidedly urban forces of recording technology and radio. Bill Malone traces the genre's ongoing fascination with the cowboy to the same nineteenth-century sources that produced twentieth-century commercial country music, such as changes to American life after the Civil War, industrialization and a developing market economy, urbanization, wage labor, migration and dislocation, and later nostalgia for a supposedly "simpler" society.[76]

Within this larger context of the folk culture–mass culture mixture in country music, Parton provides a fascinating case study for understanding this cultural tension because she is one of the most commercially success country musicians of all time. She generates a great deal of mass culture in the form of mass-marketed products, from albums to tours to Dollywood. Yet, at the same time, she continues to use her life story to insist on her organic connection to the folk music roots of country music.

Ultimately, it is in Parton's enactment of gender that she troubles the larger categories of folk and mass, authenticity and the market. Her gender performance challenges the category of gender as well, instead of leaving her trapped in the stereotypical imagery of class and gender that she invokes. Parton's work is transgressive not simply because she exposes gender as a set of socially constructed practices and behaviors (hers is just more elaborate but everyone else's is just as artificial), but because her gender performance is deeply contextualized in terms of country music themes and history. Scholars have shown how gender role stereotypes are often defined by their opposite, as a dominant version of masculinity or femininity gets defined against marginalized versions, often in terms of class or race hierarchies.[77] Again, more broadly, Parton's gender performance sheds light on this dynamic, because within white, working-class gender codes, she not only questions the distinction between a privileged "pure" versus a "fallen" version of white, working-class femininity but embodies both at once.

She places her composite version of working-class femininity in opposition to a middle-class womanhood, using a subordinated working-class femininity to critique middle-class norms.

Case Study: "Backwoods Barbie"

To substantiate how Parton's gender image has this multilayered signification, let me return to a closer reading of the "Backwoods Barbie" music video (2008). The video's visual imagery establishes links between Dolly the star and Parton as a young girl in Appalachia. As Parton sings about growing up poor and wanting to be pretty like Barbie or models in catalogues, the video opens on a childhood Parton (a role performed by a young blonde actor) as a mountain girl playing outside an approximation of her "Tennessee Mountain Home." The environments appear in black and white, while the images of Parton as the girl and as the adult are in vibrant full color, underscoring "Dolly" as spectacle. The young Parton plays with makeup she culls from nature, directly referencing stories from Parton's autobiography, as the child picks berries for lipstick and blush and uses burnt matches for eye shadow. A mother figure, pictured in black and white, looks on with amusement from the front porch. The video juxtaposes shots of the girl with a sequence of Parton walking outside that same mountain home. She is dressed in a highly campy mountain girl outfit: a tight-fitting, low-cut red gingham shirt; dangling suspenders; red gingham-trimmed pedal pusher jeans (a campy recycling of a 1950s style); red gingham-trimmed five-inch heels; and purposefully exaggerated makeup (even more than usual).

The video intercuts with these images another sequence of Parton walking down a street lined by other street performers, and the implication is that she is enacting a performance character, just like they are; they are all performers together. The fact that she is stepping on the stars of the Hollywood Walk of Fame, which includes her own star, underlines how much she is singing about her own life and her experience of stardom. Her costuming pulls in an image of prostitution, visually referencing a streetwalker, with her leopard-print, low-cut mini-dress and long, sheer pink robe and heavy makeup. The street performers she passes speak to entertainment broadly defined, a panoply from show business. They include a gold-painted man doing robot dances, a young female street busker with a guitar, a mime, a contortionist, a juggler, and celebrity blogger Perez Hilton, a well-known out gay male icon who visually references gay camp.

Like Parton, the street performers all appear in color against the black-and-white backdrop. The implication is that Parton is merely a performer, just like them, even as they might be disparaged as "circus freaks" or struggling artists. When she stops at the display window of Frederick's of Hollywood, her sad look critiquing any degradation of the lingerie-clad mannequins or use of them as stereotyped symbols of fallen women, her lyrics cajole: "I've always been misunderstood by how I look / Don't judge me by the cover, 'cause I'm a real good book." She insists that she is not as "shallow as she looks," and even "Backwoods Barbies" "deserve a second chance." The video ends with a doubled image, Parton in color in the foreground, the "Tennessee Mountain Home" in the background in black and white, the mountain mother on the front porch. The combination underscores the idea that Parton takes her girl self with her and confirms her link to the pastoral nostalgia of the sentimental mountain mother figure and the Tennessee Mountain Home.

Parton as character is both the daydreaming girl and the woman, juxtaposing the culturally validated pure childhood innocence expected of girls with the marginalized, "trashy" grown-up singer. Parton uses the privileged gender performance trope (angelic mountain girl) to salvage the disparaged one (streetwalker). Again, her juxtaposition reveals them to be equally constructed gender performances. Through her mass media popular culture expression, Parton articulates her own history and links it to a larger history: a mountain past that functions as an imagined community and an idealized region. However, it is precisely because of modernity and mass culture that "Dolly Parton" as multimedia superstar can never fully return to that past—either her own or the mythic one she inscribes by using idealized images of Appalachia—because she is too famous to "go home" again to childhood innocence.

To address the song musically, in very general terms, "Backwoods Barbie" is a confessional, simple, direct song that focuses more attention on the text than on the music. It functions more as a statement than an artistic display, which means that her thematic message is foregrounded. That is fitting since the piece is her fullest articulation in song about her infamous media image, as she pleas for listeners to "take me as I am." Parton engineers the whole piece to be transparently "simple" and is in full control of her voice, its direct projection of the text, and the stripped down instrumental parts. Several specific aspects of the song focus attention on the words and singing rather than on the music. Parton sings on her own, with no instruments doubling her part, and she is only ever doubled with backups of her own voice. She delivers much of her text in a recitation-like tone. The music is strikingly simple, with little of real melodic or instrumental interest, such that there is no distraction from the text and message. A "boom-chicka-boom" rhythm is maintained throughout, with no deviations from the simple duple rhythm. During the instrumental interlude, the guitar merely outlines the same chords of the preceding music. The piece's range is quite limited, as Parton remains within an octave, and she also limits the decorative turns, twists, and flourishes that she often applies to melodies (and is known for doing) and does not use any upward modulation. These features would allow audiences easily to sing along, such as those fans who might identify with her. The song thus foregrounds Parton's statement about her media image.[78] It also underlines the theme of return, as Parton returned to her original sound for this song, deploying the same kind of instrumental backup and accompanying style of her earliest songs (whereas her album prior to this one, *Those Were the Days* [2005], was composed of her covers of 1960s and 1970s folk and pop songs, singing with some of the original artists).

Although Parton wrote "Backwoods Barbie" for the *9 to 5* Broadway musical (2008), she infuses well-known aspects of her own autobiography here and in the sixteen other new songs she wrote for the show, merging the "Doralee" character with Parton's own life narratives to a greater extent than in the earlier film version, which was famous for slamming workplace discrimination and sexual harassment. Linking herself and Doralee, Parton asserted, "It's all about people judging you by how you look. The way I look is just a country girl's idea of glam. In *9 to 5*, they make fun of Doralee because they think she looks like a tramp and has to be sleeping with the boss, who pretends she is." Defending her image against stereotypical assumptions, Parton also compared herself to the Barbie image, playing both sides of that stereotype by upholding the objectified image but emphasizing its artificiality. Discussing the song "Backwoods Barbie," Parton says, "We released it as a single on Barbie's 50th birthday. It couldn't have been better timing. Me and Barbie look pretty good for our age—I'm a bit older—and we're both made out of plastic."[79]

The "Backwoods Barbie" song and video thus epitomize how Parton bridges folk and mass culture. It is significant that Parton finds "natural," "authentic" inspiration for her love of makeup (a girl finding berries in the woods for blush to make her "country girl's idea of glam"). She adds to that a mass culture inspiration (Hollywood models, women in catalogues). In the midst of this layering of mass culture and autobiography, Parton writes the song as an unadorned, straightforward, traditional country music song rather than country pop, and she musically references the folk roots of the country genre. Her song mixes folk and mass culture just as her rhetoric tries to balance them, resolving the folk-mass (real-fake) tension by claiming both things are true: she is both real and fake at the same time. She suggests there is a folk origin to the mass culture aspects of her work, implying that the two categories are related and spring from the same organic folk sources. To detail Parton's own elaborate case of gender performance as both genuine and fake, I turn in the next chapter to a closer exploration of the earliest stage of her career, when she was forming her gendered media image and her reaction to gender stereotypes. I explore the longer cultural context for the hillbilly trope she uses and precisely how she depicts her own version of that trope.

Notes

1. Parton, *Dolly*, 309.

2. Following popular music studies, I use the term "genre" to refer to the category of country music, although musicology terminology would refer to it more specifically as a "style" of vernacular music. See Echard, *Neil Young*, 43–45.

3. A portion of my Parton argument in this chapter appeared in article form in Edwards, "'Backwoods Barbie'"; Edwards, "Mass Art"; and Edwards, "Country Music and Class."

4. Nash, *Dolly*; Cardwell, *Words and Music*; Miller, *Smart Blonde*.

5. For key articles and book chapters, see Wilson, "Mountains"; Fox, *Natural Acts*, 138–142; and Whiteley, *Women and Popular Music*, 17, 154, 158. In Cecelia Tichi's larger study of country music's "folk poetry" connection to the broader history of American thought, she richly reads Parton's "My Tennessee Mountain Home" and "Coat of Many Colors" in relation to American ideals of nature and home. Tichi, *High Lonesome*, 25–32, 49–50. See also Hardie, "Torque"; Morris, *Persistence of Sentiment*, 173–208; Hubbs, "'Jolene'"; Heidemann, "Remarkable Women"; and Holmlund, *Impossible Bodies*, 157–170.

6. Wilson, "Mountains."

7. Fox, *Natural Acts*, 138–142.

8. Whiteley proposes that Parton's gender performance reinforces a strict gender binary in country music, but recent work questions that binary in country, finding more gender nuance historically than critics once thought. Pecknold and McCusker, *Country Boys*; Whiteley, *Women and Popular Music*, 17, 154, 158.

9. See, for example, Kaplan, *Rocking*; Lewis, *Gender Politics*; Whiteley, *Women and Popular Music*, 136–151; Whiteley, *Sexing the Groove*; Halberstam, *Gaga Feminism*; and Kumari, "'Yoü and I.'"

10. Popular musicians have often used exaggeration and parody to draw attention to the artifice of gender norms. See Shugart and Waggoner, "A Bit Much."

11. Parton, *Dolly*, 309.

12. Bergman, *Camp Grounds*, 14. For example, camp performance like drag in gay male subculture has been appropriated by mainstream culture, which coopts and undermines the mode's political critiques. On camp's background, see Robertson,

Guilty Pleasures; Ross, *No Respect*; Sontag "Notes"; Meyer, *Politics*; and Newton, *Mother Camp*.

13. Morris, *Persistence of Sentiment*.

14. Sontag, "Notes."

15. Critics have often read popular feminism in Parton's pro-women songs and industry practices. Neal, *Jimmie Rodgers*, 28–107; Bufwack and Oermann, *Finding Her Voice*, 360–387; Fillingim, *Redneck Liberation*, 118, 124, 141, 143.

16. Note that throughout this book, I use limited direct quotations of song lyrics in order to stay within academic fair-use copyright guidelines. As Nadine Hubbs argues in her article on "Jolene," the lyrics can be interpreted as having a homoerotic subtext because the female speaker focuses on how she admires her female rival's beauty. Hubbs suggests that the song is subversive because it expresses homosocial or homoerotic themes, which she argues are common in country music lyrics. In contrast, Kate Heidemann suggests that the song's vocal approach and composition, as compared to Loretta Lynn's "Fist City," signals aspirations to normative white, middle-class femininity. Hubbs, "'Jolene'"; Heidemann, "Remarkable Women."

17. Neal, *Jimmie Rodgers*, 28–107.

18. "Dolly Parton Releases New Single." Parton explained why she started her own independent label: "I put it on my own label because many of the majors really didn't want me because of my age, thinking I was over. But I feel different about that. I figured the major labels are pretty much a thing of the past anyway, kind of like they thought I was. The way music is being played today, why not make all the money, if there's any money to be made. I'd rather have all of something than some of nothing. So I hired Danny Nozell to help manage me and all the things concerning me with all the new ideas. And with his knowledge of the new age and the team that he's put together, I just didn't see how I could miss."

19. For an overview of female images in country music performance, see Bufwack and Oermann, *Finding Her Voice*.

20. Ibid.; McCusker, *Lonesome Cowgirls*; Malone, *Singing Cowboys*; Malone, *Country Music U.S.A.*; Peterson, *Creating Country Music*.

21. McCusker, *Lonesome Cowgirls*, 28–49.

22. Rather interview, in *Unspoiled Country*.

23. Parton, *Dream More*, 59–60.

24. Kristine M. McCusker cites Dorothy Scarborough's use of the term "contemporary ancestors" in *A Songcatcher in the Southern Mountains* (New York: Columbia University Press, 1937). McCusker, *Lonesome Cowgirls*, 14.

25. Notably, one such press account is in the Andy Warhol interview with her, which speaks to pop art and his fascination with her kitsch excess. Moynihan and Warhol, "Dolly Parton."

26. Rogers, *Country Music Message*, 17–18.

27. *Barbara Walters Special*.

28. Ching, *Wrong's What I Do Best*.

29. Parton's break from Wagoner can be dated from either 1974, when she left his show and released "I Will Always Love You," or from the end of her contractual arrangement with him as her producer in 1976. See Flippo, "Dolly Parton."

30. "Music," *Time.*

31. Parton, *Dream More,* 53.

32. Parton, *Dolly,* 186.

33. *Nightline,* 26 November 2012.

34. Robertson, *Guilty Pleasures.*

35. Ibid., 142.

36. Bergman, *Camp Grounds,* 14.

37. George H. Lewis argues that Parton is the best example of a country performer playing a rube as tongue-in-cheek parody. Lewis, "Lap Dancer," 165.

38. Hubbs, *Rednecks, Queers, and Country Music.*

39. *Watch What Happens Live,* 17 May 2016.

40. Robertson, *Guilty Pleasures,* 145.

41. May, *Homeward Bound.*

42. Leppert and Lipsitz, "Age."

43. Edwards, *Johnny Cash and the Paradox of American Identity.*

44. Bufwack and Oermann, *Finding Her Voice.*

45. Richard Peterson has argued for "hard-core country" as the "roots of country" in the "raw" singing style, "rough" life experiences, and lack of artifice in artists like Hank Williams or Loretta Lynn. "Soft-shell country" is "sell-out" pop of the post–World War II Nashville Sound and its pop-country offspring, from Jim Reeves to Kenny Rogers and beyond. Peterson, *Creating Country Music.* Critics have examined the problematic gendering of the "hard country" discourse. Ching, *Wrong's What I Do Best*; Leppert and Lipsitz, "Age"; Sanjek, Foreword.

46. Sanjek, Foreword.

47. Zwonitzer with Hirshberg, *Will You.*

48. Morris, *Persistence of Sentiment.*

49. Ching, *Wrong's What I Do Best*; Leppert and Lipsitz, "Age"; Sanjek, Foreword.

50. Huyssen, *After the Great Divide.*

51. Neal, *Country Music,* 323.

52. Kimmel, *Manhood,* 231.

53. Malone, *Don't Get,* ix. On broader audiences, see Huber, *Linthead Stomp,* and Wolfe, "Postlude."

54. Lewis, "Tension," 209; Buckley, "Country Music."

55. Williams, *Long Revolution,* 64.

56. Modleski, *Feminism*; McRobbie, "Post-Feminism."

57. The plastic surgery question speaks to a longer scholarly conversation about fake versus real and authenticity in the genre. In my earlier articles, I argue for Parton's unique bridging of both the fake as mass culture and the real as folk culture, and how she makes that fake-real mixture her version of authenticity. Edwards, "Mass Art"; Edwards "'Backwoods Barbie.'" For other scholarly takes on this larger issue, see Wilson, "Mountains"; Peterson, *Creating Country Music*; Ching, *Wrong's What I Do Best*; Fox, *Natural Acts*; Neal, *Jimmie Rodgers*; Morris, *Persistence of Sentiment*; and Hubbs, "'Jolene.'" On Parton's plastic surgery, see Gardner, "Grit," and Edelman, "Why." In a later article, Samantha Christensen avers that Parton

has a conflicted feminist identity because she advocates women's empowerment but participates in feminine beauty ideals. Christensen, "'Where It Counts I'm Real': The Complexities of Dolly Parton's Feminist Voice," in *Walking the Line: Country Music Lyricists and American Culture*, ed. Thomas Alan Holmes and Roxanne Harde (Lanham, Md.: Lexington Books, 2013), 163–174. Rebecca Scofield contends that Parton uses plastic surgery to symbolize rural authenticity but contradicts it with her dieting practices (starvation, food wasting) that oppose her own rural background (mountain poverty, food insecurity). Rebecca Scofield, "'Nipped, Tucked, or Sucked': Dolly Parton and the Construction of the Authentic Body," *Journal of Popular Culture* 49, no. 3 (June 2016): 660–677. Kathleen Rowe lists Parton among performers, such as Arnold Schwarzenegger, Sylvester Stallone, and Tammy Faye Bakker, who feature bodily exaggeration that can be read in potentially socially disruptive ways. Rowe, *Unruly*, 33.

58. *The Tonight Show Starring Johnny Carson*, 19 January 1977; *The Tonight Show Starring Johnny Carson*, 17 February 1977.

59. As I discuss in chapter 5, I would analogize Parton to Lady Gaga in some ways. For a reading of Gaga as a paradigm of gender fluidity, see Halberstam, *Gaga Feminism*.

60. Parton, *Dolly*, 56–57.

61. Quotation is from Bufwack and Oermann, *Finding Her Voice*, 362.

62. Lipsitz, *Time Passages*, 22, 3.

63. Parton, *Dolly*, 65–67.

64. Ibid., 311.

65. Hall and Whannel, *Popular Arts*, 269–283.

66. Marshall, *Celebrity*, 186, 198; Shank, "'That Wild.'"

67. Richard Dyer has argued that twentieth-century star images attempt to resolve the ideological contradictions in capitalism and modernity. I suggest that Parton's star image attempts to resolve a particular contradiction in that context, the folk versus mass culture tension in country music. Dyer, *Stars*.

68. Ching, *Wrong's What I Do Best*; Peterson, *Creating Country Music*; Jensen, *Nashville Sound*; Fox, "Jukebox of History"; Pecknold, *Selling Sound*; McCusker and Pecknold, *A Boy Named Sue*.

69. While rooted in folk culture, country music has always been commercial from the start, thus the market-versus-purity binary in country music authenticity narratives is a fantasy not based on historical fact. Malone, *Singing Cowboys*, 68; Fox, *Real Country*.

70. Ching, *Wrong's What I Do Best*; Peterson, *Creating Country Music*; Jensen, *Nashville Sound*; Pecknold, *Selling Sound*; Fox, "Jukebox of History," 54. My use of the term "modernity" refers to the conditions of social life stemming from the rise of capitalism and industrialization.

71. Ching, *Wrong's What I Do Best*; Jensen, *Nashville Sound*, 15; Pecknold, *Selling Sound*.

72. As historian Bill C. Malone has shown, folk music did involve commercial relations and was always simultaneously folk and popular; song collectors and academics in the late nineteenth and early twentieth centuries imposed a conception of

a somehow "pure" folk music in opposition to commercial music. Malone, *Singing Cowboys*, 68.

73. Filene, *Romancing the Folk*.

74. For fuller discussion of this issue in Pecknold, see my review of her book *Selling Sound* in *Journal of American Studies* 44, no. 1 (April 2010): E13.

75. In the "Reflections" track on that album, Cash says, "We aren't sorry for the modern sounds and modern arrangements on classics like 'I Ride an Old Paint' or 'The Streets of Laredo'; after all, they were meant to be heard on twentieth-century record players and transistor radios! For today that same west wind is blowing, although buckboards and saddles are lying out there turning to dust or crumbling from dry rot."

76. Malone, *Singing Cowboys*, 7.

77. For an overview of emphasized femininity as a gender stereotype, see Connell, *Masculinities*, and Kimmel, *Gendered Society*.

78. My thanks to my colleagues musicologists Denise Von Glahn and Michael Broyles for discussing Parton's music with me.

79. Haun, "Dolly."

My Tennessee Mountain Home
Early Parton and Authenticity Narratives

Well, it's a compliment to me. I mean we were really Hill. Billies.
To me that's not an insult. We were just mountain people.
We were really redneck, roughneck, hillbilly people. And I'm
proud of it. "White trash!" I am. People always say "Aren't you
insulted when people call you white trash?" I say, "Well it depends
on who's calling me white trash and how they mean it."

—Dolly Parton

Parton has both questioned and embodied her hillbilly tramp image since the
early stages of her career, and she has observed how her hyperbolic image itself
has helped her establish a career in the first place. She notes the complicated cultural politics involved in that trope, as I discuss below in a cultural history of the
hillbilly. The way Parton frames the early stages of her career reflects the gender
performance model I have been tracing, in which she uplifts a negative image of
femininity by linking it to a positive one. As she began to develop her signature
campy image more fully during her early solo albums in the 1970s, for example,
she was transgressive because she recuperated the hillbilly tramp by joining it
with the innocent mountain girl image. Even at this early stage of her career,

she pointed out double standards in which male performers could sing about sex and appear virile while female singers were criticized as loose or promiscuous if they did so. Even prior to that, however, she was already using campy and ironic elements in her imagery as a performer in high school. Parton both uses and critiques the trope of female singers as sex objects, and the payoff is that through her ironic exaggeration, she is not trapped by the images of excessive femininity that she invokes, instead making them campy and transgressive. Further, she uses her references to her folk culture and life story to justify her gender critiques.

In this chapter, I trace the story of her gender performance in this early period of her career, from her earliest professional performances in 1956 at age ten up until the first album she produced herself, *New Harvest . . . First Gathering* (1977), after she left Porter Wagoner and began charting her crossover musical direction. In particular, I address her use of hillbilly imagery in a case study reading of her autobiographical album, *My Tennessee Mountain Home* (1973), which represents a key early treatment of that figure, and I analyze the gender themes in her song lyrics during this period. I also place her treatment of the hillbilly trope in the context of a longer cultural history of that figure. In summary, this era includes her start in 1956 on the *Cas Walker Show* in Knoxville, her teenage efforts to expand her singing and songwriting opportunities in Nashville, her early solo efforts with producer Fred Foster, and her stint as the "girl singer" on *The Porter Wagoner Show* (1967–1974). That era includes her duets with Wagoner; her famous solo albums during that time, such as *Joshua* (1971), *Coat of Many Colors* (1971), *My Tennessee Mountain Home*, and *Jolene* (1974); her departure from Wagoner's show in 1974 and her release of "I Will Always Love You"; and her last work with Wagoner credited as her producer (1976). Clearly the most important developments in her career came after she moved to Nashville permanently at age eighteen in 1964, but her earlier childhood and teenaged professional efforts form a relevant backdrop for her later career.

During this era, Parton's media image evolved from "girl singer" to her signature Daisy Mae ironic tramp look, but it is important to clarify that even some of her earlier performances included some of these ironic elements, since she was purposefully doing things like teasing her hair up in an outdated style in order to get attention. Her musical output in this period makes important arguments about the mountain pastoral and her country music authenticity claims; it features famous, popular autobiographical songs about her childhood in the Smoky Mountains that are both celebrations of the pastoral and rejections of any false nostalgia for poverty or idealizations of rural mountain culture. Her lyrics from this era also focus thematic attention on gender relations; it is her autobiographical lyrics about Appalachia that provide the foundation for her gender themes, because they use that homegrown wisdom idea to justify her arguments for female agency in a popular feminism vein.

While her gender politics are at times thorny, with a few songs perceived to have antifeminist elements, such as holding mistresses responsible for straying husbands (most famously in "Jolene"), the overwhelming majority of Parton songs critique sexual double standards and gendered stereotypes. She decries how pregnant unwed mothers were treated as social outcasts while the fathers denied any responsibility, or how women desperate to earn a living resorted to prostitution while the men involved did not face the same social vilification. In playful answer songs to the battle of the sexes, Parton calls out cheating husbands, insisting that women are smart enough to realize what is happening and seize their own freedom if they choose to stray or to leave their husbands. Some of her most incendiary songs are positive portraits of female characters who express their own sexual desires, articulating female sexuality in ways that reject middle-class domesticity in terms of chasteness or propriety.

In terms of the larger gender tropes I have been tracing in her work, Parton's songs in this period of career begin to formulate both her version of the mountain girl and her unusual version of the tramp. Some of her early songs idealize the mountain girl, but others include critiques of that romanticization, instead noting the hard domestic labor of the mountain women she saw around her and the gendered inequities they had to contend with, from straying husbands to frequent pregnancies to struggles for income. She began to include more songs about the tramp or fallen woman as she progressed in her songwriting. Her lyrics increasingly question the social ostracism of the tramp figure, often by challenging how men involved in sexual relationships with promiscuous women or prostitutes are not held socially accountable in the same way. As part of her gender themes, her songs also question depictions of female promiscuity in general, decrying how women are blamed for being sexually active while men are not. Most transgressive is her positive portrayal of women talking about their own sexual desires, because she normalizes the idea that women can express and control their own sexuality.

Importantly, the core of the rich, highly patterned, and often-repeated mythology that Parton has developed out of her life story is found here in the earliest period of her career and with famed albums like *My Tennessee Mountain Home*. Of course, her "authenticity narrative" of her Appalachian roots and her gender themes would find even fuller expression in her later autobiography as part of her promotion for her *Heartsongs* album (1994) and her refocusing more on country music elements after her pop crossover period. For example, as I discuss in chapter 4, it would take until her autobiography for Parton to tell her full story of "finding God" and believing that he wanted her to play music and be a "sexual being," making a stunning religious justification for female sexuality and for her ambitious music career. Meanwhile, in her songwriting in this earlier era, Parton suggests that just as male singers could sing about sexual desire, female singers should be able to do the same; she legitimates female sexuality, either by normalizing it or by linking it to a sympathetic natural world in her mountain home setting.

Biographical Contexts

A key background context for this epoch of Parton's career is her earliest career breakthrough in which she was associated with Wagoner, her departure from that show, and her efforts to create crossover solo opportunities for herself. After she left her work with producer Fred Foster at Monument for Porter Wagoner and RCA, Parton's first successes came via Wagoner duets, with hits such as "Holding on to Nothin'" (1968) and an award as the Country Music Association's (CMA) Vocal Group of the Year (1968). Parton's efforts to generate solo hits during this time were at first not as successful, with Parton's first solo single for RCA, "Just Because I'm a Woman" (1968), only reaching number seventeen on the country charts.

Attempting to produce a bigger hit, Wagoner persuaded a reluctant Parton to cover "Muleskinner Blues" (1970), a Jimmie Rodgers hit that went to number three on the country charts and received a Grammy nomination. Parton changed the lyrics to depict a female muledriver, and she used a full band and a whip-cracking sound effect, as well as her yodeling. There had already been many male covers of the song, but Rose Maddox was the only woman to have earlier covered the song with her family band, Maddox Brothers and Rose (1948). In her version, Parton sang, "I'm a *lady* muleskinner," and she wrote a new verse at the end about a waitress angry because her man is taking her money, calling him a "no-good man" and saying she would prefer to go be a muleskinner. As Jocelyn Neal has demonstrated, Parton bucked "girl singer" conventions by yodeling, hollering aloud, and using a two-finger wolf whistle, and her cover song was received as empowering for women and a protofeminist statement in the context of second-wave feminism at that time.[1] Neal argues that Parton's cover would have been interpreted in terms of country traditionalism and epitomized the elements of classic country music in the sense that it referenced country music traditions, incorporated pop music as well as the crossover Nashville Sound, and explored social issues, here gender roles.[2]

Parton went on to have many successful solo singles and albums, writing a number of her most famous songs during this period to increasing success. She was named CMA Female Vocalist of the Year in 1975 and 1976. During the 1974–1976 period, Parton was already charting her own musical direction more fully, having left Wagoner's television and road show in 1974. While she characterizes the process in her autobiography as finishing out her contractual obligation to Wagoner as her producer in 1976, some observers have argued that she was slowly planning her break with him, since she wanted to produce her own music in her own vision and incorporate more pop and rock.[3] Parton formed her own touring Traveling Family Band (1974–1976), which included siblings and cousins, but decided she needed to disband that "incarnation" of herself in 1976 in order to move in a new musical direction, incorporating more of the pop and rock crossover elements into her music and look.[4] She had her own syndicated television show, *Dolly!*, which ran during the 1976–1977 season in 130 markets, with 9 million viewers each week. Shot at Opryland, it had Parton often covering pop music and hosting guests, many from other genres. While it was meant to broaden her appeal beyond a country fan base, it only lasted one season, and Parton requested a release from her contract since she felt the show was gimmicky and did not represent her accurately or allow her to launch her crossover career. She said, "It wasn't capturing me the way I really am."[5]

She famously made a series of major career changes in 1976, going to meet with RCA executives in New York to ask for their support for her crossover into pop while maintaining her country fan base, and she received their assurances. They told her they were far more invested in keeping her than in keeping Wagoner. Beyond suffering Wagoner's $3 million lawsuit against her, which was settled for $1 million, Parton also discovered that Wagoner had misled her when he implied that RCA would not want to keep her as a recording artist without him. She signed with Hollywood manager Sandy Gallin, of Katz-Gallin, in 1976, and her new management helped her form her new band, which she dubbed Gypsy Fever (1977–1979), featuring musicians who could play country, rock, pop, and any other genre in which Parton wanted to express herself. For the first time, Parton was able fully to self-produce her own album separately from Wagoner, instead coproducing with her new musical director, Gregg Perry, *New Harvest . . . First Gathering*. That album included the song "Applejack," on which Parton had a number of famous traditional country performers singing backup, including Roy Acuff, Kitty Wells, Chet Atkins, Minnie Pearl, Ernest Tubb, Grandpa Jones, Ramona Jones, Carl and Pearl Butler, Wilma Lee and Stoney Cooper, the Willis Brothers, Bashful Brother Oswald, Joe and Rose Lee Maphis, Kirk McGee, Hubert Gregory and the Fruit Jar Drinkers, Johnny Wright, her road manager (and former Wagoner Show Wagonmasters band member) Don Warden, and her parents, Lee and Avie Lee Parton. Some observers argued that the star-studded song was Parton's effort to buffer her from criticisms that she was leaving country behind and abandoning Nashville. Parton then entered fully into her highly successful pop crossover efforts with *Here You Come Again* (1977), which reached platinum status, selling over a million copies.

Gender Performance History and Media Image

In terms of Parton's evolving gender performance during this early era of her career, she engaged with several different kinds of gender tropes and images common in country music performance history. In her stage persona and image, she incorporated various aspects of the mountain girl, the girl singer, a glitzier and more sexualized show queen image, and even some elements of rock style in her Gypsy Fever incarnation, all prior to her more glamorous pop crossover look. She also incorporated her own camp and ironic aspects throughout this time in distinctive ways.

What is particularly telling about the evolution of her gender performance is how Parton gradually merged elements of the mountain girl image with elements of her more sexualized, "town tramp" image, and how she used her autobiographical songs and narratives to bring those two opposing images together. Again, what Parton did to balance the mountain girl and town tramp elements is distinctive, because even during this early period, she domesticated the tramp image through her autobiographical narratives, explaining the "trashy" element as a beauty image from her childhood. Thus, she distanced herself from the trashiness and insisted that her use of it was authentic and proved that she had not sold out.

In later autobiographical accounts, and thus as part of her image construction, Parton says she identified as a tomboy during her childhood, a gender performance she marks as entirely in keeping with her mountain farm upbringing, running in the woods and roughhousing with her brothers. Parton observes that she moved out of her tomboy phase as a preteen, when she was eager to wear cosmetics, which she had to hide from her disapproving father and to improvise from readily available materials like berries and matches. While she began singing professionally with the Cas Walker show at age ten, Parton had been singing as a group with her sisters in churches prior to that time, and she had also sometimes appeared on Walker's show with school classmates since age eight. She recalls that when she began singing as a regular on his show, she was no longer embodying a tomboy persona during her Walker performances, and she expresses her awareness of dressing for audience reaction. For example, she describes consciously donning ragged clothes to look like a "mountain waif" on trips to Knoxville when she used to busk on the street when not singing on the Walker television and radio show. She later penned the song "Nickels and Dimes," co-written with her brother Floyd, about that experience.

As a teen, she wanted to wear flashy makeup and tight clothes. She describes as "trashy" her inspiration for her clothes and makeup choices, suggesting that the look epitomizes a southern, white, working-class, "redneck" or "hillbilly" sensibility, with big hair and lots of makeup. However, she seems fully aware of how her performance persona during that time was explicitly a performance; as I discussed earlier, in high school, she incorporated camp elements into her look in order to get attention and to stand out from others, as when she teased her hair up higher in an outdated style. That look is campy in the sense that it consciously recycles an outmoded style, thus drawing attention to itself as an ostentatious piece of artifice and creating ironic distance. Also while in high school, she designed some of her own flashy clothes, and her mother helped make them, ranging from bell bottoms to dresses, jeans, and shirts, and her classmates remember that she was always know for wearing tight clothes and short dresses, while she did not wear low-cut dresses at that time. Nash argues that Parton had begun to develop her "look" by her junior year of high school and more fully by her senior year, and that she also favored the bouffant hairdo because she wanted to appear taller than her five feet size. While some of her Cas Walker bandmates argue that she did begin wearing wigs during her teen years, and that she always wore tight clothes and short skirts, others insist that she had not yet fully incorporated wigs into her look. Parton herself marks her early time after moving to Nashville as the time when she began experimenting more with wigs.[6] While the exact dating of her Parton "look" does not matter, it is important to establish that she was already authoring her own look, not later handlers or producers.

After Parton moved to Nashville, she continued to try teased up hair and tight clothes, but she had not yet fully developed her signature look of the campy country girl sexpot. During her time with producer Fred Foster, he advised her on clothes, hair, and makeup, even hiring a theater teacher to train her in self-presentation and in clearer enunciation, although Foster has also insisted that Parton is the one who developed her own image. In his liner notes for her album with him as producer, *Hello, I'm Dolly* (1967), Foster compares her to Jean Harlowe and Marilyn Monroe, already framing her as a fantasy version of femininity, dubbing her a mysterious sex symbol and linking her to movie stars.[7] These comments reflect a gendered marketing, although the album cover photo places her in a more subdued image and setting. On the cover, she is posed under a willow tree as she stares at the camera, the cover picture a close-up of her face, with a slight smile, wearing an orange turtleneck shirt and white jacket, her hair teased up somewhat but appearing more natural than in later incarnations.

When she went on Wagoner's show, she was framed as the girl singer who wore respectable cocktail dresses that were demure but tightly fitted. She gradually incorporated more glitzy, flashy elements, such as the rhinestones Wagoner himself was so known for, and using more wigs and elaborate hair and makeup. When Wagoner later attempted to claim some credit for her image, Parton and others insisted that she had created her own image. Parton argued that Wagoner simply gave her the salary that let her fulfill her personal ideas for her clothes and look: "I don't know what people mean about Porter creatin' my sex image. All he did for me was put me on television, and I just showed it off. He didn't try to mold me into any kind of image. He just happened to like me as a person and the way I was. Plus he happened to know I was stubborn, and I dressed as I wanted to. But anyway, I guess because of him, I got to makin' enough money where I could buy the things."[8] In such disavowals of Wagoner as a controlling influence, Parton adamantly insists on the sincerity and authenticity of her look, claiming that she is expressing who she is and how she chooses to look. For Parton, the sincerity always grounds the flashy, "fake" look.

Other industry executives corroborate Parton's view of her own self-creation while also noting the difference between the image and the real person. In an interview, Foster explains, "She was always very, very smart. She has created the Dolly persona, and it works for her—kind of like Diamond Lil or a modern-day Mae West. She created that image. If you ever get serious with Dolly and sit down and talk to her, she's slightly different. She's the salt of the earth. Dolly is a very spiritual girl."[9] Foster notes her ability to cross over into different genres and compete with Hollywood movie stars, even while maintaining her sincerity as "salt of the earth." In a similar interview, Bob Beckham, who was the president of Combine Music, insists on her own self-creation: "I don't think anybody molded Dolly's sex symbol image except Dolly. I think she knew what she had and she knew what the hell she was gonna do with it, and she did it. And I'm sure that Porter must have given her some pointers along the way." Beckham avers, "I don't think anybody molded Dolly's image any more than Dolly did, 'cause she is a very smart little gal. Damn smart. And she knew the more controversy and the more talk that went on about Dolly at one point, the better it was for Dolly."[10] Such comments encapsulate the purposeful performance element and the way Parton has managed her media image and her interactions with the press—as well as the common diminutive "girl singer" rhetoric.

Parton's sexualized look in the 1970s had both similarities to and important differences from some of her female contemporaries. At that time in the 1970s, Loretta Lynn was embodying the mountain girl, albeit one who was willing to speak up for herself and was not sexualized in the way Parton was, while Tammy Wynette was performing iterations of the girl singer, with glamorous though not highly sexualized images incorporated. Kenny Rogers's duet partner Dottie West did incorporate a bit more of a sexualized image into her look, albeit somewhat later, as did Crystal Gayle.

One country artist who provides a key point of comparison with Parton during this epoch is Jeannie C. Riley. Diane Pecknold argues convincingly that Riley in the early 1970s embodied a hillbilly sexpot image of working-class whiteness, used as a backward sexualized foil in the sense that she symbolized a working-class otherness that upheld the norm of middle-class conformist womanhood and propriety at the time, embodying sexual promiscuity as a negative example that would uphold its opposite, middle-class respectability. As Anthony Harkins observes, working-class whiteness, like working-class blackness, was often sexualized and used to express race, class, and gender stereotypes.[11] Pecknold notes that Riley objected to the way Music Row executives wanted her to embody the characters in her songs and wear short gold lamé miniskirts, turning her into a symbol of sexualized, working-class whiteness, and she later changed labels because she wanted to sing Christian music and embrace a new image that was Christian. Pecknold argues that Riley was a precursor to Parton in the sense that she embodied a working-class sexualized image before Parton had fully developed her own "ironically trashy Daisy Mae persona" and was still just beginning as Wagoner's "girl singer."[12] Pecknold reads Riley as critiquing a gendered double standard and working-class stereotypes but not having access to middle-class white womanhood and respectability.

Both female performers are similar in that they were often conflated with the female characters they sang about, encouraging a superimposition of their autobiographies and their characters, and their personas were of outspoken, working-class sexualized women. Parton even did a cover of Riley's signature song, "Harper Valley PTA" (1968), as did many other female country singers, because of its popularity, with Riley's version reaching number one on the country and pop charts. Parton's version appeared on her album *In the Good Old Days (When Times Were Bad)* (1969). Other singers who covered that song include Loretta Lynn, Norma Jean, Dottie West, Lynn Anderson, and Jeannie Seely. Written by Tom T. Hall, the song imagines the female speaker's widowed mother incurring the wrath of respectable middle-class society when the PTA complains about her wearing miniskirts and dating men. The woman goes and confronts the PTA, pointing out their hypocritical behavior in which the so-called respectable citizens are running around engaging in affairs and drinking. Pecknold notes that the song critiques double standards and middle-class mores as hypocritical, but that Riley in performance was often positioned as an embodiment of the very sexualized working-class stereotype the song critiques, presented as a miniskirted, hard-living sex symbol.[13]

However, Parton is significantly different from Riley in some important ways. Parton fashioned and chose her own image, while Riley had her image imposed on her. Parton creates an exaggeration in her image and a campy aspect that generates an ironic distance from the stereotype she performs, such that she is commenting on it rather than being controlled by it. Parton's ironic construction of her own image aggressively calls the stereotype of the sexualized, white, working-class woman into question, drawing attention to how it is artificial and arbitrary. Her ironic image shows how much more transgressive Parton is in this context; she takes the sexualized images that were imposed on female performers around her and instead uses them ironically, which creates her own space for self-expression and resistance to those stereotypes. She gains freedom through the hyperbole. While Parton has also often been framed in performance in similarly stereotypical ways, as when Wagoner would introduce her as the "pretty little girl singer" or a male peer would introduce her with a "boob joke," Parton often turns the tables on that framing by emphasizing irony in her own performance or by making an ironic "boob joke" herself.

Album Covers and Gender Performance

Her album covers from this period capture her gradual image and style evolution.[14] Her earliest duet and solo albums with Wagoner feature imagery of her that is more subdued and demure. Although her dresses are tight-fitting and the covers feature wigs teased up somewhat, they are not incredibly high as they would be later. She gazes off to the side or to the camera in a more demure way. Her first album with Wagoner, the duet album *Just Between You and Me* (1968), features them both in red turtlenecks, arms circled around each other in a side hug, grinning broadly. Her hair is teased up, which only seems in keeping with his blond pompadour, but the effect is one of slight exaggeration, not full campiness. On her first solo album with him as her producer, *Just Because I'm a Woman* (1968), Parton wears a tight-fitting, cocktail-length white dress with long sleeves, her arms held out to her sides, palms upward, a warm smile on her face, as if entreating the audience to be sympathetic with her. Their next duet album, *Just the Two of Us* (1968), has her matching him again, in white jackets, both gazing off to high camera left, playfully smiling and suggesting warm camaraderie. The cover of her second solo album, *In the Good Old Days*, pictures a mid-shot of Parton from the shoulders up, her blonde wig somewhat teased but still comparatively understated, a long-sleeved red dress with turtle-neck collar. Their third duet album, *Always, Always* (1969), pictures Wagoner in his signature red Nudie suit with rhinestones and images of cactus plants and covered wagons, signifying his name and his Wagonmasters band. They are singing into the microphone, as if in a scene from his television show, and Parton stands with her hands clasped in front of her chastely, in a green, tight-fitting, sleeveless dress with a white yolk collar.

However, beginning with the album cover of her next solo effort, *My Blue Ridge Mountain Boy* (1969), Parton starts to appear more sexualized and begins using more exaggeration and campy irony in her look. Her media image also starts to incorporate more references to her Appalachian childhood and mountain settings. This album cover frames Parton in a suggestive pose, lying on a couch in the foreground as if daydreaming, raising her pinky finger in her mouth, wearing a blue flowered dress, bouffant hairdo, and pronounced eyeshadow, eyeliner, and lipstick. The upper part of the album cover has a picture of her husband, Carl Dean; while he is not listed by name on the album, Parton later revealed that it was her reclusive husband on the cover.[15] He appears here as a youthful, handsome mountain man in front of a mountain cabin, dressed in a red plaid shirt, sitting on a large cut tree log.

In keeping with this campier trend, her following solo album, *The Fairest of Them All* (1970), references fairytale images and more aggressively emphasizes a ridiculously tall bouffant wig, more makeup, and a humorously overdone image. Parton stands in the camera left foreground and stares at an image of herself in a mirror as the cover alludes to Snow White. Parton wears an elaborate pink gown with taffeta, her image in the mirror almost overwhelmed by a large flower arrangement. The pious images from the earlier albums have given way to camp, and this mirrored image exhibits a knowingness about made-up images, mythologies, and fairytales, and the idea that Parton is watching herself being watched.

As John Berger theorizes of Western visual culture, women are positioned as the sexualized objects offered up for male consumption. For Berger, women watch themselves being watched and hence develop a split subjectivity, taking on the position of both the observer and the observed, looking through the stereotypical male gaze at themselves as an object, seeing themselves as how the unseen male observer would view them.[16] Parton gazing at herself as a camp image here mimics that dynamic. However, Berger also notes that some women return the gaze, looking back at the unseen male observer, complicating the male gaze that frames the image and instead claiming some kind of female agency. Here, Parton is staring back at the watcher in the mirror with a knowingness that returns the male gaze disruptively.

Other solo albums from this period likewise picture her with a big blonde wig and full makeup, creating a campy effect, such as in the Monument compilation *As Long as I Live* (1970), *The Best of Dolly Parton* (1970), and the Monument compilation *The World of Dolly Parton* (1972). Her duet albums in this period show her with bigger hair but are not as campy as her solo album covers; Parton and Wagoner look like part of a showy family portrait in coordinated outfits for the most part, in *Once More* (1970), *Two of a Kind* (1971), and *The Best of Porter Wagoner & Dolly Parton* (1971).

Some of her albums from this time also begin to incorporate imagery from her childhood, which increases the references to her life story and her mountain girl upbringing. These include matched childhood pictures of Wagoner and Parton (*Porter Wayne and Dolly Rebecca* [1970]), her performing for her hometown crowd at her live concert in Sevierville for the Wagoner-produced Dolly Parton Day (*A Real Live Dolly* [1970]), and the childhood painted image of her in the coat her mother made her from scraps in *Coat of Many Colors* (1971). On the cover of *Joshua* (1971), Parton is actually pictured in an imagined scene in the mountains, painted to look as if she is standing outside facing a cabin door, confronting her mountain man, who is pictured from the back, standing in the doorway in the foreground of the image. Her hands on her hips, she wears jeans and a shirt and is pictured like a community member going about her everyday life in the mountains.

One exception to this album cover imagery is her more demure and reserved gospel album cover, *Golden Streets of Glory* (1971). On the left side of the album cover, a painting of a golden road stretches to the horizon. On the right, Parton in a photograph looks through a window, as if gazing at a path leading to religious salvation, wearing a long blonde wig and less makeup.

In her subsequent duets album with Wagoner, *We Found It*, Parton is explicitly campy, dressed in a blue suit that matches his, her elaborate wig very large, with long hair on the sides and back, and hair in the front swooped up and pulled back, with blue ribbons tied into hair ringlets on the side. They are looking at each other and smiling, and the overall effect is quite campy cheesiness. Other albums from this time period likewise indicate a recognizable version of her signature look. The basic duet portrait covers are more campy than they had been in the past: matching portraits with matching big hair on *Together Always* (1972), *Love and Music* (1973), and *Porter 'N' Dolly* (1974), Wagoner's red cactus Nudie suit joined by Parton's butterfly-bedecked gown. She began developing her butterfly symbol imagery in the early 1970s, as also featured on her *Love Is Like a Butterfly* (1974) solo album cover, with an elaborate butterfly image and a glamorous shot of her in big wig and red gown in the center.

Some of the album covers from this era are also more sexualized. For their duet album, *Burning the Midnight Oil* (1972), Wagoner and Parton are pictured separately, as if pining for each other at the midnight hour or recovering after a breakup. Parton sits in a rocking chair in front of a fire, somberly gazing at a picture in her hands, while Wagoner in a separate picture stares off into the distance, a note and tissues in front of him. On the cover of the *Touch Your Woman* (1972) album, Parton is sitting on a bed, surrounded by pillows, staring at the camera knowingly, as if embodying her title song, which thematizes the female character's sexual desire and urges the man to give attention to his wife. For *The Bargain Store* (1975), Parton is pictured outside a storefront window, heavily made up with a high blonde wig, staring to the edge of the camera with a defensive look as if embodying the title character of the song, a woman being judged by a double standard because she has slept with men and is seen as "fallen."

In an even campier image, her solo album *Bubbling Over* (1973) features Parton's head shooting up from a pool of water and another image of her standing in a long, flowered gown and big hair, outdoors by the poolside. The effect of the image is Parton as floating head doubled by a small Parton figure that almost looks like a small Barbie doll. Another particularly odd image has a picture of Parton's head literally contained by Wagoner's, as if he has symbolically suffused and contains her, while she sings his songs on *My Favorite Songwriter, Porter Wagoner* (1972). She has her recognizable tall blonde wig and long hair, blue eyeshadow and black eyebrows, eyeliner, and light red lipstick, a black dress, and black choker necklace with a white butterfly on it.

In this context, the stark cover for *My Tennessee Mountain Home* stands out even more, because it pictures her childhood Locust Ridge cabin and front porch (one of the succession of cabins in which her family lived in her youth), from the foothills of the Smoky Mountains, a landscape portrait of her hardscrabble upbringing with no people in the image. The gritty realism of the photograph underscores her authenticity claims on that album, where she sings about her life experiences as a way to ground her style of country music influenced by folk and traditional music. The realism claims of that album significantly downplay the campy effect of some other albums from that period.

On the cover of her second "best of" RCA compilation solo album, *Best of Dolly Parton* (1975), we see a full articulation of her signature look. She includes mountain girl elements, with a red, homespun, patterned blouse and a wooden plank fence wall behind her, setting her in nature. Also present are elements of her campy "white trash tramp" look, replete with hoop earrings, exaggerated blue eyeshadow and red lipstick, and a platinum blonde wig that is teased up high into a large bouffant. The other duets album from this period, *Say Forever You'll Be Mine* (1975), returns to the matching staid portraiture model. Her solo albums leading up to *New Harvest . . . First Gathering*, meanwhile, keep reiterating the same signature Parton imagery: long blonde wig, hoop earrings, sometimes a bandana in her hair, often pictured in outdoor, pastoral, rustic scenes (*The Seeker* and *We Used To* [1975], *All I Can Do* [1976]). *New Harvest . . . First Gathering* implies her intention to maintain the same imagery she had already established on previous solo albums. Here, Parton sits in a truck, dressed in denim, a blue bandana, and heavy makeup in her familiar overdone "tramp" aesthetic.

Her Wagoner show incarnation would fit her into girl singer domesticity but with a flashiness and glitz thrown into the mix. She writes that their old album covers picture the two of them in very similar clothes, hairstyles, and cheesy smiles; she then creates distance between Wagoner's styling choices and her own self-expression by saying in her autobiography that it is funny "how your tastes change."[17] Thus, by the time of her articulation of her signature look in the early and middle 1970s, she could be seen as an expression of campy female sexuality combined with mountain girl, country bumpkin innocence that buffers the sex-pot image. While she has gone on to adapt that image to different contexts since then, as I detail in later chapters, the foundation of the image remains the same.

Autobiographical Authenticity:
Tennessee Mountain Home

While developing her stage persona during this early period of her career, Parton was also further fashioning her autobiographical stories, strongly linking her persona to her life story. Parton's treatment of the pastoral and of her own autobiographical narratives of her mountain origins is multilayered. At times, she is nostalgic for her mountain home. At other times, she eschews easy nostalgia and instead depicts the gritty realism of how hard mountain life could be in the midst of stark material conditions and crushing poverty. She often balances the depiction of harsh conditions by focusing on how familial love offset the material hardships, yet she conveys experiences of being bullied for being poor, her father struggling with illiteracy, and various compensatory discourses, like religion, nostalgia for a "simpler" time, escapism, and domesticity. She frequently describes "choosing to be poor" as a mental state and choosing not to be as an attitude (as in "Coat of Many Colors").

Her fullest expression of that mountain context appears on *My Tennessee Mountain Home*, her self-written concept album about her Smoky Mountain childhood context and her eleventh solo studio album. Parton explicitly frames it as an autobiographical portrait of her desire to leave the mountains and make it as a country music star, and her subsequent nostalgia for the "simpler time" of that childhood she has left behind, even though she is proud of reaching her dreams of stardom. The album's depiction of an impoverished East Tennessee mountain context is largely positive, imagining an idyllic space of warm, encircling nature; parental love and care; siblings and family offering support and companionship; and hard-working country folks like her parents, who supported and believed in her.

However, it also includes critiques of false romanticization in moments of gritty realism that depict the hard labor and bruising poverty involved in these circumstances. It imagines that the incredibly hard-working mountain people like her father would be rewarded in heaven, as would regional leaders like the doctor who faithfully delivered her and countless others ("half the babies" in East Tennessee) in treacherous, isolated rural mountain conditions, immortalized in the song "Dr. Robert F. Thomas." While not many of the songs include explicit gender themes, some do reference her career dreams and how she left her home and family to pursue them, establishing that independent effort as the conflict that keeps her from returning to the pastoral idyll, implicitly making her reject any gender role expectations of marrying a mountain boy, having children, and remaining in the mountains, even though her family supports her dreams. She also makes references to female virtue and "being good," that is, not being led astray by the temptations of the big city.

In the album's conflation of the speaker with Parton's own life story, we see the kind of presentation of the self as a spokesperson for a mountain childhood, as if Parton is depicting a universalized experience of an idealized Appalachian upbringing, as well as the heroic working-class she celebrates in song, symbols of a "simpler time," with Appalachia as premodern purity and the people as "contemporary ancestors." Parton here positions herself as a participant observer, something akin to what theorist Antonio Gramsci postulated as an "organic intellectual," a class organizer who speaks for an entire group of people.[18] The way some folk singers have been presented as organic intellectuals, like a Woody Guthrie–style proletarian folk hero, or a leader organizing their class, is also relevant here. However, that presentation of her as an organic intellectual has sometimes taken problematic forms, as when she has been reductively conflated with an Appalachian, white, working-class femininity. Witness Linda Ronstadt's comments about Parton and their *Trio* albums, in which she claims Parton is an "authentic voice" for an Appalachian working class.[19] Here, however, Parton is offering a testimony of this virtuous, innocent "Other," and she sings as someone who has proven her credibility as a member of that group, perfectly mimicking how country music wants a pure authenticity to claim as its roots, even while the listeners move further and further away from that context and the imagined southern, white, working-class audience is not the same as the actual larger audience.

The song that makes the harshest critique of impoverished conditions is "In the Good Old Days (When Times Were Bad)," which appeared on a previous album of the same name. The song lauds good memories of familial love but says the speaker would never want to return to those hard times. Parton focuses attention on the bleak living conditions of rural mountain poverty and refuses any effort to romanticize or be nostalgic for that experience. The lyrics describe backbreaking work in the fields, from sunup to sundown, with the children going to bed hungry, watching their father worked to his limit and their mother suffering and ill when they could not afford a doctor. Nature is an antagonist here, as they would have to stand by helplessly when a hailstorm dashed their crops or the wind blew snow into their cabin through cracks in the walls, awakening them to ice on the floor. The speaker finds the memories invaluable but rejects the idea of ever returning to that experience, saying, there is "no amount of money" she would accept to take those memories from her but also no sum would make her "go back and live through it again."

Parton adds another layer to her mountain portrait with another song on the album, "Better Part of Life," which is more focused on positive memories and actually critiques a negative view of mountain life. She even seems to respond to her own moment of critique from "In the Good Old Days," because in "Better Part of Life," she writes that her mountain childhood was fun and full of good memories of simpler times, "back when they say times was bad." This more upbeat song imagines a family with five children reuniting and remembering the better times "left behind," like swimming in the swimming hole or getting drunk on homemade wine, the speaker dreaming of being a "singin' star" and her family believing in her. However, the song ends on a note of melancholy. She expresses the desire to go back to those good times but notes the existential angst of time passing and not being able to reclaim the past, since she cannot return to those moments because "time moves on and nothin' lasts."

A number of songs on the album work to link Parton's life story to her "authenticity" and sincerity claims. She aggressively frames the album as autobiographical and explicitly makes truth claims in it by using details from her own life. The degree to which her autobiography has taken on a self-sustaining mythological dimension is evident in how Parton interweaves factual accounts of her childhood with poetic license in this album. The album is almost a blueprint for her later full autobiography.

Parton emphasizes the autobiographical truth claims of *My Tennessee Mountain Home* by starting the album with her reading of "The Letter," her first letter home to her family upon her arrival in Nashville after graduating from high school. She gives the date of the letter, June 2, 1964, and includes all of her mixed emotions from that time. There, she says she is homesick and misses her family, and that she did not realized how much she would miss the shouts and energy of a house full of siblings. She notes that "Nashville is not exactly what I thought it was gonna be," but she still must follow her dreams of stardom as a singer and songwriter, and she vows she will "be good just like I promised you." She reassures them that she has found some opportunities and will be able to support herself. In her later autobiography, Parton notes that in this initial letter, she was downplaying how homesick she was and how much she was struggling to support herself and even eat during her early days after moving to Nashville. Here, the letter sets the tone of the album as ambitious and hopeful, and it firmly grounds her musical career efforts in a justifying narrative of virtuous mountaineer childhood.

The album's songs go on to balance the positive and negative elements of her childhood. Many naturalize key elements of what Parton identifies as her Appalachian context, such as a large, loving family; a closeness with nature; the ritual of church-going; and music and singing ringing out over the hills ("I Remember," "Old Black Kettle," "Daddy's Working Boots," "Dr. Robert F. Thomas," "My Tennessee Mountain Home"). However, some songs register the hard work involved in impoverished conditions in the mountains ("Old Black Kettle," "Daddy's Working Boots," "Dr. Robert F. Thomas"), even though that toil is offset by loving family memories and the emphasis on the Edenic qualities of the virtuous pastoral over and against the fallen, corrupt influences of the city. A trilogy of songs at the end express a wistfulness about the speaker's inability to return back home to the "simpler" time of childhood innocence and a pastoral ideal, impossible to recapture because of the passage of time and the fact that the speaker has left to follow her own dreams ("Wrong Direction Home," "Back Home," "Better Part of Life"). The album concludes with a closing frame that refocuses on Parton leaving to find her dreams and then succeeding, breaking through at RCA, recounted in "Down on Music Row." Thus, the narrative frame returns to bookend her opening letter of a young woman attempting to achieve her dreams by depicting her achieving those dreams in the closing song.

Of the songs that emphasize the positive elements, the title song most notably encapsulates her celebration of the mountain pastoral. An audience favorite, Parton features it prominently in her touring performances (framing her section of her classic mountain songs during that portion of her concerts) and at Dollywood, where she has a replica of that particular Locust Ridge cabin as pictured on the cover of the album. The gospel-tinged chorus celebrates the elements of nature and home, where "life is as peaceful as a baby's sigh." The lyrics set the scene of the speaker sitting on the front porch, watching kids play in nature, with June bugs and fireflies, the setting seeming to feature the smell of honeysuckle and the music of songbirds and crickets, as well as memories of walking home from Sunday church stealing a kiss from her boyfriend when her parents are not watching (the line written in the second person, "you might steal a kiss or two," so that the audience can imagine being youngsters in that setting, walking home "with the one you love"). The song categorizes all of the elements included as natural, such as music, church, the wilderness, children growing up, and expanding families reproducing themselves. All appear as an inherent part of this mountain upbringing and context, as if encapsulating an entire way of life that is universalized here with the implication that anyone growing up in the mountains during that time would have shared such experiences. Parton invites listeners to share in her mythologized, romanticized nostalgia for this setting. Likewise, "I Remember" paints a picture of idyllic nature linked to a loving family and music. The speaker recalls her mother and father "most of all" in a "country home filled with love," with her mother singing and her father making the children homemade toys, surrounded by a pastoral wonderland of golden wheat fields, sugarcane, and songbirds, and a moral upbringing in which the parents taught the children "right from wrong."

Of the songs that include a more critical element, many elaborate on difficult labor conditions in a way that complicates any easy celebration of the mountain pastoral. "I Remember" includes a hint of the hardships involved because the speaker's parents pray that they would live to see their children grow up, implying that they could easily not achieve that goal. "Old Black Kettle" celebrates how the speaker's mother would use that kettle and bemoans how the simpler way of life is vanishing, but it nevertheless registers the hard work her mother had to do in the home. "Daddy's Working Boots" lauds how hard the speaker's father worked on the farm or at jobs in order to support the family, and the boots are worn and beat up from the toil, just like he is. The speaker offers a religious and moral victory for him, praying that the hard-working father will get "golden boots" in heaven when his time comes. The lyrics celebrate how the working man's boots gave him his foundation of hard work, which also served as the bedrock of their family. While such songs imagine heavenly rewards as compensation for suffering, they nevertheless offer realism in their depiction of difficult labor conditions.

The three songs that express regret inject a note of melancholy into the pastoral celebration, emphasizing the inability to return home because of the passage of time and the decline of a way of life. These songs imply that mountain life is inevitably vanishing with the influx of modern civilization, the trappings of modernity, like technology and industrialization, pushing out older lifeways tied to the agricultural and the pastoral. The speaker often deflects her desire for the unattainable memory of home into the future, as if these complex yearnings and emotional responses to cultural change will find their solution at some point in the coming days. Cecelia Tichi has argued that Parton's framing of home in "My Tennessee Mountain Home" relates to a long-running cultural tradition of agrarian ideals of nature, from Crèvecoeur onward, and an Emersonian idea of authenticity; she also notes that country songs in this vein express the yearning to return home and the impossibility of doing so, since the idea of home itself is mythic and impossible to achieve.[20]

In "Wrong Direction Home," the speaker regrets leaving her family and her mountain home, rhapsodizing about memories that are as "sweet as mountain honey." She has left to follow her dream and finds herself far from home and the familiar, wanting to return home. In a light allusion to Dorothy in *The Wizard of Oz*, Parton sings that "there's no place like home." But the implication is that home is not even like home, because she cannot return to that idealized space of nostalgia. Her dreams have taken her in the "wrong direction," but she displaces her hope into the future, hoping she will get back home sometime soon, where her family waits for her.

In "Back Home," the speaker does return home after many years to see her mother and father. Her mother has written a letter asking her to come home because she is lonely with all her children gone. Having left to pursue her dreams and always wishing to return home, the speaker leaves a corrupted, polluted city and finally returns home, but the implication is that the respite from modern city life in this pastoral idyll will only be a temporary one, and the idealized pastoral space itself has changed, as none of the children are there any more. While "Better Part of Life" imagines that it is the singer's music career dreams that have left her bereft of her idealized mountain past, the album's closing song, about winning over Music Row, makes those music dreams the triumphal closing to the narrative frame.

Indeed, "Down on Music Row" contributes to the mythologizing function of this album, because it imagines Parton's success as a kind of magical act, simplifying her own narrative by imagining that she makes it her first day in town, persevering through rejections by impressing Chet Atkins and Bob Ferguson at RCA. Parton takes poetic license here, implying that she came into town, fresh off the bus, and got power players to see her potential, which is not what actually happened. A teenaged Parton, of course, had already spent years trying to break through, had released recordings prior to that time, and was signed to a publishing deal by Buddy Killen at Tree Publishing.

In Parton's musical output from this period more broadly, some of Parton's songs from other albums likewise reinforce the positive nostalgia for a pastoral ideal, while others add in both the nostalgia and the more critical realism for the difficult living conditions. In "Will He Be Waiting for Me" (1972), Parton describes a woman who returns looking for the mountain man she left behind, wondering if he will still want her back. The mountain setting represents purity and innocence, as does her lost love, as she walks a mountain path to find him and describes how "the smell of mountain laurel fills the air with sweet perfume." In a more complex vision, Parton writes in "The Greatest Days of All" (1972) that there was "some good and some bad" in the mountain childhood the speaker describes. She remembers a country upbringing in nature, surrounded by whippoorwills, hummingbirds, and a garden, which she places in stark contrast to the busy, alienating city sidewalks and noise. However, she nonetheless recalls the negative elements of the past as well, such as a leaky roof, rats, and insects ruining her clothes. She resolves the tension between the good and bad memories by suggesting that together they combine to form the most important and best period of her life, as the song title describes. Thus, Parton's autobiographical songs about her childhood in the Smoky Mountains are both celebrations of the pastoral and rejections of any false nostalgia for poverty or idealizations of rural mountain culture.

Hillbilly Deluxe: Critical Histories

Parton's use of the hillbilly cultural trope is nuanced and reflects a long cultural history of hillbilly images and stereotypes, both positive and negative, in US popular culture, including music, comic strips, films, and television. The well-known history of the hillbilly term in country music involves explicit efforts by record executives during the mass commercialization of country music in the 1920s to draw on hillbilly images and an association with a southern, white, working-class mountain folk culture. Later, by the postwar 1940s, the industry rejected the "hillbilly" music moniker as derogatory and moved to use "country and western" or "country" instead, although there were still some widespread uses of the term "hillbilly music" into the 1950s.

As part of barn dance radio practices of the 1930s, John Lair, in his promotional efforts for *National Barn Dance* for WLS in Chicago, famously created a positive stereotype of the mountain girl when he made up the persona of Linda Parker (performed by actor and nightclub singer Jeanne Muenich) as the

"Little Sunbonnet Girl," a carefully created image. She could innocently sing "mountain songs," which often involved stories of the sentimental mountain mother left at home when her children migrated to the city. As for his mountain girl, he insisted on her as a symbol of traditional values, rural folk culture, and a premodern, romanticized sense of a simpler time and place. He would later object to other images of hillbillies circulating in relation to country music, arguing that he did not want negative stereotypes associated with his constructed image of cultural innocence and wholesomeness. Lair made this image distinct from the hillbilly image, which he viewed as a low-class stereotype, while, in contrast, the Grand Ole Opry included more degraded hillbilly stereotypes and images. As Kristine McCusker demonstrates, the *National Barn Dance*'s rural-to-urban and South-to-North migrants (a significant part of their audience) could articulate their nostalgia for mother and home through this music, even while they adjusted to their new, urban context via this imagined community on the radio.[21]

The hillbilly stereotype became popular in comic strips beginning in the 1930s, with series such as Paul Webb's *The Mountain Boys* (1934–1958); Billy DeBeck's *Snuffy Smith* (1934–1944), which grew out of his existing comic strip, *Barney Google*; and Al Capp's *Li'l Abner* (1934–1977). Some observers, like Lair, objected to what they saw as demeaning caricatures. Lair explicitly rejected Al Capp's comics.

In his history of the hillbilly trope in US culture, Anthony Harkins argues that the hillbilly trope since 1900 has signified both negative stereotypes (backwardness, ignorance, savagery) and positive ideas (folk culture, ruggedness, independence, devotion to family and home), and both a rejection and an embrace of white, working-class southerners as "Other," indicating struggles over the meanings of race, class, gender, and mass culture. Because the trope has always been an ambivalent one, it has done different kinds of cultural work at different times, often as a way for audiences to define American identity and to contend with the social changes of modernity and urbanization, technology, and the growth of capitalism. For Harkins, the hillbilly figure let a mainstream, middle-class, white audience romanticize the past but also recommit to modernity, because it offered a negative caricature of premodern, uncivilized society.[22]

The *Li'l Abner* hillbilly image is particularly relevant to Parton, because some observers saw her voluptuous, blonde country bumpkin image as her adaptation of the well-known Daisy Mae Scragg (later Yokum) character from the Capp comic strip. Parton would later pose as Daisy Mae explicitly in a pinup poster from 1978, wearing the polka-dotted Daisy Mae shirt and short shorts, lying in a haystack. Harkins argues that the Capp strip was popular because audiences used it during the Depression to imagine a simpler time and place. While handsome Abner Yokum (the name was Capp's combination of "yokel" and "hokum") embodied a mountain innocence, virtuousness, and pioneer hardiness, his parents were portrayed as almost subhuman, simian, backward mountain folk who were not taken in by materialism but who were not recognizably modern. Beautiful Daisy Mae, meanwhile, wore her signature polka-dot peasant blouse; a very short, cropped skirt; and no shoes. Capp emphasized her voluptuous figure, which led to pop culture responses to her such as pinup girl paintings of her on military airplanes. Capp portrayed her as a hard-working woman determined to get her man, who continually chased Abner, wanting to marry him and finally getting her wish in 1952. One lasting influence the comic strip had is Capp's creation of Sadie Hawkins Day, where the Dogpatch, Kentucky, women could marry any man they captured. This notion led to Sadie Hawkins Day dances in high schools beginning in the 1930s, which Harkins notes could challenge gender decorum and the idea of feminine deference but nevertheless reinforced stereotypes linking "impoverished southern mountaineers and aggressive and aberrant sexuality."[23]

Daisy Mae was portrayed as stereotypically virtuous in the sense that she was only after one man and rejected the advances of other men, but she was also sexualized and objectified, reinforcing an idea of women as sexualized objects. The comic strips would depict a male-dominated mountain culture of female subordination, where the women had to work because the men would not. Harkins argues, "Images of hillbilly families and kin networks could be used both to challenge supposed norms of male breadwinners and submissive female domesticity and to uphold these 'traditional' gender roles by negative example."[24] These hillbilly gender images were seen as the exception that proved the norm.

The use of the hillbilly trope as innocent nostalgia in television shows in the 1960s, such as *Andy Griffith* and *The Beverly Hillbillies*, might continue more recently in the "hicksploitation" genre on reality TV. Series ranging from *Buckwild* to *Here Comes Honey Boo Boo* to *Redneck Island* and *My Big Redneck Vacation* gaze upon working-class, white, rural subcultures as symbols of an imagined pastoral premodern simplicity or sensationalized stereotypes of "white trash," which the outsider tourist gaze frames as abject. These shows also often frame the hicksploitation subjects as overtly racist. In that television genre, "redneck" becomes shorthand for racism, as stereotypical images of "white trash" are often deployed as symbols of racism in US popular culture, sometimes as foils to categorize other white, working-class characters as less stereotypical.[25]

In music, Harkins notes how some country artists, like Dwight Yoakam, Marty Stuart, and BR 5–49, since the 1980s have embraced the hillbilly term to signify neo-traditionalist authenticity and links to folk music—which is ironic because in 1930s incarnations, for example, it was used in opposition to the authenticity of folk music.[26] Others, like psychobilly band Southern Culture on the Skids, have used the trope ironically (with kitsch songs like "White Trash"). Some mainstream country artists have used it in an ironic way that nonetheless claims the burlesque abjection, as with Blake Shelton's "Hillbilly Bone" (2010), which ridicules pretentious put-downs of a white working class by claiming the hillbilly identity, with an atavistic rendering of it as a genetic generational legacy.

In Parton's version of the hillbilly, she links it to cultural preservation. Dollywood and her associated tourist ventures in Pigeon Forge market hillbilly culture as a tourist destination yet value local folk culture and the preservation of mountain folk practices, most noticeably in Craftsman's Valley in Dollywood, where working mountain artists can teach tourists folk crafts. Thus Parton offers both the kitschy mass media fantasy of the hillbilly or mountaineer and also the practicing folk culture version. The so-called fake and the so-called real are both present at once, and both are equally true, just as her juxtaposition of the two reflects how the categories of mass and folk are never that clearly delineated from the outset. She solves the tension between them by linking the mass culture to the folk source. Ironically, the more she builds up the mountain tourist destinations and theme park venues, the more she may push out the earlier mountain culture and lifeways in the area, although again, that preexisting culture was never "pure" or noncommercial to begin with, of course.

Her own descriptions of the Dollywood hillbillies illustrate these dynamics. In her autobiography, she insists, "I'm proud of being from the South. At least rednecks and hillbillies are interesting." Thus, she implicitly acknowledges the "trash" and "bad taste" stereotypes, but she claims the identity position underneath the stereotypes and attributes positive qualities to real people. She notes that some tourists may go to Dollywood merely out of interest in her, but she demurs that she is only the most "famous hillbilly," and she sees the theme park as a way to honor her "real people" and celebrate their mountain spirit. She goes on to explain her conception of Dollywood in relation to the hillbilly concept, emphasizing that "real people" work there who are "real hillbillies," many of whom are related to her, and that you can watch them do what they "do best," such as make music or other items such as soap, quilts, or dulcimers. She admits that her praise of Dollywood sounds like "a commercial," but she demurs that she lauds the park because she is proud of it, which she readily confesses.[27]

Parton lends humanity to the "real hillbillies" behind the stereotypes, celebrating them as hard-working artisans and grouping herself with them, identifying with them and embracing the category of "hillbilly," reclaiming it and uplifting the meaning of it. Likewise, she sometimes calls them "skillbillies," another reclamation of the hillbilly trope in which she refers to them as skilled artisans. At the same time, she essentializes them, because she suggests that what they "do best" is their folk crafts. Still, she does not consign them to the status of "contemporary ancestors" but rather views them as "real people" and her own relatives who work with her. She ends on a both/and note, because she notes that she is, in effect, delivering an advertisement, yet she insists that it does not matter because she is expressing her sincere sentiments of pride. Thus, the most fake (a commercial pitch) is the most real (because she is sincere in her heart). Her comment encapsulates the rhetoric she uses to set up her Dolly Parton persona.

Harkins notes that during the Depression-era height of the hillbilly image, some southern mountain people rejected it as a demeaning caricature. Some embraced a positive version of it as rugged independence. Others ambivalently used it, recognizing the urban derision and negative stereotype circulated by patronizing outsiders but deploying it to make money and even spur more interest in the region's folk heritage, helping more locals see the value of mountain folk customs and skills.[28]

I contend that Parton's approach is to emphasize the positive image of the hillbilly or mountaineer. In her jokes about being "hillbilly trash," she is also reclaiming the negative caricature and turning it into an authenticity argument, meaning she says do not react to trash as negative because she has sincere intentions. Her commercial efforts might fall into the ambivalent category of recognizing how some tourists might play into negative stereotypes in their consumption of her image, but she is profiting from it. Further, she might be able to spur more interest in her local folk culture. Parton's use of exaggerated "rube" humor and slapstick also functions like a burlesque that critiques the outsider tourist gaze that would frame them as abject stereotypes of "white trash."

Parton, in creating her mass culture fantasy of her folk culture roots, draws on a long history of the hillbilly image as both pure source and fallen stereotype in country music history. The multivalent trope meditates on race, class, gender,

mass culture, and modernity—specifically what the processes of industrialization, urbanization, and market capitalism did to previous lifeways and folk cultures. Parton engages with the fantasy of an unspoiled premodern past, the idea
that country music is the literal life expression of simpler folks and times, and she
is presented as if she is speaking that experience in a pure way.

Crucially, Parton's hillbilly image is a critical one, in her combination of the
hillbilly tramp and the mountain girl. She turns the Daisy Mae–type voluptuous
mountain girl image into knowing camp and irony. Unlike other female country
singers who were her contemporaries, Parton's response to her sexualization by
the country music industry was not an uncomfortable embodiment of it but
rather ironic distance that she created through exaggeration, kitsch, and a knowing campiness, using the images and escaping entrapment. Harkins argues that
the hillbilly is the "white Other" through which larger cultural anxieties about
race, class, and gender can be staged.[29] Here, Parton seizes that "white Other"
and turns it into a gender parody, both tramp and pure at once. Ultimately, she
insists that viewers should not accept a negative tramp stereotype nor should
they judge her by a stereotypical appearance; rather, they should instead separate
outside appearance and inner emotions and values.

In relationship to the country music genre as a whole, then, Parton's oeuvre
comments on how the hillbilly trope has been either demonized in country
music in order to claim middle-class respectability for the genre or framed positively to recuperate working-class abjection. Country music's treatment of the
hillbilly also fits into larger authenticity narratives that frame the South as a site
of rural folk exceptionalism. Similarly, southern studies scholars have critiqued
the way US popular culture more generally reinforces narratives of southern
exceptionalism.[30] In her important book on country music's authenticity claims,
Pamela Fox has cogently detailed how rusticity has served as a figure for authenticity in country music since 1930s barn dance programming, and how it is
gendered; for male performers, the rustic hillbilly stereotype was shameful and
feminized, while for women through the postwar period, rusticity framed them
as guardians of rural folk culture and conventional domesticity. In part of her
chapter on the female country star memoir in the 1980s and 1990s, Fox argues
that the gender performance of stars like Loretta Lynn, Tammy Wynette, Dolly
Parton, and others allows them simultaneous identification with rusticity (such
as the abject figure of the hillbilly) and disavowal of it to try to appear modern.
Fox avers that Parton reclaims the poor white trash subject position and shows
that she knows gender is performative. Again, Fox argues that Parton gets out

from under class-based objectification but is trapped by gender objectification because her gender performance does not rise to the level of critical parody.[31]

In reference to this scholarly discussion, I would concur with the idea that Parton identifies with rusticity and distances herself from certain stereotypes of it. However, as I have been detailing in this study, I diverge by contending that some aspects of Parton's gender performance are transgressive and do achieve critical parody, precisely through her use of camp. I also read Parton through a different lens, arguing for the specific model I see of Parton's gender performance, where she plays a particular marginalized version of femininity off of a dominant one in order to gain cultural power. That model has evolved over the course of her full career and in different contexts, ranging from Hollywood film to new media models of stardom.

Porter's Hard Country: Gender and Class

In broader terms, Dolly Parton's relationship to Porter Wagoner's performance persona raises complicated questions of gender and class. In Barbara Ching's important arguments about masculinity and class, male "hard country" stars like Porter Wagoner, George Jones, and Merle Haggard perform masculinity as abject white "redneck trash" in a way that critiques an outsider tourist gaze. In her discussion of class, Ching uses Pierre Bourdieu's theories of taste as a class marker along with his concept of cultural capital, that is, high cultural knowledge an actor uses for social and financial advantage.[32] Building on Bourdieu's contention that taste hierarchies are actually versions of class hierarchies in which subjective "good taste" corresponds to "higher" class values, Ching argues that male hard country singers use burlesque to recuperate their own class abjection, meaning that when the dominant culture belittles them as "bad taste," they use a burlesque performance of the "trashy" or "low" to claim their own position and push back against dominant norms and hierarchies. Ching argues that female singers like Parton, Loretta Lynn, and Tammy Wynette do not enact hard country in this kind of male burlesque model because they are mostly singing about women triumphing and succeeding, often over disappointing husbands, rather than about a "hard country" embrace of "bad taste."[33] In contrast, Richard Peterson and others have suggested that Parton does at times express "hard-core" country styles in a more general sense.[34] Nadine Hubbs, in her vital study of Gretchen Wilson's "Redneck Woman," has demonstrated how Wilson appropriates male "hard country" artists' performance of masculinity to reclaim white, working-class, female subjectivity against the abjection projected onto it by middle-class discourse.[35]

Parton's parodic burlesque is its own case. However, I suggest that Parton does use some elements of burlesque in that sense, as in a display of "bad taste" to critique a cultural hierarchy, especially in her duets with Wagoner. There, they both use a key performance of sincerity, which Wagoner said his mentor Red Foley taught him to do convincingly.[36]

When Parton delivers her famous tag line, "it takes a lot of money to look this cheap," she claims a high culture ironic knowledge of her look as "cheap." Yet she also parodies the cheapness in a way that critiques that stereotype and the cultural hierarchy on which it is based, all while linking her "both/and" rhetoric of sincerity and irony to her authenticity narratives. Thus she at times uses burlesque as a comic mode that can undermine cultural ideals by violating standards of good taste. In cultural expression such as her jokes about her breasts, Parton uses humor to defuse misogyny. However, she also invokes a different burlesque tradition, a theatrical one, to recuperate class and gender abjection, for instance, through her identification with Mae West and the theatrical burlesque tradition, as I detail in chapter 3.

Along the same lines as Peterson's hard-/soft-style model, Ching explains why Wagoner as a solo artist fits a "hard country" model. The term was first used pejoratively in 1970, but the style it retroactively refers to was evident by the mid-1960s.[37] For Ching, hard country is evident in Wagoner songs such as "A Satisfied Mind" (his chart-topping 1955 single). That song imagines a moral compensation for poverty, suggesting that rich men do not have satisfaction, whereas the suffering, impoverished, working-class speaker does. However, the suffering in the speaker's voice belies any moral or symbolic satisfaction. Wagoner's version of Bill Anderson's "The Cold Hard Facts of Life" (1967) was popular (number two on the country chart). The lyrics describe a male narrator speaking from prison; he has killed his wife and her lover because he came home a day early, went to the liquor store for champagne, and overhears another man buying alcohol to go cheat with a woman whose husband is out of town. It is only when the speaker watches the man turning into his own driveway that he realizes it is his wife who is cheating, and he kills both his wife and the other man with a knife. He imagines he will "go to hell" or "rot here in the cell." The final line is, "who taught who the cold hard facts of life?" emphasizing the suffering male speaker who blames the female cheater. But since he has murdered her, the song ends with some degree of ambiguity about which bleak facts are being underscored.

That song features male working-class aggression and possessiveness of women as compensation for working-class status, with murderous responses to female infidelity and a claimed moral justification for that response. Wagoner appears as the abject working-class male subject who projects a "sincerity contract" to the audience and relatability to working-class fans. As Ching argues, his speaking position is to return the demeaning tourist gaze by claiming his own "bad taste," abject position. She notes that Wagoner identified his own "low" positioning on purpose: "I don't try to do anything for the uptown people."[38] Wagoner also embraced the fact that people put him down for being "hard country."[39] She notes that Porter's final riddle in that song toys with the patronizing listener who might simply take the question literally when instead it is figurative and participates in an imaginative tradition where the song is exploring the concept of suffering rather than merely describing it literally.[40]

While Parton does not express suffering manhood in the way Wagoner does, she does establish a relationship between his persona and hers, not only through their duets but also in her album of Wagoner compositions, *My Favorite Songwriter: Porter Wagoner* (1972). In her duets with Wagoner, Parton often sings about female and male characters who are discussing the challenges of relationships, the work that goes into marriages, or the conflicts that arise around issues such as jealousy, division of labor, drinking, infidelity, and emotional intimacy or neglect. Likewise, some of their duets address tragic stories of families suffering hardships or despair. They depict a bleak human condition, where hardships indicate a harsh environment, chance and risk play a huge role in life, and characters appeal to religious faith as a salve to grief. Wagoner often takes the role of the jealous man, encapsulating a suffering manhood. Parton often takes the role of the wife who questions how she is treated and speaks up for herself in the marriage. Some songs plead for the mate not to leave, such as "Please Don't Stop Loving Me" and "Say Forever You'll Be Mine," both of which beg for steadfastness in love but, given how they worry that the mate may not prove faithful, also suggest uncertainty and fear about fidelity and the stability of love.

On her Wagoner tribute album, a tragic and resigned depiction of suffering dominates. Her album (number thirty-three on the country chart) includes a cover of his song "What Ain't to Be, Just Might Happen," which he had released as a popular single (number eight on the country chart) on his album of the same name (1972). While "What Ain't to Be, Just Might Happen" is a rollicking, up-tempo song, it expresses an idea of fate and then undercuts that idea. The speaker contends that if a relationship is fated, it will happen, but yet there is still a chance it could happen anyway, even if it is not fated. It decries love that put the speaker on a fourteen-story ledge in the past, and it argues that there is no use worrying about love because it just happens: "What is to be will be and what ain't to be just might happen." While the song might appear to be an optimistic ode to the possibilities of love even when it is not fated, it is also a bleaker look at chance winning out over fate, which leaves meaning in life more arbitrary and unpredictable.

Other songs on the album lament lost love. In "Lonely Comin' Down," the speaker awakens in a strange place and feels disassociated from the speaker's own image in the mirror (now a "strange face") and looks for a mate but instead finds an empty bed and cries, "And then I felt the lonely comin' down." Bereft, the speaker does not think it will ever be possible to find another. The introduction to the song includes Parton humming, spare instrumentation and production, and a lilting piano fill. The song's effect is one of suffering and sadness. In similar lost love laments, "Comes and Goes" yearns for lost love, as does "Oh, He's Everywhere," where the speaker is haunted by the memory of a lost love. In "Still on Your Mind," the female speaker laments that her man cannot forget another woman he still loves, while on "He Left Me Love," the speaker says her dead lover left her with eternal love and memories.

The album also hits other standard country themes, such as rural loss and nostalgia and religious comfort for earthly suffering. "Do You Hear the Robins Sing" is a pastoral lament, with the speaker decrying as artificial the AstroTurf lawns and tall buildings of the big city, instead celebrating the nature of country lanes, willow trees, and butterflies. The speaker queries the listener: "Is all the beauty in your world this artificial thing?" In a standard use of religion as consolation, two religious songs imagine that suffering will end in heaven. "The Bird That Never Flew" offers a recitation in which the speaker watches a bird with no wings but in death is given wings of gold to fly to heaven. In "When I Sing for Him," the speaker says singing praise songs helps her feel God's presence, and she looks forward to singing for him in heaven.

In contrast, one song takes the woman's half in working-class gender relations. "Washday Blues" decries how the speaker's man uses his money to dress her in finery to show her off but then has no money left to offset her domestic labor. In spoken lines at the end, she says she wishes she could hire herself a maid, because she spends all of her time doing laundry. While she looks like a country "princess" in a calico dress on Saturday, by Monday morning wash day, she looks "like a lady hobo." The speaker thus objects to unrewarded domestic labor and also expresses aspirational class desires, wanting to be a princess but actually suggesting that she will be stuck as a "lady hobo," which is slightly burlesque in the sense of claiming the "low Other" subject position.

Parton's Lyrics and Gender Themes

Parton's own songwriting offers a range of gender depictions, with two notable recurring critiques: she decries sexual double standards for women, and she questions mountain girl idealizations while reframing the hillbilly tramp positively. In her solo efforts, Parton's songs about gender politics often take a stance in line with popular feminism. Famously, in "Bargain Store" (1975), the speaker refers to herself as "used merchandise" because she has been damaged by a previous relationship. The song was banned by some radio stations that interpreted the line "you can easily afford the price" as referring to prostitution. Parton implicitly avers that fallen women should not be outcast and stigmatized for a sexual double standard. In "My Blue Ridge Mountain Boy," a country girl leaves the mountains and her boyfriend for New Orleans. As she struggles there and becomes a prostitute, she looks back longingly on the mountain boy she left behind, who has since married another woman. While the song suggests an inevitable tragedy for the woman, it also criticizes the men who hire her as a prostitute, saying "the men here ain't warm and tender" like the mountain boys were. In addition to figuring country purity versus city corruption, the song also opposes the tragic fallen woman, portrayed sympathetically, with the harshness of the men in the city.

Similarly, a number of Parton's songs decry double standards or urge sympathy for the fallen woman. In "Mama Say a Prayer" (1969), a country girl asks her mother back home to pray for her; she has been tempted by unkind men in the city, because "lonely makes it easy for a good girl to go wrong," and "the goodnight kisses I get now are cruel and so demanding." "Daddy's Moonshine Still" (1971) explains why a young woman turned to prostitution and implicitly asks the listener for sympathy for her plight. Her father's moonshine ruined the family as two brothers died trying to run alcohol across state lines. The young woman leaves and becomes a prostitute, sending her mother money; she says, "at least it took me far away." The story ends tragically as the father dies from alcoholism and the mother dies too, leaving the rest of the family haunted by memories.

Decrying the stigma of unwed pregnancy and motherhood, Parton critiques men who leave women pregnant or suffering. Famously in the folk lament "Down from Dover," which first appeared on *The Fairest of Them All* and was frequently reissued on other albums, a pregnant woman cries for her lover to come down from Dover and join her; she realizes he is not coming when the baby is stillborn. Some Parton songs slam a man who left the speaker for another woman, such as "Mine" (1969), while others describe tragic experiences in which a woman sleeps with a man and becomes pregnant but is abandoned. In "Love Isn't Free," when a young man denies paternity, a young woman goes to a home for unwed mothers; her daughter later suffers in an orphanage, becoming the one "who's paying for love," not the man who has left them. Seeking comfort in such a situation, an unwed pregnant woman returns from the city to a country boy who still loves her in "Home for Pete's Sake" (1969), written by Rudy Preston. "The Bridge" (1968) criticizes the man who walked out on the pregnant female speaker; she jumps from a bridge and commits suicide, as if being a pregnant unwed mother would be a fate worse than death.

Parton expresses more incendiary ideas about female sexuality in her song-writing. She attacks the sexual double standard in "Just Because I'm a Woman" (1968) (number seventeen on the country singles chart), questioning why men are not condemned for sex before marriage but women are. The female speaker says a man will sleep with a woman but then look for "an angel" to marry, which persecutes the woman he slept with and left; she is now looked upon as fallen, with a ruined reputation. The female speaker reminds her male interlocutor that they have both slept with others before marriage, saying her actions and his should be seen equally, rather than the woman taking all the blame. Parton writes, "My mistakes are no worse than yours / Just because I'm a woman." Parton later said the song was inspired by her husband's extremely jealous reaction to finding out she had slept with other men before him. Parton does slightly buffer the song's critique, perhaps domesticating the message somewhat by linking it to her own autobiography. She links her discussion of female sexuality to a nonthreatening, domesticated marriage situation because in the song, the speaker is currently married. Parton also suggests monogamy in the past situation, saying that when the female speaker had sex before, she thought the man in question would stay with her, but he abandoned her. While it is a qualified idea, Parton nonetheless expresses a condemnation of sexual double standards and suggests a transgressive idea of female sexual freedom in that context. In a similar song, "It Ain't Fair That It Ain't," Parton likewise condemns a double standard in which a woman sleeps with a man who then leaves her.

Parton also writes about female sexuality in more explicit terms, depicting characters who express their sexual desires, as in "The Last One to Touch Me"

(1971) and "The Fire's Still Burning" (1971). Other Parton songs entreat male characters to give female characters respect or affection, questioning men who do not ("The Little Things" [1967]). Some suggest that the men should leave if they cannot give the women the love they want ("Don't Let It Trouble Your Mind" [1969]). "Touch Your Woman" (1972) urges male listeners to give their women sexual affection, linking physical to emotional intimacy. In "Don't Let It Trouble Your Mind," the female speaker says her man should leave if he does not love her. She would prefer to be alone than with someone who "doesn't love me," and she objects to him putting her down, "a-thinking you're above me." Some songs implore the man to accept the woman as she is ("Just the Way I Am" [1970]) or not to be overly possessive lest she leave him ("When Possession Gets Too Strong" [1970]).

However, alongside those forceful critiques, other songs warn female listeners about the costs to them of sexual double standards, as in "The Company You Keep," co-written with Bill Owens. That song is a standard prohibition against promiscuity, but it suggests that the men who engage in promiscuous behavior will not pay the same price as women. The speaker warns a female family member not to ruin her reputation through promiscuity, implying that it would also reflect poorly on the family.

Parton's playful answer songs to the battle of the sexes assert female agency in a popular feminism vein and censure gendered double standards against women. *Hello, I'm Dolly*, which reached eleventh on the country albums chart, rereleased her previous singles "Dumb Blonde" (written by Curly Putman) and "Something Fishy," both of which had been top-twenty-five hits previously on the country singles chart. The speaker in "Dumb Blonde" talks back to a cheating husband, who attempts to deny his infidelity; she slams stereotypes that she is unintelligent based on her appearance. In "Something Fishy," her previous single (top twenty on the country charts), Parton uses the trope of a female speaker rejecting her husband's infidelity. The chorus insists, "There's something fishy goin' on," because the husband's frequent fishing trips seem suspicious, as does the lipstick on his shirt. Speaking to the absent husband, the speaker threatens her own act of infidelity: "Some night when you come home and discover that I'm gone," he will be left the one wondering about "something fishy goin' on."

Parton similarly uses joke songs to condemn an inequitable gendered division of labor as well as women being expected to do domestic labor. She denounces a man who does not work and instead lives off of his wife's labors in "He's a Go Getter" (1969). The speaker describes a neighbor who lets his wife work while he plays checkers and jokes with his male friends, all of them living off of their own wives for income. He is a "go getter," meaning "he'll go get her" when she gets off of work, because he refuses to work. A similar song, "You Ole Handy Man" (1967), rebukes a male character who will not help with domestic labor, suggesting that men who do not contribute to the household labor are not living up to their responsibilities. The novelty joke song "I'll Oilwells Love You" (1968) treats gold digging satirically, suggesting that the speaker wants the oilman's money, and they will marry and live happily ever after because "oil's well that ends well." While the song seems an excuse for punning and wordplay, it nevertheless undermines the ideal of a happy marriage, implying that marriage could simply refer to an arrangement of convenience or that the ideal of domesticity does not match a more problematic reality within the institution of marriage and in the context of economic inequality.

In a cheating song theme, Parton covers a range of gender issues and responses. A number of songs slam the male cheater, such as "Fresh Out of Forgiveness," "I'm Fed up with You," "The Monkey's Tale," and "You Can't Reach Me Anymore." "You're Gonna Be Sorry" (1968) lightly references the Ernest Tubbs hit "Walking the Floor over You." The female speaker tells the straying male, "You'll walk the floor and you'll call my name, but I ain't gonna hear you," meaning since he is out cheating, she is going to leave him. Some songs more elaborately critique straying men, making a deeper argument about the effect on women. In "Daddy" (1969), which Parton later claimed was semi-autobiographical, the speaker begs her father not to leave her mother for a younger woman (younger than the daughter, even), because "you've taken her best years, so don't leave her now." The daughter cites her mother's hard labor to support him and their family, suggesting that if the mother's beauty has faded, it was from "working for you." In "Daddy Come and Get Me" (1970), a woman is put in a mental institution by a man who is leaving her for another woman; she wants her father to come and save her. In some songs, a woman holds onto memories even though her man has cheated or left her for another woman ("Mine," "Walls of My Mind," "Mission Chapel Memories") or even forgives him for hurting her ("As Long as I Love"). Several Parton songs threaten female violence in response to male cheating. In "J. J. Sneed" (1971), written by Parton and her aunt Dorothy Jo Hope, the female speaker laments that her outlaw lover, with whom she robbed and killed, has left her for an evil woman "with a painted face and pretty sweet disguise"; the singer says she intends to murder him for leaving her. In some, it is the woman who has strayed and asks forgiveness ("Love Is Only as Strong [as Your Weakest Moment]") or regrets cheating ("Loneliness Found Me").

In depictions of women and gender politics involving mistresses, some of Parton's songs have an antifeminist slant, blaming the other woman rather than the straying man. In "She Never Met a Man (She Didn't Like)" (1971), the speaker pleads with her man not to leave her for another woman to whom he will be just "a new acquaintance in the night." Placing blame on the other woman, the speaker asks the man not to let the other woman "ruin our lives." That song shares similarities with "Jolene," because the speaker begs another woman not to take her man and blames her, as if absolving the husband for any responsibility. Other lyrics focus on female betrayal of other women. In "Traveling Man" (1971), a young woman castigates her mother for leaving with the man she herself was going to run off with; she laments that she never knew her father and tells the mother, "I really don't think I ever knowed you either."

Many Parton songs explore intersecting class and gender critiques through romance narratives. In "Robert" (1970), the class bias of a previous generation affects the next. A rich boy has a crush on a girl, but she says he does not realize that they are siblings, because her mother was the poor girl that his rich father left behind. Even more forcefully, in "Chicken Every Sunday" (1971), written by Charlie Craig and Betty Craig, the speaker advocates working-class pride in response to negative social reactions to dating across class lines. A boy's family will not allow him to date the speaker because she is "lower class." Her mother insists she not let him or his family shame her, because "you're just as good as him," and "we won't take no sass off of them." The speaker expresses her own class pride and lauds her family's activities, like Sunday chicken dinner, the preacher visiting, and her father taking them to a picnic and Saturday movies in town. She concludes that if that is what lower class is, "then I'm glad that's what I am." Meanwhile, one notable Parton song critiques class stereotypes but reinforces gendered ones. The speaker in "A Little at a Time" (1972) is a working woman with a small weekly paycheck who can only pay off her credit debts a little at a time. She is "looking for that rich man I might find" but must support herself in the meantime and live off of credit. The idea that she needs to find a rich husband to save her clearly plays into stereotypes. However, her sense that she cannot make ends meet on her own paycheck is an implicit indictment of gendered pay inequities in which she would not be given the "family wage."

On the topic of the prospect for successful marriages or relationships, Parton does have a number of solo songs that idealize relationships, as epitomized by "Love Is Like a Butterfly." Porter Wagoner claims that he urged Parton to write more love songs rather than songs about her mountain experiences, because he felt more listeners could relate to a more universal theme. Some of her love songs are standard romantic fare with clichés about the need for faithfulness and stability in marriages. She also released songs that took the opposite stance, however. Parton covered the Bobby Braddock and Curly Putman song "D-I-V-O-R-C-E" in 1969, a hit Tammy Wynette song in 1968 (Wynette's version reached the top of the country chart). The song discusses divorce from the wife's perspective, with the word spelled out to shield the couple's young son from understanding that the parents are uncoupling.

Finally, some songs debate the difficulties of balancing marriage and career. One particular song offers an intriguing case study that contrasts sharply with her autobiographical narratives. In "False Eyelashes" (1968), written by Bob Tubert and Demetrius Tapp, the female speaker has given up family and a boy who loved her for empty fame on "the wrong side of the world," the foolhardiness of her venture signified by her fake eyelashes and "a tube of cheap lipstick" along with worn high heels and an ill-fitting dress. While the speaker's disillusionment critiques a harsh music industry, the song otherwise is not in keeping with Parton's image, in which she uses her fake appearance to play off of her underlying "real" sincerity. The song also implies that the woman should have married the man and stayed at home rather than seeking an ill-fated singing career.

Parton's own life trajectory bucks that narrative as well, since she continually insisted that she could do both, be married and have her singing career. The degree to which she was departing from social norms at the time is evident in the ongoing rumors about her nontraditional marriage to Carl Dean, in which some used to suggest that he did not exist or that it was not a real marriage, while Parton insisted on the validity of her personal model of marriage. The song "False Eyelashes" and its departure from Parton's persona serve to highlight the tenets of her own character as a counter example.

As I examine in the following chapter, during the next stage of her career, Parton would further develop that persona and interweave it with a range of media texts. In particular, her entrance onto a much bigger media platform in Hollywood films changed her image. Parton's status as a multimedia superstar added significant new components to her gender performance.

Notes

1. Neal, *Jimmie Rodgers*, 28–30.
2. Neal, *Country Music*, 256–258.
3. Nash, *Dolly*, 164.

4. Parton, *Dolly*, 180.

5. Nash, *Dolly*, 157.

6. Ibid., 50–51.

7. Cardwell, *Words and Music*, 21.

8. Nash, *Dolly*, 69.

9. Cardwell, *Words and Music*, 17.

10. Nash, *Dolly*, 69.

11. Harkins, *Hillbilly*.

12. Pecknold, "Negotiating Gender," 153–157.

13. Ibid.

14. Her official website, DollyParton.com, includes all of her album covers.

15. Oermann, *Behind*, 141–142.

16. Berger, *Ways*.

17. Parton, *Dolly*, 168.

18. Gramsci, *Selections*, 453.

19. Gundersen, "'Trio.'"

20. Tichi, *High Lonesome*, 25–30, 45–50.

21. McCusker, *Lonesome Cowgirls*.

22. Harkins, *Hillbilly*, 140.

23. Ibid., 138.

24. Ibid., 8.

25. Newitz and Wray, *White Trash*, 1–14.

26. Harkins, *Hillbilly*, 101.

27. Parton, *Dolly*, 308.

28. Harkins, *Hillbilly*, 139.

29. Ibid., 7.

30. See Greeson, *Our South*; Bone, *Postsouthern*; McPherson, *Reconstructing Dixie*; Smith, *Purple America*; and Romine, *Real South*.

31. Fox, *Natural Acts*, 138–142. Fox adapts Judith Butler's theories of gender performativity to include race and argue for this identification and disavowal model. Fox, *Natural Acts*, 7–8.

32. Ching, *Wrong's What I Do Best*. Nadine Hubbs discusses how Gretchen Wilson garners cultural capital for a "redneck" subject position. Hubbs, "'Redneck Woman.'" See especially her application of sociologist Beverly Skeggs's class models of "cultural exchange-value," in which individuals borrow from race, class, gender, and sexuality subject positions in order to garner power in Western political and symbolic economies. Skeggs, *Formations of Class and Gender: Becoming Respectable* (London: Sage, 1997); *Class, Self, Culture* (London: Routledge, 2004).

33. Ching, *Wrong's What I Do Best*.

34. Peterson, *Creating Country Music*, 153.

35. Hubbs, "'Redneck Woman.'"

36. Nash, *Dolly*.

37. Ching, *Wrong's What I Do Best*, 5.

38. "An Interview with Porter Wagoner."

39. Peterson, *Creating Country Music*, 150–156.

40. Ching, *Wrong's What I Do Best*, 15.

Parton's Crossover and Film Stardom

The "Hillbilly Mae West"

I look one way and am another. It makes for a good combination.
I always think of her, the Dolly image, like a ventriloquist does his
dummy. I have fun with it. I think, "What will I do with her this
year to surprise people; what will she wear; what will she say?"

—Dolly Parton

I'm gonna be Mae West, not Dolly Parton. I've watched all
her films. I've always thought she was great. And we're not
that different as far as our attitude and our personality.

—Dolly Parton

Dolly Parton frames her self-conscious fashioning of her own image as a character, a persona she can inhabit, a tool she uses to garner audience interest in
her performances, whether on the musical stage, television, or a film screen.
Parton's Hollywood film stardom in particular has allowed her to engage in ever
more elaborate formulations of her persona. For example, her fervent statement
that she dreamed of playing Mae West should come as no surprise.

Some of West's brand of campiness has found its way into Parton's image, and the ironic, sexualized camp she references from West sheds light on how Parton created her own star image. Indeed, Parton used West's screen persona as one guiding compass during her efforts to become a film star. As actors, both became known for a sexualized screen persona. West's drawling "come hither" lines are as iconic as Parton's giggled vamping. Both also used irony to control that image. Where they differ is that Parton's gendered image is very specific to country music performance history, with her mountain girl and hillbilly tramp. Yet when Parton began to shock some of her country audiences during her crossover period in the 1970s and 1980s with more provocative costumes and banter, some of her most combustible looks were direct quotations of West, homages to West's hairstyle and dresses. Since the 1980s, Parton has talked about wanting to play West in a television biopic.[1] Although that idea has never come to fruition, Parton has long been interested in embodying the West persona, in "being Mae West."

Parton's screen performance moments that most echo West involve her combination of gendered risqué humor and camp. Parton, like West, delivers precise, sophisticated jokes that depend on the speaker framing herself as a sexualized object but at the same time seizing an ironic distance from her own objectification. When asked to explain the source of her fascination with West, Parton muses that she always identified with West's style and manner as an actor onstage and onscreen. In particular, in Parton's role as the madam in *The Best Little Whorehouse in Texas* (1982), she explicitly mimicked West's look with her gowns and wigs and also channeled West's screen persona and delivery, including signature one-liners. West's most famous tag lines were, "Why don't you come up sometime and see me?" and "Is that a gun in your pocket or are you just happy to see me?" In *The Best Little Whorehouse in Texas*, Parton made an homage to West when she delivered the line, "Come see me, boys." Meanwhile, Parton's country bumpkin sexpot secretary character in *9 to 5* (1980) rejects her male boss's advances with, "I'm going to change you from a rooster to a hen with one shot," a line Parton said she took from her own life but which also echoes the West brand of sexualized camp. As a speaker, Parton claims a sexpot status but also an ironic distance from that image; she speaks from outside of that objectification dynamic, making fun of it.

The comparison between Parton and West is a vital one because it illustrates how Parton uses camp and irony and how she went about becoming a film star.

Parton's careful shaping of her own star image sheds light on models of celebrity and film stardom in US media history. The analogy also speaks to gendered power dynamics in the entertainment industry. However, they differ in important ways, because West arguably ended her career having lost control over her own image, instead appearing in films that made fun of her, what Pamela Robertson dubs a "tragic camp artifact."[2] In contrast, Parton has managed to exercise her own agency and maintain control over her own image.

In this chapter, I analyze the evolution of Parton's gender performance and construction of authenticity in her media image and music in the crossover period of her career, covering the late 1970s through the mid-1990s. I assess how her gender performance became more complex during this era, with a new balance between her "fake" appearance and "real" personality. I pay particular attention to her career juncture that sparked journalistic debates about authenticity at the time—her pop crossover in the late 1970s and early 1980s, featuring such hit albums as *Here You Come Again* (1977) and *Heartbreaker* (1978). Some Nashville insiders protested that she had abandoned country music and Music Row, while Parton contended that she would take country with her into other mass media contexts.[3] This chapter traces the story of her gender performance from her efforts to go solo (1976); her first self-produced country album where she tried to layer in more pop elements, *New Harvest . . . First Gathering* (1977); through her subsequent string of fully crossover pop albums and her Kenny Rogers duets. I include in this era her 1980s and 1990s Hollywood film career, her Dollywood launch (1986), and her evolving musical performances up until just before she began reemphasizing her country roots in the mid- to late 1990s, in albums like *Heartsongs* (1994) and notably *Hungry Again* (1998).

After elaborating on her biography in terms of her career trajectory with her films, television shows, and albums during this period, I focus on two case studies. The first is how her 1985 "Real Love" tour with Kenny Rogers epitomized the dynamics of her gender performance and stage persona during that time; in concert footage from that tour, the animated Parton stalks Rogers, vamps around the stage, and amplifies her burlesque elements with some explicit visual references to Mae West. The second is how her screen role in *The Best Little Whorehouse in Texas* showcases her use of camp, her homage to West, and her own version of an ironic, sexualized star image. I also discuss how her other film and television work during this epoch helped shape her persona and reflects on larger ideas of stardom in US culture.

Career Contexts on Screen

Parton's specific gender performance adjustments during this period signal her efforts to buttonhook a mainstream audience, summit record charts in a variety of categories, and elevate her mass culture appeal. She began amplifying the sexualized elements of her look and persona, but in a more glamorous, contemporary way, to target a larger mass audience. In her stage costuming, she incorporated more sophisticated dresses, including low-cut gowns, shorter wigs, and chic accessories. She retained key parts of her mountain girl persona, particularly her use of autobiographical narratives in her self-presentation, but her references to gendered images from country music history were slightly more muted and leavened by contemporary images. In sum, her gender performance continued to balance the mountain girl and town tramp elements, but she added in glamorous images to the sexualized part of her persona, such as Hollywood star codes, while still using the sincerity of her mountain girl autobiography to domesticate the more sexualized image. In addition, she started adding in direct references to sexualized star personas from film, like that of Mae West, thereby increasing her level of knowing irony and parody, creating a distance from the sexualized image through exaggeration.

Indeed, her film and television stardom during this period fundamentally impacted her image, just as her country authenticity tropes illuminate common notions of stardom, or star discourse. Film theorist Richard Dyer has argued that star images serve to resolve larger ideological contradictions involving, for example, tensions in society between a supposed meritocracy versus class hierarchies or unequal access. The "star made good" story appears to resolve that contradiction by suggesting one can be self-made because a celebrity appears to use some extraordinary talent to gain fame, fortune, and class status.[4] I have already discussed how Parton's persona reconciles opposed ideas in country music history, notably the folk, real, and pure versus the mass, fake, and manufactured. In her film persona, she reconciles those binaries in similar ways, but she adds another layer of complexity to her media image, notably with her increased use of camp and sexualized images on film. Parton is often perceived as if she is just playing a version of herself onscreen, but the way she incorporates her own authenticity narrative into her star image is quite complex.

For example, Parton's television context is enduring and integral to her career. As a country star working on TV since age ten, Parton already had a media image that consciously engaged with TV performance codes, influencing her signature look and her ability to engage TV audiences with her projections of sincerity. However, the earlier television codes she addressed were particular to syndicated country music television. In this crossover moment of her career, Parton began to engage with a broader set of codes. While her first variety show of her own, *Dolly!* (1976–1977), was still a syndicated show, it did attempt to incorporate some crossover elements. Meanwhile, her second eponymous series, *Dolly* (1987–1988), was a network show on ABC and a fully crossover program, in the sense that it was intended to reach a broad, nationwide audience, although it was canceled after one year due to declining ratings. Also during this period, she starred in TV films that showcased aspects of her autobiography and persona in a crossover context, ranging from *Smoky Mountain Christmas* (1986) to *Unlikely Angel* (1996).

Through her wealth of appearances, Parton illuminates how country music and southern stereotypes can signify in both television and film. In this crossover moment, Parton risks becoming a caricature of a hillbilly tramp for broader outsider audiences, some of whom might laugh at the stereotype and use it to reinforce negative southern, white, working-class stereotypes. However, because Parton incorporates nuanced camp and irony, she defuses that potential putdown, often by making jokes about her appearance before others do. She deflects any possible criticism by using her country music mode of address, that is, a projection of sincerity.

Some of her famous talk show interviews from this period illustrate how Parton was adapting her persona along those lines, as in her first two interviews on Johnny Carson's *The Tonight Show* (January and February 1977) and a Barbara Walters interview (December 1977).[5] There, she presented herself and her autobiography using sincerity codes familiar to country music audiences but more novel and engaging to mass audiences. In his initial responses to her, Carson framed her as a native informant about Appalachia and country music. On her first visit, Carson famously became spellbound by her life story and treated her as if she was an endearingly quaint manifestation of the "contemporary ancestor," or the voice of a supposedly simpler time. In the interview, Carson candidly discusses "Dolly Parton" jokes with her. She retells several "boob jokes" other country musicians and comedians made about her, using cornpone humor that reflects a barn dance rube humor influence, jokes that would be familiar in a Grand Ole Opry setting. Carson then calls her "zaftig." Not sure she would know that term, he asks what term they would use where she grew up; she replies, "healthy." She is about to respond to rumors about whether or not her breasts are real when he interrupts and says, "I have certain guidelines on this show, but I would give about a year's pay to peek under there." His infamous, oft-quoted line evokes laughter from his audience, but his joke is much more direct than the corny ones she had been repeating. He responds to her projection of earnest truthfulness, but he also makes jokes at her expense, implying that the audience would understand his humor more than she would.

In contrast, when Carson invited Parton to return the next month for a second interview, he framed her as a witty participant-observer who could also be recognizable to a broader general audience. In that interview, they both joke in a more ironic way about her appearance. Parton delivers one of her standard one-liners: "I enjoy the way I look, but it's a joke," as if to make sure that the audience understands that her look is meant to be ironic.

Similarly, in the Barbara Walters interview, Walters at first handles Parton like an innocent documentary subject and only gradually begins to shift her approach, later treating Parton as a knowledgeable interviewee who exhibits sophistication and irony. Walters questions if Parton is a hillbilly. Parton replies that she is, but she goes on to give a multilayered description of her own hillbilly look. She explains her image as a "gimmick," knowingly a cartoon look, like Daisy Mae. Responding to an implicit class critique, or outsider put-down of her as "white trash," she tells Walters she believes in having "country class" (claiming dignity for the hillbilly identity position) so that she is not looked down upon or ridiculed.

As I discuss in chapter 5, Parton's more recent TV appearances maintain a balance of sincerity and irony but more explicitly incorporate her ironic elements, as when she has adapted her persona to a reality TV context that requires a knowing performance of the self, one she is perfectly suited to do.[6] Parton has replicated that same dynamic in appearances with talk show hosts up through Jimmy Fallon on the current incarnation of *The Tonight Show.* In recent guest visits there, she projects a campy, sexualized image, replete with "boob jokes," and Fallon happily plays cheeky games with her and tries on her wigs. But she nevertheless still deploys her country sincerity mode of address. Fallon listens transfixed whenever she tells her "down home" mountain stories, fascinated by her as if she is a witness of a supposedly purer way of life.[7] Parton has sometimes been described as being able to charm people so thoroughly with her folksiness that they will accept the most outlandish stories from her.[8] However, it would be more accurate to say that Parton has a highly calibrated stage persona, mashing up irony and sincerity, plastic and pure, her rhetoric of fake and real.

Musical Crossover Controversy and
"Dolly Parton" as a Character

It is important to analyze Parton's specific crossover moment in 1977 and 1978 more closely for how it reveals her evolution as she attempted to reposition herself to adapt her sound and image to a broader mass audience. In her late 1970s–1990s epoch, her pop crossover albums tried to present her as hip and contemporary, suitable for a vaster audience. She utilized different stylistic elements of classic country but also incorporated more features of other genres, such as R&B and disco. In addition to writing some pop songs that focused on more general themes, like love and relationships, she continued to write songs that market her specific version of critical rural nostalgia. As she did in her earlier, formative stage of her career, Parton during this crossover era continued to tie her articulation of popular feminism to her autobiographical narratives, as if domesticating her gender ideas and making them less potentially threatening to some audiences by rooting them in her life story. During this epoch, she brought mass culture, folk culture, and gender themes together when she linked popular feminism and mountain folk culture and expressed it in a high circulation, mass culture form.

The steps she took to launch that pop music crossover, particularly in 1977 and 1978, disclose her careful navigation of her music and her self-presentation as a character. Having ended her family band, her new management helped her put together her Gypsy Fever band. By May 1977, she had already abandoned her brief experimentation with a gypsy image of hoop earrings and bandanas. She made a deal with new manager Sandy Gallin that she would produce *New Harvest . . . First Gathering* (coproduced with her musical director Gregg Perry), but that if the album was not a major sales success, she would agree to let Gallin get an outside producer on the next album. *New Harvest* did receive strong critical reviews and some sales success, topping the country charts for one week and reaching number seventy-one on the pop chart. However, it was not the substantial success in both country and pop that they were seeking. Thus, Gallin brought in Gary Klein to produce *Here You Come Again*. Klein then coproduced *Heartbreaker* with Parton, an album distinctive for demonstrating more easy-listening and disco influences.

During 1977–1978, Parton boosted her mainstream media exposure. Her high-profile guest appearances included the Carson and Walters interviews, as well as a spot on Mac Davis's TV special and musical tour. In other efforts that targeted a broad audience, she cohosted Mike Douglas's talk show with him for a week, appeared on Cher's variety show, and was a celebrity on *Hollywood Squares*. Likewise, Parton made triumphant trips to New York City, lauded at concerts attended by everyone from Andy Warhol to Jane Fonda. During one concert tour in 1978, where Eddie Rabbitt was opening for her, Mayor Ed Koch gave her the key to the city, she did a show at the Palladium, and there was a party in her honor at Studio 54.

While Parton was amplifying her multimedia presence, some of the more sexualized media images of her sparked controversy, most notably her "Daisy Mae in the haystack" poster (1978), her *Playboy* cover (1978), and the racy *Rolling Stone* interview with Chet Flippo (1977).[9] In the *Rolling Stone* story, she told dirty jokes and appeared in the dual pictorial with Arnold Schwarzenegger, photographed by Annie Leibovitz. The pictures emphasized hypermasculinity as well as hyperfemininity in several playful images. One photograph features Parton standing in front of Schwarzenegger as he flexes his bare muscles behind her. She wears an iteration of her familiar look: a gaudy pink-and-white sequined jumpsuit, a rose in her hair, exaggerated makeup and long platinum blonde wig, garish jewelry and fingernails. The pose emphasizes her breasts as well as his muscles, but the image also makes her appear superimposed in front of him, as if it is a trick doubled image in which his arms could at first appear to be hers. That juxtaposition adds a critical element to the image, drawing attention to the pose as an artificial one and even slightly defamiliarizing their bodily appearances.

Parton's suddenly more incendiary appearance did spark some backlash in Nashville. Parton altered her costuming during this crossover period, wearing shorter wigs and more contemporary, low-cut dresses and outfits. Biographer Alanna Nash argues that Parton's first public low-cut gown was on Cher's TV special in 1978 and that it surprised country audiences, running counter to Parton's former well-known efforts to cover up her bust, albeit in skin-tight dresses.[10]

While country audiences still supported Parton (she even won the CMA Entertainer of the Year Award in 1978), Parton's crossover efforts prompted fierce press and industry debates about authenticity. The criticism of country stars for doing crossover pop and watering down or betraying "pure" country music is a familiar one, still evident today in ambivalent responses to Taylor Swift "going pop" with her critically and commercially successful album *1989* (2014) and to Shania Twain's earlier country-pop albums. Of course, that objection is problematic because the genre boundaries are blurry to begin with and are based on arbitrary and shifting distinctions, just as the country "purity" narrative is a subjective one.

Some Nashville industry insiders worried at the time that Parton was being sold as a degraded sex symbol not aware of how she was being exploited, while others insisted she was in charge of her own image and would eventually discern how to win mass appeal but keep country roots. Since journalist Nash was writing her Parton biography precisely at that time, she reported on the industry uproar about Parton "going pop and Hollywood." Nash herself bemoans what she views as Parton's loss of authenticity in her performances and interviews after 1977. Comparing her own interviews with Parton from 1977 versus 1978, Nash contends, "Dolly has another image to work on, one that will let her young, newly acquired hip fans know that she's just kidding when she wears all her sequined trappings."[11] Concerned Parton was blindly being taken advantage of by others, Nash cites critics who worried Parton was being hoodwinked by Hollywood and New York entertainment executives; perhaps Parton was too desperate to turn herself into a joke before others could, enclosing herself in an increasingly self-parodic mask, with a sexualized image that exploited and degraded her without Parton realizing it. Many fretted that her Los Angeles management team exerted a deleterious influence, and that producer Mike Post had turned her touring show into Las Vegas–style plastic sheen, as when Post had Parton turn her classic "down home" songs into a brisk medley rather than performing those songs in their entirety. Parton still often performs a medley version in concerts today.

Nash bemoans the loss of what she asserts were Parton's more spontaneous and "authentic" performances prior to the Los Angeles influence. Revisiting this question years later, in a 2002 update to the biography, Nash suggests that Parton's ultimately long-running entertainment industry success and promotion of country music settled that earlier debate in Parton's favor, proving that she was in control of her own image. As Nash notes, some of the earlier controversy occurred because Parton was the most famous established female country star to go pop at that time.[12]

My own view in this kind of debate about Parton's identity is that Parton has always had a degree of self-awareness and parody in her performance. During this period of her career, she was simply adapting her performance codes to different contexts and carefully fashioning them, from her early work in syndicated country music television to Hollywood films. It would not be accurate to say that an earlier persona was purely "her" and more natural and authentic, as compared to the more Hollywood glam crossover image she projected beginning in the late 1970s. Rather, she traded syndicated country music television modes of address for more mass-appeal network television and Hollywood film codes. As I discuss more fully in the final sections of this chapter, this kind of varying performance of the self based on media context defines star discourse. The contention by some observers that the folk Parton was the more real Parton is a problematic claim, because it repeats the familiar country music "authenticity" narrative that values a subjective distinction of folk purity over manufactured sheen. The point is that the music and the image are all created pieces of cultural expression; one kind is not inherently "purer" than the other.

Nash goes so far as to suggest that Parton has played herself as a character for so long that she has become that character, and that there is nothing underneath the image; she cites other journalists and Nashville industry insiders expressing similar concerns.[13] Other observers have likewise raised that issue. For example, in an interview for a Biography channel Parton documentary (2006), Kathy Mattea recounts trying to talk with Parton backstage at the Grand Ole Opry, as other female performers would chat and let their guard down, being themselves. Mattea insists that Parton would not "let down the mask," leaving Mattea to wonder about the costs of maintaining that character 24–7 and never being able to leave it behind and simply "be normal."[14]

However, Parton refers to her own persona as a character in quite sophisticated ways, suggesting that since the artificiality of show business prompts people to play themselves as characters, she is merely exaggerating her persona more obviously than others. Parton discusses "Dolly Parton" as a character she plays, an explicit persona she inhabits. In the telling passage I used as an epigraph for this chapter, Parton explains, "I look one way and am another. It makes for a good combination. I always think of her, the Dolly image, like a ventriloquist does his dummy."[15] Parton uses her fake appearance versus real sincerity distinction; she uses the fake "Dolly image" as an entry point for the presentation of her talent, knowingly shocking audiences in order to draw their attention to her artistic expression. She argues, "The whole purpose of the image was a gimmick to catch people's attention and then to let them know there was a person underneath it that did sing, write songs, and was very serious about her music," with the audience needing to "get over the shock of my image before they can get real serious about my music." Detailing how she positions her "Dolly image" as a character, Parton suggests that she never takes off her makeup and only wants to be seen in character, precisely to maintain that character identity for her fans. She observes that if fans saw her without her makeup and costuming, "It would've been a disappointment, even though you might not realize it. Because the character would have died, and characters do not die."[16]

Indeed, Parton's stage persona has always been a knowing character. Her "Dolly image" has its own mythology and signature look, its own camp icon status, and its own longevity, with the life story mythology, well-worn and polished like a stone, helping to keep the character alive permanently in narrative. Further commenting on her use of a fakeness rhetoric and applying it to all of show business, Parton observes of her image: "It's ridiculous, but it's fun. It's just the way I choose to enjoy the business. . . . I could choose to be very stylish if I chose to be, but I would never stoop so low as to be fashionable. . . . Show business is a big fake, anyway the biggest part of it. So I choose to do the fake part in a joyful way. . . . I don't want to look like everybody else, I don't want to be like everyone else, 'cause I'm not."[17] Parton here claims her own distinctiveness for her hyperbolic fake persona. As I discuss in chapter 5, it is Parton's long history of carefully turning herself into a character that makes her perfectly suited for reality TV appearances in which she is asked to play herself as a role.

Case Study: The "Real Love" Tour

Perhaps the best specific example of how Parton presents herself as a character in performance during this era is her 1985 "Real Love" tour with Kenny Rogers, which epitomized her evolving stage persona and gender performance. As an HBO documentary of a tour concert captures, she includes a solo set that nods to her past country performances as well as a duet set with Rogers that places her more firmly in a crossover pop context.[18] In this section, I provide a close textual analysis of the concert; in my next section, I provide fuller context for that tour with a discussion of her albums and recordings during this time to show specifically how she was addressing broader crossover musical contexts. The tour was designed to support Parton's crossover efforts after her initial successes with albums like *Here You Come Again, Heartbreaker, Great Balls of Fire* (1979), and *Dolly, Dolly, Dolly* (1980), as well as her film soundtracks, *9 to 5* (1981) and *Rhinestone* (1984). In teaming with Rogers, she was targeting continued success on country, pop, and adult contemporary charts.

During this tour, Parton amplified certain parts of her stage persona as she tried to appeal to a mass audience. The concert footage demonstrates how she retained some components of her "country bumpkin" mountain girl persona but sometimes downplayed those aspects to a greater degree, while she glamorized her sexualized tramp part of her image to fit a more mainstream mass culture context. Opening with the Parton solo set, followed by a Rogers solo set, the concert concludes with their duet segment. During the concluding duets, Parton highlights the sexualized tramp aspect of her look, bouncing her hips and engaging in risqué stage banter with Rogers. In her costuming, she mimics a Mae West style she also used in *The Best Little Whorehouse in Texas*, here with a long, skin-tight, low-cut black ball gown with a high leg slit, and a blond wig styled much like West's signature look. However, Parton also underscores a more sophisticated projection of irony, in the sense that she deploys a multilayered vision of glamor and elaborate banter with Rogers. Meanwhile, in her solo section, her mountain girl persona is a bigger part of her performance, alongside the sexualized tramp image. She plays her banjo for certain songs (like "Appalachian Memories") and wears a country-themed stage costume, a tight yellow, low-cut dress with rhinestones and a Western shirt design, with a tassel-fringed skirt and a long blonde wig. In both costumes, she maintains her exaggerated makeup, multicolored eyeshadow, excessively long red nails, and five-inch heels.

Here, Parton balances her mountain girl and hillbilly tramp imagery in a new commercial setting, as she tried to extend her crossover appeal to pop audiences by building on her earlier successful duets with Rogers. Specifically, their duet "Real Love," which topped the country chart, was their follow-up to their signature hit duet "Islands in the Stream" (1983), a song that proved the crossover appeal of both artists. "Islands in the Stream" became a platinum-selling single that topped four *Billboard* charts: country, pop, adult contemporary, and Hot 100. The ongoing appeal of "Islands in the Stream" has continued; decades later, Country Music Television (CMT) named it the top country duet of all time. After recording it, Parton and Rogers would collaborate over the next five years on three albums, two world tours, and four TV specials, becoming closely associated with each other in the public imagination. In his autobiography, Rogers notes how fans still ask him "where's Dolly," as if the two should always perform together. The cultural reception of their duets was gendered, with audiences interpreting them as a romantic couple onstage even though they publicly denied any involvement. Rogers describes Parton in performance as a force of nature, noting that she almost bowled him over onstage on the "Real Love" tour. They were choreographed to walk around opposite sides of the circular stage and meet in the middle, but she would stalk the stage so quickly that she would overtake him.[19]

The "Islands in the Stream" song and history illustrate Parton's attempts to merge genres and audiences at that time. Originally written for Rogers, the Bee Gees–penned disco song was suggested as a duet for Rogers and Parton by Barry Gibb. Musicologist Jocelyn Neal has argued that "Islands in the Stream" perfectly encapsulates countrypolitan as a musical style in the early 1980s, speaking to how disco, country, and pop were merging, with the song becoming popular in the easy-listening category too. Both singers were recording pop styles rather than classic country then, and Parton had used disco. Neal notes that the song's lyrics, instrumentation, vocal styles, and musical structure all reference countrypolitan, not traditional country, with strings, horns, synthesized sounds, a pop-style drum part, breathy vocals, rhythmic syncopation, and a distinctive prechorus (following the verse, leading to the chorus) that is one of the earliest instances of a common countrypolitan song feature and a structural marker of pop influences. Regarding Parton's singing specifically, Neal points out her use of 1980s pop-rock stylistics, as when she modulates the key when singing lead and shifts from brassy belt to a breathy sound.[20]

Both singers parlayed the song's commercial success into further albums, television specials, the tour, and a series of joint family-friendly Christmas albums and TV specials. A CBS television special promoting their album, *Once upon a Christmas* (1984), established their stage patter formula. There, Parton flirted and joked with Rogers using cornpone humor.

Meanwhile, the "Real Love" tour was designed to aid Parton on the pop charts. Her *Real Love* (1985) album had singles on the country and adult contemporary charts and received a country Grammy nomination, but it struggled more on the pop charts. Both "Real Love" and her single "Think about Love" topped the country chart, while "Real Love" also reached the pop chart (ninety-first) and the adult contemporary chart (thirteenth). Other singles had country and adult contemporary success but not pop, including "Don't Call It Love" (third on country, twelfth on adult contemporary) and "Tie Our Love (in a Double Knot)" (seventeenth on country).

As evident from the HBO special, the staging of the "Real Love" show depended on the charisma of Parton's stage persona to tie together disparate musical genres, alongside the hit Rogers pop songs that were familiar to the mainstream audience. The tour had over forty US concert dates with capacity audiences in large indoor stadium venues, including sports arenas and civic centers, followed by concerts in Australia and New Zealand. The HBO special, *Kenny and Dolly: Real Love* (1985), was recorded at a Portland, Oregon, concert date.

The concert footage encapsulates how Parton is using gender and sexuality codes to establish her star persona at that time. The documentary goes to great lengths to confirm both Parton and Rogers as stars by including fan interaction sequences; each walk through adoring crowds as they come to the stage for their solo sets. They leave together after their concluding duet set, pushing through the screaming fans. The special also includes staged, behind-the-scenes footage, with Parton and Rogers rehearsing together. As with star discourse, the behind-the-scenes footage buttresses the public persona, because the backstage footage provides the audience with greater "access," but they are still performing in their stage personas.

In the behind-the-scenes footage, Parton places more emphasis on the comic rube, country bumpkin aspect of her persona in contrast to Rogers. She flirts and jokes with Rogers, who makes fun of her cornpone jokes and seems to want to appear more sophisticated and urbane, distancing himself from her country barn dance style of humor. She sings Rogers some of what she calls her "bad songs," that is, joke songs like "I Will Oilwells Love You," then amuses him by singing his song "Blaze of Glory" with him and lip synching as a band member sings the baritone part. Parton's costuming in this footage links her more to country than do her concert costumes. In the studio, she wears a red gingham shirt and denim skirt with a cut, jagged hem, emphasizing a comedic country look. Parton claims the country sincerity mode of address as an authenticity marker when she and Rogers rehearse "The Stranger," a folk-inflected ballad Parton wrote and Rogers recorded (1984). Parton sings the song's melody, and Rogers joins in on the chorus, singing harmony. The lyrics tell the story of a straying father and husband who tries to come home again, but the speaker, here Parton as daughter, tells him not to bother the mother anymore because "you're just a stranger." In this rehearsal studio footage, Parton emphasizes her earnest sincerity during that song, abandoning her comedic irony.

In contrast, the concert footage underlines Parton's efforts to toggle between country and pop modes of address and performance. In her solo set, she tries to cohere her oeuvre through her folksy persona. The raised circular stage allows her to interact more with the audience. She opens, as she often still does in concert, with the up-tempo "Baby I'm Burning" (1978), which mixes country, pop, and disco elements. The song was a hit on multiple *Billboard* charts, speaking to the crossover elements; it topped the country chart and performed well on the dance chart (fifteenth), Hot 100 (twenty-fifth), and adult contemporary (eleventh). In keeping with some of Parton's common gender themes, the lyrics are about sexual desire, the female speaker singing, "Your eyes reflect love and desire / I see that you need me, I need you to please me." At this show, Parton shouts and claps and stalks the stage, out of breath by the end of the song, engaging the crowd as fans hand her teddy bears and roses, which she tosses to her band members in the lowered pit in the stage's inner circle. The staging also includes some typical pop elements from the era, such as a laser light show, while the HBO special has a number of campy graphics that occasionally appear, such as a stardust graphic around Parton or Parton throwing a ball of light at Rogers.

In her set, Parton continues to switch back and forth between pop crossover and classic country. When she sings "Two Doors Down," she uses a more staccato delivery; the performance highlights that song's pop and rock elements, including the electric bass line. Meanwhile, "Here You Come Again" emphasizes the pop crossover aspect of her sound, as Parton uses standard rather than Appalachian pronunciations on that song, particularly on the song's chorus. She serenades individual fans during that song. In stark contrast to her country pop songs, she includes a section of her classic country songs in a more traditional and folk style. She plays banjo on "Applejack," accompanying herself solo at the beginning of the song. On "Appalachian Memories," she foregrounds the gospel elements of the song, with backup vocalists singing in close gospel harmonies and gospel-style piano fills. In performance here, she raises her hands to the sky when singing about religious faith and hope, mimicking being in church and singing a hymn.[21]

The HBO special intercuts Parton's solo section with Rogers's in a medley of song excerpts, creating a jarring juxtaposition between Parton's traditional and Appalachian folk and Rogers's disco, rock, and pop songs. An excerpt from Parton singing "Applejack" on her banjo is followed quickly by footage of Rogers singing his disco song "She's a Mystery." The jump cut from Parton to Rogers delivers a genre whiplash effect. In her segments, Parton continues with some of her hit folk-inflected songs, such as "Coat of Many Colors," with her playing acoustic guitar, and "Jolene." The discontinuity between Parton's solo music and Rogers's suggests how important Parton's persona is in pulling all of her music together. She too has crossover disco, rock, and pop elements in some of her songs, but the segues between her songs do not seem as abrupt and out of place as they do when the scenes shift from Parton to Rogers.

The way Parton depends on her stage persona also becomes evident when she engages in stage banter with the audience or with Rogers. Notably, Parton plays up her ironic sexpot persona right before she is about to sing a gospel-inflected song, resulting in her typical, distinctive juxtaposition of sex and religion. Introducing "Appalachian Memories," she exclaims that "this song is for all the daddies in the audience," noting that the song is about her own father's brief sojourn in Detroit to find work, where he found strength in memories of home.

As a college-age male fan in the audience catcalls her, she teases him by exclaiming, "You ain't nobody's daddy" and "you've been looking up my dress ever since I came out here." The audience responds with laughter and applause.

In comparison, Rogers does not attempt to maintain different sides of a persona nor does he treat the country differently from the pop genre. He instead insistently frames himself in terms of pop stardom throughout. He tries to establish his level of success by describing himself as "one of the few" chosen to sing the pop and R&B celebrity single "We Are the World," the Lionel Richie and Michael Jackson composition that raised money for Ethiopian famine relief. He also emphasizes rock styles on songs like "A Little More Love," which features an electric guitar solo typical of the era. He effectively emphasizes a pop presentation style for his crossover country-pop hits, such as "The Gambler" (1978), "Coward of the County" (1979), and the Richie-authored "Lady" (1980). Each of those singles achieved notable crossover success, topping the Billboard country singles chart but also reaching other charts, including pop, adult contemporary, and the *Billboard* Hot 100 (which "Lady" topped for six weeks). "Lady" in particular demonstrated genre versatility, combining R&B, country, and pop.

Their concluding duets set underlines how different their stage personae are from each other. Rogers conveys a pop-rock detached coolness, while Parton continues her cornpone humor and sexpot banter. In their costuming, Rogers projects a more understated gender performance of masculinity, clad in a casual white bomber jacket, sleeves pushed up to his elbows, and black pants. Meanwhile Parton, in her black sparkling ball gown, bends to emphasize the high-cut leg slit and coyly flips her dangling earrings, her performance of femininity even more exaggerated than in her solo set. Her banter includes ad libs that reference gender politics and sexuality. In their opening duet, "We've Got Tonight," Rogers sings his opening lines from the stage, while Parton makes a splashy spotlighted entrance, singing her answering lines from offstage, reentering the arena and walking through the crowd to the stage. For the line "Who needs tomorrow," Parton laughs and ad libs, "Who needs Sheena Easton," as a joke about Rogers previously performing that duet with pop singer Easton. In their stage patter, while she flirts with Rogers or teases him for singing with someone else or for his signature singing style, he almost exclusively responds with Parton "boob jokes," which she quickly reframes ironically. When she mimics his vibrato, saying she wishes she could sing that way, Rogers quotes one of her "boob jokes" back at her, jesting that she could do that vibrato like him, but she would have to be careful not to bounce her chest or she would get "two black eyes." Parton replies, "That

Kenny Rogers, he sure is a funny rascal, huh?" encouraging the crowd's laughter and applause.

In highly gendered exchanges, their other comedic patter similarly focuses on her "boob jokes" and her ironic campy persona. Talking about the concert venue, Rogers expresses a masculinized love of sports and teases Parton's ignorance of basketball. He tells the cheering crowd it is "a thrill" to play on the same court as the NBA's Portland Trailblazers, because "I just identify with those guys a great deal." Parton's rejoinder angers the crowd: "Oh, you identify with those guys, you can't score either?" As the crowd starts to boo at her joke questioning both their team and their masculine virility, Parton apologizes, "Just a little joke there, I was only playing. That was ugly, I'm sorry, I love you, that's why I could say that," while Rogers chimes in: "You don't know nothing about basketball." Parton uses another "boob joke" to regain the crowd's sympathy: "I know enough to know I carry two of 'em around all day long." There, as the crowd laughs in response, she uses her ironic jests about her hyperbolic appearance to defuse a hostile reaction, making her own gender performance an ironic metacommentary on which they can all agree.

Some of their other stage patter focuses even more attention on Parton's sexualized appearance. One canned exchange has them joking that since they are both married, they must be careful not to be tempted by each other while on tour, the banter playing off of the audience's tendency to interpret them as a romantic couple. Commenting on her costuming, Rogers says, "That's the first time I've seen that dress, I think that's my favorite." She thanks him and makes a show of modeling the very low cut dress with the very high leg slit: "Well, I'm glad you like it, you don't think it's too much do you?" Noting the skimpiness of the garment, Rogers opines, "I don't think it's too little. Your zipper's broke on the side there." After Parton pretends to check her zipper, she launches into banter about how hard it is to belt out love songs with a handsome male singer when both of them are married, and that after several weeks on tour, "Every day my dresses get a little shorter and little lower, and here we are, both of us lonely, and Marianne [Rogers] out there somewhere." Parton references the song lyric to "We've Got to Tonight" and namechecks Rogers's wife at the time. Rogers admonishes, "Don't you start that with me." Parton demurs, "I ain't got a chance with a pretty woman like Marianne," and Rogers concludes the comedy bit with the joke that "this could very well be our last show together."

This exchange is actually a scripted repetition of a standard bit of Rogers stage patter that he used in his earlier hit duets with country singer Dottie West in the late 1970s. However, the contrast between how Parton performs gender codes and how West did is telling. While West and Rogers sang love songs together, and she wore somewhat sexualized outfits, with slightly low-cut blouses, Parton's image is so much more overtly sexualized that the contrast is striking. West's image was not exaggerated like Parton's, and she did not use Parton's ironic trashy tramp look.

In this concert, when Parton and Rogers sing a version of "Anyone Who Isn't Me Tonight," a duet Rogers and West had an earlier hit with for their album *Every Time Two Fools Collide* (1978), it offers a stark comparison between Parton and one of her contemporaries. The song, written by Julie Didier and Casey Kelly, reached number two on the *Billboard* country singles chart. In earlier concert performances, West sang the female part much more sedately and demurely than Parton does in this version, even though the former was known for her powerful voice. Parton's voice is higher, she adds more vocal embellishments, and her stage performance uses much higher energy. Introducing the song at the Portland concert, Parton conspiratorially leans into Rogers, querying, "Oh, we're going to do a Dottie West and Kenny Rogers song? I'm going to have to sing it a little different." She delivers her opening line with amplified volume, pumping her arm and laughing while stalking Rogers around the stage for the up-tempo country-pop duet: "Oh when you made love to me tonight, I thought that I had died and gone to heaven." He uses a similar performance persona in both versions, growling and increasing the rasp in his voice when he sings, "You got the kind of body that was made to give a man a lot of pleasure." Parton shakes her hips and strikes a provocative pose at Rogers's line, hamming it up when the bongo drums come in and the two singers trade lines. She swings the black and silver tassels on her dress belt and wiggles around Rogers. Parton's stage persona also exhibits an amplified energy level, evident even in comparison with Rogers's more subdued persona beside her. After Parton's hammy rendition, the duet elicits a standing ovation from the Portland audience.

Throughout the concert, Parton updates her mountain girl and hillbilly tramp elements while adding in more glamorous pop performance references. In places, she plays up ostentatious country barn dance–style humor, as when she inserts an exaggerated southern accent and giggles during "Islands in the Stream." At other times, she is at pains to underline a pop performance style, particularly in her arrangements for her country-pop songs. Meanwhile, her choreographed banter with Rogers continues to play up her sexualized image, while her own humor in response underscores her camp elements—her jokes and girlish laughter defuse the ribald humor, but she maintains her ironic, knowing campiness.

Crossover Albums

Meanwhile, as a closer textual analysis can demonstrate, Parton's albums during this period illustrate specifically how she was balancing various elements of her star persona in her music and in the imagery on her album covers. In her pop crossover albums in particular, the mountain girl component of her persona is more muted as she focused on adding in the crossover contemporary elements to her campy tramp. She does still have some lyrics that return to her Appalachian roots with the multilayered, pastoral nostalgia she uses. However, she had more new songs that focused on general, mass appeal themes of romantic love.

On *New Harvest . . . First Gathering*, as part of her first effort to combine more explicitly crossover pop and country music, her songs vary from the classic country single "Applejack" to her covers of soul classics, such as "My Love," her version of The Temptations' hit "My Girl," and Jackie Wilson's hit song "(Your Love Keeps Lifting Me) Higher and Higher." Her single "Light of a Clear Blue Morning" had greater country than pop chart success (eleven on the country chart but only eighty-seven on pop). The song was perhaps most well-known for its autobiographical framing. Parton famously recounted how she wrote the song when she drove away after having broken with Wagoner. Her line "Everything's gonna be all right / That's been all wrong" references that departure, suggesting newfound freedom and an optimistic forward movement to reach her goals for worldwide stardom.

The album is dominated by love songs, in line with Parton's attempts to reach a broader audience. Some are optimistic odes, like "How Does It Feel," where the female speaker reassures a man of her constant love. Likewise, "You Are," a rerelease from the previous album by the same name, features a female speaker expressing her undying love to her man. Several love songs detail broken hearts and lost love. In "Holdin' on to You," a woman wants to stay with a man who breaks her heart, while in "Getting in My Way," the speaker is haunted by memories of a past love. In a love lament that is more Gothic in tone, "Where Beauty Lives in Memory," a woman has lost her sense of time and reality and instead stares in the mirror, applying elaborate makeup, waiting for forty years for the man she loves who left her. She is living in a fairytale memory waiting for her charming prince to arrive. As the song concludes and she falls dead on the floor, she imagines that he has arrived to lead her away, the final image a poignant portrait of a woman abandoned by love, going crazy and dying. The song implicitly critiques fairytales that lead women to believe in a mythological

Prince Charming. To these secular love songs, Parton adds "There," a religious song celebrating heaven.

The album's cover seems calculated to reassure potentially worried country listeners that Parton was still recognizably herself, still rooted in a country genre. In keeping with her previous albums of that time, Parton appears as a country tramp. She sits in a truck, wearing a bandana, blue denim shirt, and jacket, with the long platinum blonde wig and exaggerated makeup of her signature look. As one measure of Parton's attempts to go mainstream, Nash claims that Parton also spent time during 1977 and 1978 changing her pronunciation to deemphasize her Appalachian markers.[22]

Parton established pop crossover success with *Here You Come Again*, both commercially and critically. Her first platinum album, selling over a million copies, it won a Grammy in the female country album category. Although the album faced extensive press backlash for the crossover pop, observers like Fred Foster have noted that it was odd to see such a negative reaction to Parton singing pop, since she had done so before, much earlier in her career with him at Monument.[23] The title gold-selling single signaled Parton's new course; it had success topping each of the country, pop, and adult contemporary *Billboard* music chart categories for several weeks. Firmly in the pop genre, it was written by pop hit-makers Barry Mann and Cynthia Weil. A more country-oriented single, "It's All Wrong but It's All Right," reached number one on the country chart. Parton's efforts to revise her party song "Two Doors Down" also indicate how much she was pushing for a pop crossover sound on this album, since she released a more up-tempo second version for the single and for all versions of the album after the first pressing.

The other Parton-penned songs on the album revert to some typical religious themes, most notably in "Me and Little Andy," her famously melodramatic, tragic song about a little girl of six or seven and her dog who come to the speaker's door asking to stay the night in a storm, both having been abandoned. When the girl and the dog pass away during the night, the speaker repeats the child's broken nursery rhymes and laments their loss while suggesting that both will find comfort and religious redemption in heaven. Parton's song, "God's Coloring Book," continues the religious theme with a spiritual celebration of nature and the "multicolored rainbow" as divine artistic creations filling the everyday world.

Parton was criticized because the rest of the album featured songs written by other people. She was accused of giving up her own musical vision in order to cover manufactured pop records by formulaic hit-makers. Importantly, from the point of view of genre, Parton also covered Kenny Rogers's "Sweet Music Man" here, reinforcing the country-pop crossover genre references because Rogers was likewise releasing music in that category. Rogers's version of that song originally appeared on his pop crossover album *Daytime Friends* (1977), which had country and pop chart success.[24]

Musically, the album reflects genre hybridity. Musicologist Mitchell Morris has argued that the only identifiable country elements in the song "Here You Come Again" are Parton's vocals and the timbre of the pedal steel guitar, and he reads a soft-shell country aesthetic in other songs on the album, including "It's All Wrong but It's All Right." He views "Two Doors Down," meanwhile, as a combination of country inflections in Parton's vocal, gospel in the close harmonies from the backup singers, 1970s urban music in the throbbing bass line, wah pedal, and synthesizer.[25] Producer Gary Klein only agreed to add the pedal steel guitar as a compromise to Parton because she did not wish to alienate her country fans.

In the albums that followed, Parton extended her crossover efforts but was careful to include material that would appeal to her country fan base, just as she continued to include autobiographical songs that anchored her star image to her Appalachian roots, even if those references were fewer than before. Her next album, *Heartbreaker*, was even more pop oriented, venturing into disco and adult contemporary easy listening. She released disco remixes of two songs that became popular in clubs, "Baby I'm Burning" and "I Wanna Fall in Love." Like her previous crossover effort, this album also enjoyed popular success with a mass audience. It went gold and produced the hits "Heartbreaker," written by Carole Bayer Sager, which similarly made three charts (topping country, thirty-seventh on pop, eleventh on adult contemporary), and "I Really Got the Feeling" (first on country). Once again, Parton included a number of songs written by other people, including those two hits. However, she did include some autobiographical material that delivered her sincerity address. Her autobiographical song "Nickels and Dimes," co-written with her brother Floyd Parton and inspired by her memories of busking on Knoxville street corners for change, discusses repaying with songs people who contributed to her dreams; she describes how she is thankful she has "made it" to "the big time," but she remembers her debt to people who supported her as a poor young girl hungry to succeed.

Both of those pop crossover albums, plus the next two, *Great Balls of Fire* and *Dolly, Dolly, Dolly*, feature covers with Parton dressed and posed noticeably differently than in her previous country albums. They all reframe her in a contemporary pop context, with more updated clothes and styling, and an emphasis on "hip" references to current trends like disco and neon lights. On *Here You Come Again*, a triptych of Partons strike disco poses in cuffed, dark-wash jeans and a red blouse tied at the waist as if in a club. She retains her platinum blonde wig, but in a more contemporary style. At the top of the cover is the Dolly signature logo that would decorate her subsequent RCA solo albums, similar to the "Dolly" logo on her earlier syndicated television show. *Heartbreaker* pictures her in two other disco-inspired poses. To the left of the cover, she appears as a partial image in a more modern pink dress and heels, her leg kicking into the frame as if she is dancing into view. To the right foreground, she is pictured again in the same pink dress, this time as if leaning at a bar counter with one foot on a stool, the image focused on her exposed legs. The next two albums have her whirling under a neon Dolly signature, as if dancing, and then riding a merry-go-round horse in a haze of neon lights.

Those album covers increasingly posed Parton as a pop singer, a trend even more evident when compared to a throwback Parton album that came out during that time and featured a starkly different cover. *Porter & Dolly* (1980) was an album released according to the terms of Parton's settlement with Porter Wagoner. It consisted of previously unreleased duets and some reissued duets. Infamously, Parton and Wagoner were not on speaking terms, thus the cover photo merges two separate photographs. Wagoner appears in a slightly updated hairstyle and white Nudie suit, while Parton is pictured in an elaborate long pink gown and platinum blonde wig pulled up, in an older pose. The album did indicate her country fan base's ongoing investment in her, since it performed well on the country chart (ninth).

In this epoch of Parton's career, she continued to try to gain pop chart success with new album releases, with the pop sales increasing her circulation to a higher level than she had when she was only releasing country-targeted albums on the country charts. Her next two solo albums had both country and pop chart success, although her singles continued to perform better on the country than the pop charts. *Great Balls of Fire* went gold (fourth on country, fortieth on pop) and launched the hit single "You're the Only One" (first on country, fifty-ninth on pop). *Dolly, Dolly, Dolly* likewise reached both country and pop chart approval (seventh on country but only seventy-first on pop), although the single "Old Flames Can't Hold a Candle to You" was only a country hit (first on country) and "Starting over Again" topped the country chart but did not fare as well on pop (thirty-sixth).

Parton's emerging film career clearly bolstered her subsequent record sales, creating a larger multimedia base for her stardom. Significant success characterized this period of Parton's career, with film soundtracks and other albums that gradually tapered off in the early 1990s, a time that coincided with artists such as Parton not getting as much radio airplay, as I discuss more fully in chapter 4. As her movie career began garnering attention with her *9 to 5* role, Parton released albums associated with her films alongside more crossover pop albums, with the *9 to 5* labor concept album being particularly successful critically and commercially. The gold title single topped country, pop, and adult contemporary charts, and the album topped both the country and pop charts for over ten weeks. Parton's subsequent film soundtracks had diminishing success on the country and pop charts, with the gap between major Hollywood film starring roles also measuring diminished market success for her films (twenty years passed between *Straight Talk* [1992] and *Joyful Noise* [2012]).[26] However, *Rhinestone* did speak to Parton's continued country appeal, because it mined the familiar Appalachian themes of Parton's earlier work and featured music from Parton's family members, such as brother Randy and sister Stella. Parton's nostalgic "Tennessee Homesick Blues" was a country chart-topping hit.

This period also witnessed her high-profile collaborations with other artists, some of which began to perform better than her solo albums, most notably her highly successful crossover duets with Rogers. Her *Trio* (1987) and *Trio II* albums with Linda Ronstadt and Emmylou Harris (the second was released in 1999 but recorded five years earlier) succeeded in the context of country music's turn to neotraditionalist musical styles in the late 1980s. The first album featured covers of traditional country songs with the three singing in close harmony, and was a notable commercial and critical success (it won a country Grammy, went platinum, topped the country albums chart for five weeks, and hit number six on the pop chart, with the hit single "To Know Him Is to Love Him" topping the country singles chart). Ronstadt explicitly claims Parton as "authentic Appalachian music" in the album's promotional material, positing Parton's life history as a proxy for purity and an authenticity claim for their collaboration.[27] The album's neotraditionalist style is evident in its use of instruments associated with earlier hillbilly or folk traditions, such as the autoharp associated with the Carter Family since the 1920s (Mother Maybelle Carter continued to play her autoharp into the 1960s folk revival, during tours with son-in-law Johnny Cash). Parton's other significant collaboration from this epoch is *Honky Tonk Angels* (1994) with Loretta Lynn and Tammy Wynette. The album is a nod to country music history and was a commercial success that helped revive Lynn's and Wynette's careers, particularly since all had begun struggling to get country radio airplay.

However, by the early to mid-1990s, Parton herself was growing frustrated with her lack of solo chart success and her struggles for radio airplay. Some of Parton's 1980s and early 1990s solo albums enjoyed substantial audience support, such as *Eagle When She Flies* (1991, platinum). Albums such as *White Limozeen* (1989, gold) featured hit singles like "Why'd You Come in Here Lookin' Like That," while *Slow Dancing with the Moon* (1993, platinum) generated the hit "Romeo," which had a well-known music video featuring Billy Ray Cyrus as a younger male country star presented as beefcake. Parton's Christmas albums also displayed wide appeal, both solo (*Home for Christmas*, 1990, gold) and duets with Rogers (*Once upon a Christmas*, 1984, double platinum). But with her solo album sales dropping, by 1997 Parton was between labels and went home for inspiration to write the country album *Hungry Again*, which received critical acclaim but not high sales.

Marking another transition point in her career, her solution to her dilemma was a fuller return to her authenticity narratives and to the country genre. As I discuss in the next chapter, Parton's album of "old home" songs and covers, *Heartsongs*, was a precursor to her later serious attempt to regain a country fan base with *Hungry Again*, and her successful attempts to court an Americana roots music audience with her subsequent bluegrass and Appalachian music albums.

Film and Television Personae

To detail her persona's evolution further, a closer reading of Parton's most important television and film roles during this period can capture how she fashions "Dolly Parton" as a character onscreen. Parton's newfound Hollywood stardom in the 1980s and early 1990s added further intricacy to her image, particularly since these films tended to frame her in a feminist rhetoric, as a character who explicitly critiques sexual harassment and exploitative labor conditions for women. In *9 to 5*, *The Best Little Whorehouse in Texas*, *Rhinestone*, *Steel Magnolias* (1989), and *Straight Talk*, Parton as a film actor references her own persona and engages with images of southern and Appalachian femininity in multivalent ways. In some films, she has played roles that further her media narrative with characters especially similar to her persona (*Straight Talk*, *Rhinestone*, and the TV films *A Smoky Mountain Christmas* and *Unlikely Angel*).

Beginning with the success of *9 to 5*, in which she was largely interpreted as if she were playing a version of herself, a pure "authenticity" presentation, Parton began negotiating gendered film imagery in nuanced ways. In the movie, she puts her combination of "fake" and "real" persona, the "trampy" look and the "sincere" heart, in service to a feminist critique of visual stereotypes of women and inequitable treatment of them in the business sphere, including sexual harassment. In *The Best Little Whorehouse in Texas*, she explicitly references Mae West, like she did in her "Real Love" tour, visually echoing West in her blonde wigs, makeup, and low-cut, long gowns. With her West homage, Parton performs an amplified campy knowingness that puts her in a particular kind of gendered film star tradition. In *Rhinestone*, Parton exaggerates her persona further, juxtaposing a highly stereotyped country character with the Sylvester Stallone city slicker for a fish-out-of-water story. In *Steel Magnolias*, Parton offered a more realistic performance but still tinged with her own personality and autobiography. For *Straight Talk*, Parton engaged in a less campy presentation of self in the sense that her visual image was more mainstream and contemporary, with skirt suits and high heels, but her autobiographical presentation of self as a character was increased, as she invoked aspects of her life story while playing a character dispensing folksy southern country wisdom to a broader audience, in this case a northern audience in Chicago.

In parallel developments in her television stardom, Parton experimented with how to pitch her star image on TV. While her navigation of syndicated country TV show conventions began on local television on Cas Walker's syndicated show (1956–1964), her knowledge of the genre was solidified on Wagoner's (1967–1974) and then on her own first syndicated variety series, *Dolly!*, from the same production company (Show Biz) as Wagoner's show. Company president Bill Graham pitched her the idea of her own show with a large budget at that time ($85,000 per episode), shot in Nashville, with country music guests but also a broader range of musical and acting guests. Parton's guests ranged from Tom T. Hall, Kenny Rogers, and Emmylou Harris to KC and the Sunshine Band and Anson Williams. While the program had high ratings, Parton asked to be let out of her contract, in part because she needed vocal rest under doctor's orders but in part because she did not feel the show accurately represented her. It tried to mix different modes of address, because it wanted to appeal to her country base but also start moving her in a crossover direction, targeting a wide-ranging audience. It featured some Parton songs, like "Love Is Like a Butterfly" and "I Will Always Love You," but she was also asked to sing what she viewed as ill-fitting standards, like "My Funny Valentine." Parton expressed dissatisfaction with the production company's inability to incorporate her image preferences, autobiographical narratives, musical influences, or guest stars related to her own musical interests. Parton wanted more carefully to combine her country music and pop and rock crossover elements.

However, Parton also experienced difficulties in balancing the different elements of her star persona in a TV variety show setting when she did her post-crossover second show, *Dolly*, on ABC, which was pitched as a traditional variety show, with musical segments and comedy skits. In her later autobiography, Parton drily complained that a cadre of out-of-work variety show writers, who had witnessed the decline of the genre a decade earlier, dumped all of their clichéd vaudeville material on her show. Taped in Los Angeles, the show made use of Parton's Hollywood film stardom, presenting her in a mass appeal context, with guests ranging from Burt Reynolds, Bruce Willis, Oprah Winfrey, and Tom Selleck to Kermit the Frog and Miss Piggy. A range of musical guests included Patti LaBelle, the Neville Brothers, Smokey Robinson, Tom Petty and the Heartbreakers, and Alabama. It also featured other musical guests who had worked with Parton in country and country-pop crossover contexts, including Tammy Wynette, Merle Haggard, Emmylou Harris, Linda Ronstadt, Loretta Lynn, Willie Nelson, Ricky Skaggs, Brenda Lee, Barbara Mandrell, and Mac Davis. Parton again featured "I Will Always Love You" as her closing theme, while "Baby I'm Burning" took the place of her first syndicated show's theme, "Love Is Like a Butterfly."

Parton and manager Sandy Gallin created the show and maintained creative control; Parton shifted the tone and focus halfway through the season to better express her own sensibility and maintain her ties to her country "down home" persona, with specials filmed at the Grand Ole Opry and with her family in Sevierville. With initially high and then lower ratings, the show only lasted one season. Although ABC had paid her $44 million for a two-year contract, the show failed to find a sustainable formula for combining Parton's country roots with mainstream appeal.

It is possible to discern the difference between Parton's earlier media image and her evolving image during this crossover period by comparing earlier and later television appearances. For instance, on the infamous 1988 "Nashville Memories" episode of Parton's ABC *Dolly*, where she had her first onstage reunion with Porter Wagoner since their falling out a decade earlier, Parton invited the Grand Ole Opry mainstay to appear on the Opry special, displaying the image of their reconciliation.[28] During this segment, Parton has Wagoner join her onstage. He gives her the present of an old flowered towel like the ones they used to advertise on the Wagoner show, and they joke around, much like they used to on his show. However, she is careful to point out that her current show is a network show (as opposed to his syndicated one), implicitly asserting her own power in this situation. She then has him come stand with her to watch a TV monitor with clips from her first appearance on his show in 1967. They laugh together about how young they looked then. One effect of this kind of looking back in a new context is that Parton seizes control of the frame in a different way than before—she literally reframes the earlier images by watching them on her own show. Here, Wagoner is her invited guest and functions more like the sidekick, not the other way around, and her slight dig about "network television" marks that distinction.

The comparison of the earlier image with the later one also throws into sharp contrast how her stage look had changed. In the 1967 Wagoner show image that she replays, Parton is dressed much more demurely, with a plainer, pink, cocktail-length dress; sparse jewelry; and little ornamentation. She has her hair teased up in a bouffant hairdo, but it is not as high or elaborate as it later became in her signature look. Her dress is tight-fitting, as was her custom, but it is fully covered and not revealing.

In contrast, her dress on the 1988 show is extremely glitzy, with silver tassels, abundant jewelry, sequins, and an elaborate, low-cut show-queen ball gown with a very short skirt and five-inch heels, although her makeup is still similarly elaborate. She is wearing one of her contemporary styled wigs from that era, no longer the beehive bouffant look, instead choosing a long, feathered style that would have been more common in the 1980s yet still obviously an elaborate wig. Thus, Parton has exaggerated the campy elements and chosen clothing that balances a glamorous crossover look with some country girl elements. Wagoner is wearing one of his rhinestoned Nudie suits and a more updated hairstyle, having abandoned the high pompadour for a still somewhat high feathered style. However, Parton looks glamorous in a crossover Hollywood film star vein, while Wagoner does not engage the look of hip crossover and instead fashions an image that is more specific to his country star setting.

Their gendered interaction from the Wagoner show episode also differs markedly from their interaction on Parton's show. In the older show, Wagoner is paternalistic toward her, referring to her as a "pretty little lady," and Parton defers to him. In the newer show, Wagoner seems to want to be in charge, trying to fall into their familiar onstage patter comic rhythm with him taking the lead, but she finds ways to assert herself as the one in charge, talking about her own show. She commands the narrative power to determine how she will characterize their falling out. She says that she and Wagoner had had their "problems," but that she "will always love him." Their interaction is much more as peers rather than paternalistic, with Parton seizing the upper hand, marking a different iteration of her own gendered star image.

Hollywood Star Discourse

Meanwhile, as Parton moved into the Hollywood film stardom era of her career, she adapted her existing authenticity rhetoric of "fake" look and "real" sincerity to a familiar Hollywood star discourse model, adding another layer of visual culture complexity to her gender performance and stage persona. Just as she has consistently argued that her artificial appearance does not stop audiences from seeing her "true" self underneath, which she suggests she presented for them to discern, Parton insists that her star image onscreen is the same as her personality, meaning that she is merely playing a genuine version of herself for whatever fictional character she portrays onscreen.

Parton's star image construction is distinctive, although not unique, in this context. In all of her films from this era, she is consistently framed as if she was simply playing a version of herself onscreen, much like Burt Reynolds was. Since Parton's stage persona at that time was already discussed as being a character she was playing, adding another layer of performance onscreen created further complexity to her existing star image. At the time of her crossover, she seemed to be modeling her sense of stardom explicitly on some famous Hollywood icons who themselves had elaborate star constructions. She told Alanna Nash that she wanted to be "mysterious" like Greta Garbo, meaning she wanted to leave enough mystery to compel audiences to yearn to learn more about her. She also explicitly maintains that her fame came from her playing herself as a character 24–7, and that she would never drop the character, since she thinks playing that star image is the reason she is successful. Parton characterized her acting career at the time as her effort to find the right vehicle to play herself onscreen; she argued that she was just being a personality onscreen rather than being an actor. She implies that she can only act like her existing persona, even in movies.[29]

Theorists Richard Dyer and Richard deCordova have shown that in Hollywood film, audiences continually look for traces of stars' "authentic" selves in their performances. A star's publicly available private life—splashed across tab-loids and promotional materials—and the star's film roles mutually inform each other, as if a star's performance in a film appears to reveal something about that person's personality (even though the film scenario has nothing to do with actual life).[30] Thus, when stars prompts audiences to want to learn more about them by giving media access to their "private" lives, that supporting material actually reinforces their "public" star persona. The process of manufacturing the star image glamorously becomes part of the image itself, as Dyer puts it, "like a conjuror showing you how a trick is done."[31] In that context, press cover-age and extra-textual materials about a film star purport to let fans "behind the scenes," and when media coverage offers to display to audiences the private per-son beneath the constructed public persona, it reinforces the very existence and cultural currency of that public persona, particularly when the private persona is equally constructed.

Parton fits that kind of stardom model. Press coverage of her career and her private life quickly blur the boundary between the two, and Parton encourages that collapse. Parton has long joked about being the queen of tabloid press cover-age. At one time during this period of her career, she was the third most recog-nized person in the world behind the pope and Madonna.

Parton's star image on one level fits a classic Hollywood film star model as well because her story is about succeeding through her individual talent in her "rags-to-riches" story. Dyer argues that a film star appears to be an exceptional person who becomes famous for some quality or talent, thus serving as an exemplar of individualism in a capitalist society.[32] In this model, if a star can achieve fame based on talent and merit, then the audience is encouraged to believe they too can succeed through hard work in a capitalist society (according to Dyer, thus appearing to resolve contradictions involving unequal power hierarchies within capitalism and modernity).

Parton also enacts another classic film star feature because she uses her rheto-ric of fake versus real in a way that is similar to a star rhetoric of extraordinary versus ordinary. According to film theorist John Ellis, stars must balance between being extraordinary (some talent or quality makes them exceptional, unreach-able, thus seen in glamorous, larger-than-life surroundings) but also ordinary (relatable, in close proximity to the viewer because they want the same things everyday people want, often described in terms of the personal, such as home, family, marriage, and happiness for their children).[33] The extraordinary/ordi-nary binary is also akin to a public/private split.[34] If stars seem too glamorous or remote, the audience can become alienated, while if they seem too familiar or ordinary, they can lose the star effect. The star pose requires a balance of the two. Hence, a peek into the star's private life in behind-the-scenes coverage reinforces the star persona in these terms as well, particularly because that coverage is often trying to reinforce the idea that the person is a star. Ellis argues that TV drives fans to magazines and secondary materials to see if the personality of the performer is the same as the character they see every week on television, while tabloid coverage spurs audiences to go to films to give them a sense of the star as a unified narrative persona.[35]

In the case of Parton, this extraordinary/ordinary stardom rhetoric maps onto her existing star persona of fake (extraordinary, glamorous, ostentatious, outsized, gaudy appearance) and real (ordinary, relatable, a simple country girl, sincere, "down home"). She underscores the idea that her talent makes her succeed in a way that specifically balances the fake and the real. She says, "The thing that's always worked for me is the fact that I look so totally artificial, but am so totally real. It gives me something to work against. I have to overcome myself. I have to prove how good I am."[36] Her fake/real rhetoric is also her variation on the foundational country music genre rhetoric of manufactured versus pure. In a later CNN interview with Larry King, Parton argued that "country music is just simple stories, ordinary stories about ordinary people often told in an extraordinary way."[37] In response to his queries, she was trying to explain how she had become so famous for singing country music and why the genre enjoys such widespread popularity. While Parton was not explicitly drawing links between different kinds of stardom rhetorics, of course, her point about country music using this ordinary versus extraordinary rhetoric is telling.

We see a series of related ideas meeting up in her star image. The fake, extraordinary, mass culture, modernity side of the binary is balanced against the real, ordinary, folk culture, premodern side of the binary, and Parton uses her star image to mediate between the two sets of ideas. Meanwhile, as I discuss in fuller case studies in the following sections, the cultural work her gender performance does in each of her films is more specific and places her in relationship to feminism.

9 to 5 and Other Odd Jobs

The film 9 to 5 places Parton in an explicitly feminist context, and because of how it uses her stage persona onscreen, it links the Parton persona to the film's gender critique. At the time of its release, 9 to 5 was seen as promoting a feminist effort to gain workplace reform, and it actually sparked union organizing.[38] The wish-fulfillment fantasy about secretaries who get revenge on their abusive boss was obviously a "woman's power" message film like many others of that women's movement's epoch. But it is distinctive because it helped prompt workplace reforms. In the film, when the women kidnap their boss and run the office themselves, they institute equal pay for equal job levels, a daycare center, part-time schedules, and job-sharing and flexible hours. Director and co-writer Colin Higgins did extensive research with an organization of clerical workers. After the film's release, that group became a union called District 925. In a measure of cultural longevity, the film later generated the Broadway musical version (2008) as well as a twenty-fifth anniversary DVD release (2006). In the DVD commentary track, producer and star Jane Fonda attributes the film's lasting success to its "historical synchronicity": "It's a comedy, but it exposed issues that office workers had been trying to get on the map for a long time. The movie showed that they were real, you know, so it was the beginning of them starting to do something about it. I mean, it really started a movement." Discussing the film's politics, Parton links the gender commentary to a class critique, noting that working women and men both might wish to rebel against a bad boss. She tartly observes, "Whether you're a man or a woman, if the boss is a prick, you wish you could do something to him." Indeed, the film's reception speaks to a cross-gender, class-based appeal, with co-writer Patricia Resnick registering surprise over the film's appeal to a broad demographic, including men and teens. She attributed its success to broader frustrations with power hierarchies.[39]

Working in the film's feminist vein, Parton famously composed the Oscar-nominated, Grammy-winning hit title song on set, drawing on the background material as inspiration and using her fake fingernails for percussion. That song became part of her working-class concept LP record, 9 to 5 and Other Odd Jobs (1980). Both her song and her performance won widespread critical acclaim (two Grammy awards and another nomination, a People's Choice award for the title song, and three Golden Globe nominations, for both music and acting). In the song itself, Parton incorporates pop-influenced features such as a horn section, syncopated rhythms, and the song's immediately recognizable electric bass line.

Parton's description of her creative process incorporates the feminist statement of the film; it also reinforces her own "hillbilly tramp" persona. On the commentary track, describing the song composition process, Parton reveals that she had all the women acting in the film sing together on the record; she wrote the song on set because she was listening to the characterizations and ideas in the film for inspiration. Of using her outlandish fake fingernails as her rhythm section, Parton says they sounded like a typewriter to her and inspired the song. She "plays her fingernails" to get this typewriter sound, which signifies secretaries toiling away. She jokes, "You've gotta have falsies to do this, and the nails have to be artificial as well." Here, Parton turns the composition story into another example of one of her "boob jokes" that creates ironic distance and parody in her gender performance.

In the film's central condemnation of gender discrimination, each of the three main female characters face discrimination and difficult labor conditions in what is a paternalistic working environment. The film's plot follows the three secretaries as they kidnap their "sexist, egotistical, lying, hypocritical bigot" boss, Franklin Hart Jr. (Dabney Coleman). They hold him hostage, running an office of the intentionally nondescript Consolidated Companies in his absence. When they ultimately institute the series of reforms to improve gender equity and workplace conditions, they manage to succeed in spite of his attempts at retaliation. Hart's assistant, Violet Newsted (Lily Tomlin), a widow with four children, is unable to rise in the corporation in spite of her seniority and the fact that she trained Hart herself. After garnering the promotion over her, Hart continually passes her over for promotions and steals her ideas. Idealistic new employee Judy Bernly (Fonda), forced to find work because her husband left her for his much younger secretary, faces Hart's constant ridicule. Sweet-natured "country girl" Doralee Rhodes (Parton) is the object of the married Hart's aggressive sexual advances, which she thwarts, but he spreads the rumor that she is his mistress. Due to gender stereotypes about her voluptuous appearance and promiscuity, her coworkers believe him. As the film begins, Doralee struggles with the social ostracism that results. In her storyline, the film critiques gender stereotypes about women's appearances and underscores her innocence and competence on the job.

As the women face discrimination, the film examines a number of possible responses, from fantasy resolutions to farcical violence. It uses imagined surreal fantasy solutions as a vehicle for satire. In a drug-fueled dream sequence, sparked when the women gather to smoke pot and commiserate, each imagines revenge fantasies that flip the power hierarchy with their male boss. Judy visualizes hunting him down, shooting him, and mounting his head on a wall. Doralee imagines becoming a cowgirl boss (on the commentary track, Fonda says Parton looks like "Barbara Stanwyck with boobs") and making Hart play "secretary" while she ropes, hogties, and roasts him on a spit. Violet reverses a fairytale image of female innocence by imagining herself as a demented Snow White; she poisons Hart's coffee and then catapults him out of the office window with an ejector chair, while animated woodland animals look on approvingly.

Following the fantasy sequence, when the women engage in an actual violent response, by kidnapping Hart and holding him hostage, the film's tone maintains the slapstick farce, suggesting that while they do undertake these actions, it is not a realistic strategy for social justice. When Violet sees Hart unconscious on the floor of his office, she assumes she must have mistakenly acted on her coffee fantasy and poisoned him, and the women engage in a farcical cover up, trying to hide what they think is his dead body and seizing the wrong one at the hospital. When Hart wakes up (he had merely fallen from his chair) and discovers what they had been doing, he makes a sexual threat, saying he will send them to jail unless Doralee agrees to sleep with him. It is in response to this sexual threat that they kidnap him and hold him hostage, later blackmailing him when they discover he has been embezzling, until he escapes. In a carnivalesque dynamic, the women run the office without him and no one notices his absence. The film levels a stronger gender critique when it has the women's workplace reforms result in a major jump in productivity for the company. When the CEO arrives to congratulate the office, an escaped Hart appears and takes credit for the women's reforms. The women ultimately win a modified victory, because while the male boss once again takes credit for their labor, his reward actually sends him away on an undesirable promotion out of the country, leaving the women freed from him and with their reforms in place at the office.

Thus, the film makes clear feminist critiques of gender themes ranging from sexual harassment to structural gender discrimination in the workplace. While the slapstick fantasy sequences and violence are not offered as viable solutions, the workplace reforms are. Again, it is notable that the film prompted actual workplace reforms along those lines.

Parton's gender performance in 9 to 5 places her camp performance in new contexts. In this film, she is presented as a version of herself, with an emphasis on her earnest realism in her portrayal. The character reinforces Parton's familiar fake-real rhetoric, because while she is misjudged for her exaggerated appearance, her heartfelt sincerity is presented as her "true" self.

The collapse between her character and her own autobiography is reinforced by contextual material about the film. In the DVD commentary, producer Fonda recounts how she wanted to cast Parton because she met her on a plane and exclaimed, "She *is* Doralee!" She went to Parton's concert in New York City and was convinced that Parton was the embodiment of this character. Fonda's idea for the film also involved tailoring the script to each of the three leads. When discussing her casting, Sandy Gallin told Parton the producers merely wanted her to be herself onscreen rather than act, because the part is "exactly" like her.[40]

The film and its subsequent iterations gave Parton perhaps one of her most widely circulated platforms for articulating her media persona and adapting it to Hollywood stardom models. Parton later explicitly interwove her own autobiography with the new songs she wrote for the Broadway version, reflecting the close ties between her persona and the film, just as she joked about her legacy being tied with the film's: "I've worked that 9 to 5 job for 30 years now."[41] The film also inspired a television series version (running from 1982–1983 on ABC and 1986–1988 in syndication), starring Parton's younger sister Rachel Dennison in the Parton role. While the Broadway musical opened in 2009 (after it premiered in Los Angeles in 2008), then closed after five months, it continued on in a national touring version (2010). Because of the film's gender themes and social critiques, it also provided a key backdrop for Parton's own gender performance. Meanwhile, if 9 to 5's effect on Parton's star persona was to claim her for feminism, her second film, *The Best Little Whorehouse in Texas*, offers a much more multifarious case of gender politics.

Case Study: *The Best Little Whorehouse in Texas*

Parton's role in *The Best Little Whorehouse in Texas* gave her a setting in which to amplify her ironic, feminist camp effects by doing an explicit homage to Mae West. While the film critiques some gender stereotypes, it nonetheless reinforces others in its conservative romance narrative resolution. On one level, it cites feminist arguments for the decriminalization of prostitution. It rewrites a familiar, gendered Hollywood film script by widening the definition of who can count as the heroine and claiming humanity for the socially ostracized "fallen woman." Parton's character even cites religious arguments: "Jesus was very good to Mary Magdalene, the fallen woman." Yet on another level, the resolution reiterates a common film trope in which the male character legitimates and reforms the female "hooker with the heart of gold" by marrying her, restoring a gender hierarchy within a romance plot. The film's thematic content affects Parton's performance of her persona in the sense that, again, her persona is frequently conflated with her film characters, such that Parton's film roles can potentially impact audience reception of her to some degree—as when Parton worried that her fans might respond disapprovingly to her playing a madam.[42]

Most relevant to how Parton's gender performance evolves during this period is precisely how she channels Mae West. Parton's performance is an explicit West homage delivered as camp farce. Both her gown and hair are similar to West's signature look. Parton wears a series of low-cut, floor-length, sequined gowns, with platinum blonde wigs styled up, with ringlets. As Parton bounces her hips and calls out "Howdy boys!" or "Y'all come back now, y'hear," her characterization of the film madam echoes a version of West's film persona, with West's knowing double entendres and ribald wit. Parton differs from West, of course, in that she filters this dynamic through her country persona, but she similarly explicitly puts her star persona into relationship with a film gender trope of the knowingness of the prostitute character.

The film's plot follows the efforts of Madam Miss Mona Stangley (Parton) to keep her infamous Texas brothel, the "Chicken Ranch," in business. Based on the true story of a legal bordello in La Grange, Texas, the film grew out of the earlier Broadway musical (1978), which drew on an article from *Playboy* (1974). In the film version, set in Gilbert, Texas, the brothel is illegal, and Miss Mona was a former prostitute there.

The film establishes its campy, farcical tone from the outset as Jim Nabors narrates, playing deputy sheriff Fred Wilkins. It opens on Nabors looking at old pictures of the more than half-century-old brothel. Famous for playing Gomer Pyle on *The Andy Griffith Show* and channeling hillbilly tropes of naiveté in his persona, Nabors smiles to the audience and intones in direct address to the camera: "It was the nicest little whorehouse that you ever saw." The film thus establishes the parodic tone by juxtaposing his country bumpkin star persona with a knowing, bawdy humor. Nabors establishes the film's doubled treatment of the brothel as a paternalistic institution; he suggests that it is sinful but yet an accepted tradition, "like a home away from home," immoral but also full of "fine upstanding citizens," like Miss Mona, who mean well. He insists that she "saw the house as a Texas institution and aimed to keep it that way," as each generation of men sends their sons to visit the ranch, which is so named because farmers paid in poultry during the Great Depression.

For her part, Parton's character critiques pimps as "bloodsuckers" and claims that she is creating better working conditions for herself and her fellow "working girls" who just want to "make a living." The film implies that while respectable society impugns her, most characters see the brothel as "boys will be boys" immorality that is part of patriarchal culture, integrated into the system, as when Mona queries, "You mean to tell me the cows don't enjoy a little time off when the bull goes out to another pasture?" Within the film, in a television news story covering the ranch controversy, an elderly townswoman says she does not mind her husband frequenting the brothel and cites the 1970s context of the women's movement and the sexual revolution since the 1960s, saying, "Nowadays women enjoy doing that sort of things themselves, so I've been told." While the scene attempts to mine humor by implying that the elderly woman says the opposite of what she would have been expected to say, it nevertheless delivers a feminist critique. A reporter notes that feminists were supporting a bill already in the state legislature for the decriminalization of prostitution, and that they were arguing with fundamentalists and traditionalists about the issue. While the film does not actually critique how that patriarchal culture generates the system of prostitution and exploits women, it does castigate the hypocrisy of citizens who condemn female sex workers but not their male customers.

The film satirizes politicians for keeping the illegal house of prostitution open. The mayor, senators, and governor are either customers or look the other way, as does sheriff Ed Earl Dodd (Burt Reynolds) because he has been secretly dating Mona for years. The governor only orders it closed when a television reporter, Melvin P. Thorpe (Dom DeLuise), creates a media scandal by falsely accusing Ed Earl of accepting bribes and the ranch of being a front for organized crime. As the governor ignores Ed Earl's pleas on Mona's behalf, the film spins that resolution as the governor hypocritically caving to polls. In the film's concluding "happy" scene, Ed Earl decides to run for the state legislature himself and proposes to Mona, in spite of any social approbation. The film ends with them driving off into the sunset and the narrator intoning that Ed Earl was elected and they were happily married.

The film's resolution centers on how the sheriff learns to grapple with gender role stereotypes. He goes from subconsciously reinforcing negative stereotypes of "fallen women" to rejecting those stereotypes eventually. His moment of negative stereotyping comes when he confronts Mona about reneging when she had earlier agreed to close the brothel temporarily. In reply, she castigates him for his gendered opportunistic behavior, for essentially keeping her as a mistress on the side while he maintains a respectable relationship with a woman in town. Mona contends that he has his affair with her yet strings along Dulcie Mae (Lois Nettleton), a cafe owner in town: "You use me as your mistress, you use damn

Dulcie Mae as your in-town wife" and "play weekend daddy" with Dulcie Mae's son. She damningly concludes by questioning his attempts to enact a certain version of masculinity: "You ain't never going to be more than you are right now, a chicken shit sheriff in a chicken shit town," playing at "being a man" and a cowboy. He retorts by excoriating her using gender stereotypes, saying "it's a helluva lot better than being a whore." After he storms off, the film implies that he changes his attitude after retreating to a pastoral landscape, standing all night in a farm field in contemplation, as if recentering on his values; his self-reflection prompts him to declare his love for Miss Mona in spite of the social stigma.

The film's gender politics follow Ed Earl's evolution. When Ed Earl later describes Mona to the Texas governor as a tax-paying, civic-minded, good citizen and business owner who provides a service and is accepted by their community, the film implies a distinction between a "respectable madam" and a "vilified whore." When he calls Mona a "whore," the male hero suddenly reinforces the stereotype of her degradation, and it is that slur that he tries to rectify by the film's conclusion. While his pleas to the governor are to no avail, he engages in masculine posturing in defense of Mona by decking hypocritical reporter Thorpe, who was in the capitol with a marching bands and signs saying "Citizens for a Whore Free Society."

As it slams political hypocrisy and educates the sheriff, the film does imply that the good-old-boy culture it satirizes is a version of patriarchal culture that generates this dynamic of prostitution, replete with political corruption. However, on another level, the film celebrates the brothel as a good-old-boy haven and tweaks critics of that dynamic, particularly via the musical numbers and titillation of those scenes at the ranch. The marriage plot resolution places Miss Mona in a different status, relegating her madam role to the past, turning her into a partially legitimated symbol of middle-class domesticity; it implies that Texas politicians and voters would not care about her past because they would largely still support such ranches if they could, their paternalism making it all "business as usual."

It is important to note how the movie makes use of the star persona dynamic in which both Reynolds and Parton appear exactly the same as their personas, the good old boy and the sweet hillbilly tramp, both consciously playing their personas as their characters. The film uses that trope to make metatheatrical jokes and to connect their characters in the film to their larger stardoms, garnering thematic mileage out of the association and the audience's knowledge of both stars. Reynolds plays the Texas cowboy sheriff using self-parody of his screen persona as the good old boy. Nabors as narrator characterizes him as humorously conceited: "Everybody liked Ed Earl, especially Ed Earl."

In one scene that emphasizes these personas, Parton and Reynolds perform a duet Parton wrote for the film, "Sneakin' Around." They dance around his bedroom, teasing each other and playing up their personas. Reynolds mugs to the camera as the playful rascal and Parton giggles as the knowing yet sincere country sexpot. The scene includes risqué comedy, as Parton's character wears black lingerie just ordered from Frederick's of Hollywood; she tries to get him to wear some racy underwear she ordered him, which he refuses to do, but she threatens to leave so he complies. Throughout the scene, Reynolds makes several "boob jokes" and stares at Parton's breasts. The film sends up her cheesecake and his beefcake images as meta references to them beyond their film roles. He enacts some physical comedy bits, including pratfalls and pulling himself around a door as if he is being dragged away, and he mugs to the camera when Deputy Fred comically interrupts them by knocking on the door. The scene is played as slapstick farce.

Mae West Madam

Parton's Mae West imagery in this film is important to the camp effects here, as is Parton's knowingness in playing a fictional prostitute while incorporating an exaggerated version of that imagery into her own star persona. Parton drew analogies between herself and West in interviews.[43] To detail this case more thoroughly, let me explain the West model.

In her discussion of feminist camp, theorist Pamela Robertson argues that Mae West drew on a tradition of subversive theatrical burlesque popular from roughly the 1860s to 1930s. This tradition included parodic exaggerations of gender that transgressively challenged norms, often via a comic inversion of the bourgeois world using slang, puns, and gender masquerade.[44] Robertson details how West did female-female impersonation by referencing famous female impersonator acts (with her use of the comic dame figure and double entendres). For Robertson, West deployed feminist camp to articulate a disruptive female sexuality that was provocative and knowing, and that showed her character and her "self" to be equally performances.

Again, I read Parton as engaged in a similar kind of knowing performance of the self as character, albeit one that has to be understood in terms of country music performance history, as she layers in her country girl trope (echoes of the mountain girl purity) over the town tramp imagery. When Parton uses exaggerated prostitute imagery in her own look and then plays a version of herself in this fictional character of a film madam, in effect she is satirizing how she as a female performer (any woman on stage) could be viewed as a sexual object and associated with prostitution.

The Mae West references here are campy in the sense that Parton recycles an older style (1930s West) and reframes it in a new context (the 1970s into the early 1980s during the women's movement). Parton uses ironic exaggeration to critique gender norms and stereotypes, targeting false propriety and social denigration of female sex workers. West herself likewise recycled 1890s styles in her 1930s films to critique gender and propriety norms in the 1930s.

West was censored and even arrested for the risqué stage plays she wrote. She authored her Diamond Lil character as a racy woman from the 1890s in her stage play of the same name (1928). She then revived the character in different plays and films several times in her career, including in *She Done Him Wrong* (1933) with Cary Grant, playing a bawdy barroom singer renamed Lady Lou. In that film, she delivered her signature line, "Why don't you come up sometime and *see* me?" and then delivered more variations of the "Come up and see me sometime" line in her next film with Grant, *I'm No Angel* (1933). She also was associated with a similarly provocative signature line, "Is that a gun in your pocket, or are you just glad to see me?" A version of that line appeared in her later film *Sextette* (1978). Robertson asserts that West incorporated prostitute images and parodied that dynamic through exaggeration, thus satirizing the association of women on stage and in the audience with prostitution. Robertson finds that West's camp changed over time, as her "awarish-ness" about her own manipulation of sexual objectification in the 1930s became misogynistic grotesque camp at her expense when West was trotted back out as a pitiful camp artifact in the 1970s.[45] "Awarish-ness" is what Robertson finds in the burlesque theatrical tradition of female performers who are different from women performing in girlie shows, tableaux vivants, and the ballet, because of the female performer's "awareness of her own 'awarishness'—the directness of her address and her complicity in her own sexual objectification."[46]

Parton's persona has often been directly compared to West's Diamond Lil character. However, I contend that Parton has escaped the same fate as West because she continues to control her own media image and has the cultural power to continue to make music and other media more on her own terms than

West was able to do at the end of her career. Nevertheless, Parton could be seen to reference the same kind of burlesque trope of "awarish-ness."

West was challenging sexual mores and explicitly writing incendiary material that allowed women to be sexual beings, explored drag, or supported gay and lesbian rights, and she was trying to seize control of how she signified in a sexualized stage and screen setting. Over her career, to differing degrees in different contexts, Parton is also challenging sexual mores and trying to seize control of how she signifies as a camp sex object. In Parton's case, the sexual objectification has remained in quotation marks because of the complexity of her camp performance.

For example, in Parton's first scene in *The Best Little Whorehouse in Texas*, the camera frames her as a sexual object in the classic style of the male gaze of Hollywood cinema, but her camp effect breaks up that gendered dynamic to a certain degree. In film theorist Laura Mulvey's foundational argument, classic Hollywood cinema makes women the passive sexual object and men the active heroic subject and screen surrogate for the viewer, such that the camera gazes at the objectified woman in much the same way a stereotypical male gaze would look at her, voyeuristically, focused on the pleasure in looking.[47] For Mulvey, avant-garde cinema would break up that objectifying effect, but she also allows that multiple gazes and accompanying gender ideologies can be present and can complicate the film frame even in classic Hollywood cinema and by extension, more recent mainstream Hollywood films. In this case, I contend that Parton's camp performance, because it adds the ironic distance to her gender performance, has the effect of disrupting the objectifying male gaze of the camera. While the film certainly fetishizes her body, purposefully including her breasts in almost every shot of her, her own camp performance nevertheless disrupts the camera's stereotypical male gaze. She returns the gaze in an exaggerated, knowing way, breaking up the gender dynamics.

As a case in point, Parton's introductory scene begins with a close-up of her character's red, peep-toe high heels walking toward the big central staircase on the second floor, starting down the stairs. When she reaches the central landing at the top of the staircase, we see a close-up shot of her stopping to adjust her red floor-length dress hem over her shoes. The camera cuts to the male patrons and female coworkers at the bottom of the stairs, all of whom stare up at the sight of Parton's character, mouths agape. The men doff their cowboy hats, as if mimicking an imagined audience's spectator role. The camera pans slowly up her body, and the low-angle camera shot frames Parton as she momentarily stands silently, presented as the film's central spectacle. In that shot, she is dressed ostentatiously, standing out in comparison to the other characters, and they all cede to her power as the central figure in that setting. She wears a stereotypical madam's costume, a gaudy long red gown with sequins and taffeta on the shoulders and a long taffeta train, the fishtail gown very low cut, the tightly fitted top emphasizing her cleavage. Her hair and makeup are similarly garish; she wears a platinum blonde wig styled up with ringlets, large red earrings, long red nails, gaudy fake diamond rings, and a large amount of makeup, including bright red lipstick, rouge, blue eyeshadow, and copious mascara.

While that kind of shot exemplifies the objectifying male gaze of cinema, the scene moves quickly into camp performance, as she winks and sings while walking down the stairs and bouncing her hips. The scene underscores how Parton is delivering a Mae West–style routine. She sings "A Lil' Ole Bitty Pissant Country Place," and the song characterizes the brothel as having "just lots of good will and maybe one small thrill" but with "nothin' dirty goin' on." The scene's jocular tone matches the film's claim that the house is an accepted institution, with mild immorality but not socially unacceptable behavior. In the musical number, with the men and women around her making up the chorus and dancing and singing the up-tempo song, Parton's character sweeps through the ranch, recounting her house rules to protect her "girls" and keep them "ladylike," singing "nobody messes with my girls." The song continues over a montage of the house; Parton sings while appearing in different gowns in different rooms, orienting the audience to this fictional space. She ends the song by introducing the male visitors to her "girls," exclaiming, "Well, howdy boys!" to a group of arriving men. In this final sequence of the musical number, she wears an ostentatious, long, black, low-cut gown with silver sequins and a feathered train, carrying a large feather burlesque-style fan. She bounces her hips and yells "yah" as she sweeps the fan to end the song. Significantly, while Parton directly echoes a burlesque performer and also Mae West in this scene, the other women are not framed as campily as she is, because her camp effect is directly related to her existing star persona.

The point here is that Parton looks almost how she usually looks, with the exception of the especially low-cut gowns and the lingerie. The concluding scene for the entire film echoes this earlier scene, further reinforcing an analogy between Parton and the character. In the film's final scene, Parton as Mona again walks down the central staircase, this time to a deserted house, clad in a gray cowgirl dress with fringe and a cowboy hat, the style more demure and covered up than her earlier low-cut gowns, in line with the more subdued clothes the character wears around town when not at the house. When Ed Earl arrives and proposes, she suddenly sings "I Will Always Love You" in response (since she initially wants to refuse him for fear of harming his political career, until he convinces her otherwise). There, the film breaks into an extra-textual reference to Parton via one of her signature songs, which cannot help but signify much more broadly than the fictional confines of the film. That moment puts her star persona front and center in the movie. Ultimately, the film concludes by restoring the original framing of her as the cheerful, good-time madam because it ends with a montage of the characters taken from footage of the earlier bustling opening scene of the movie. Only one shot is a new one. In the film's final shot, we see a cartoonish iris-in shot (it goes from a full frame down to focusing on a circle around her, the rest of the screen blacked out) of Parton in her black, sequined, Mae West–style gown again. However, this time she says in direct address to the camera, "Y'all come back now, y'hear," implicating the audience in her star persona.

The film's extra-textual marketing material also draws on her camp effects by blurring the line between her fictional character and her star persona, creating resonances with all the different ways Parton's star persona signifies to audiences. In a behind-the-scenes short about the making of the film, included on the later DVD edition, both Parton and Reynolds draw links between their lives and characters. Parton discusses the controversy around her taking the racy role. When the interviewer asks if her fans would "accept her in the role of a whorehouse madam," Parton registers the risk she took: "I think it's a big responsibility, I think we have to protect our public as far as what we're doing. So I gave it a lot of thought and I talked to my folks about it and I saw it as a story about life, a way to show that these people have personalities, these people have reasons for being what they are." Parton makes the case for her close relationship with her fans and her protection of her own star image. In her discussion of how the film culls sympathy for the female prostitutes, she cites the "Hard Candy Christmas" scene in the house, where the women are leaving the closed brothel, some revealed to be mothers worried about the children they are trying to support. She says she uses her own life experiences to empathize with her character: "When I thought about it, I thought well, well, this person, this lady, this madam, she is me, because I am just full of life and love and energy for all kinds of people, I have sampled enough of everything in life to say that I have lived. This lady, this character that I am playin', although I didn't own a whorehouse, if I had not been as fortunate as I am, who knows what I could have been."[48] She draws the analogy between her life and character, and she does so in part because as a female actor, she will be compared to the character and judged for playing a racy part. She asks for empathy for the fallen woman, suggesting that others could be in that situation if they did not have economic recourse. Indeed, the film asks for sympathy for Mona by giving her the backstory of having been a child who bounced around the foster care system and never had a family.

The gendering of these filmic and extra-textual expectations is clear. Even given how both actors play themselves as characters, the gendered politics of reception for their film work differ significantly. As a male performer, Reynolds does not face that stigma. He cites his own southern sheriff father as inspiration for his role. In film outtakes, Parton and Reynolds use the same personae when filming and when not filming, with similar banter, "boob jokes," and interactions, that is, reinforcing the idea that they are merely playing versions of their star personae on screen.

Parton actually makes a much larger claim for the cultural work she was attempting to do with this film role, saying she wanted to find a way to make her country music accessible to a mass audience. She observes,

> I think I know what my audience wants from me, now that we have gone through all these things together. And I depend on the audience a lot. And the songs in this movie are more *me* and more what I have been *trying* to do, all the routes I had to take to try to get to a place to where *my music*, the simple version of my music, the country flavor of my music, would be accepted by a broad audience. So I think that I have really accomplished a great deal of things with this movie.[49]

Her comments reveal how she sees the film as a mass audience vehicle for her music and, implicitly, how she sees her own star persona as just such a vehicle— all methods for gaining the attention of a mass audience to get them invested in her music. She also explicitly stakes a genre claim for country music here and makes the case for why she did her crossover pop music while retaining her country foundation, meaning that she wanted to circulate her country music more broadly using that tactic. Her discussion indicates that she was concerned about audience support and media access, and that she was frustrated with her struggle for creative freedom in terms of making different kinds of music.

Camp Politics

In my analysis of Parton's camp image, I am arguing that she uses parody in a transgressive way, and it is worth tracing out further the cultural politics of camp in Parton's performances. Let me briefly elaborate on how my reading of Parton contributes to scholarly discussions of camp.[50] Several cultural theorists have cited Parton in passing to support their larger arguments about gay camp, feminist camp, drag, or embodiment.[51] However, in much of that literature, scholars invoke her as an emblematic example but only in a cursory way, giving a quick read of her to support a broader argument. I have tried to show how it is important to account in a much fuller way for the nuances and changes in Parton's use of camp across time and contexts.

In a key argument, theorist Carole-Ann Tyler uses Parton as an example in order to suggest that drag is not necessarily or always subversive, rather, some drag performances reproduce stereotypes and could be seen as conservative.[52] I agree with Tyler's larger point about potential conservative elements in camp and drag, since their political effects, as critic David Bergman has shown, depend on their context.[53] However, I disagree with Tyler's reading of Parton.

In a brief analysis of Parton, Tyler claims that Parton's working-class performance might only appear "campy" if viewed from a white, middle-class perspective. She means that white, working-class audiences might actually see it as a realistic version of womanhood that fits working-class norms. Her point is that some drag performances use classist and racist stereotypes in order to make it clear that they are ironic, that is, different from white, middle-class norms of femininity. While I agree with Tyler that some camp traffics in such stereotypes, I contend that Parton's does not.

As I discuss more fully in chapter 5 when I address fan responses to her, Parton's working-class country audience is well aware of the insider joke and the obvious exaggeration she is making. Parton's camp would be understood in a country music performance context as an obviously exaggerated parody, not as a realistic portrayal of white, working-class femininity. Working-class audiences familiar with country music would know she is making a joke.

Parton references her own past ("a country girl's idea of glam") and authenticity narrative to ground a parody that was always about recycling out-of-date styles as camp and artifice, such as her knowing use of out-of-date teased hair, dresses, and shoes, exaggerated as artifice, as an attention-grabbing style. I read that movement as liberatory, a challenge to the idea that gender codes are natural or inherently true, undermining their seeming naturalness through excessive repetition and hyperbolic style. Of course, the way such camp signifies politically depends on context. Robertson, in her study of feminist camp, maintains that it can be both critique and containment; camp can take past taste and recode it in new contexts, re-historicizing it, as a form of what she calls "productive anachronism" and "recycling."[54]

Parton's performance in effect comments on how gender works culturally, with theorist Judith Butler's work being an obvious cultural theory parallel. Butler argues that gender is performative in the sense that gender expression, such as everyday gestures, behaviors, and enactments, creates gender identity, thus gender is socially constructed; there is no preexisting "natural" gender. She cites drag as an obvious example.[55] Parton's camp performances, ironic distancing, and combinations of different gendered personae (including a Mae West female-female impersonation reference) lend proof to this idea that gender itself is performative.

Ultimately, Parton's gender performance is transgressive because she uses feminist camp to imply that she is in drag all the time—and that everyone else is too. Parton's camp effect also needs to be understood in terms of specific sociohistorical contexts and how it changes over time. The 1970s contexts of Parton's crossover and alterations to the music industry at this time are important for understanding the social history context. As the industry evolved in the 1970s, audiences became fragmented into niche markets, and a growing number of genres and subgenres emerged and gained popularity. The social movements of the time also influenced Parton's reception, as her labor concept album and film work for 9 to 5 struck a chord in audiences in conjunction with the second-wave feminist movement. Likewise, some of her disco releases and dance remixes during that decade and the 1980s were taken up in the context of the gay and lesbian rights movement, with Parton becoming a gay camp icon alongside other singers popular at the time, such as Cher. Gloria Steinem interviewed Parton and named her as one of the Ms. Women of the Year (1986), a feminist celebration of her even though she had often claimed not to be engaged with the middle-class women's movement. Steinem said Parton was chosen to be honored because she had seized the platform of her own fame to reclaim gendered imagery, contending that Parton "has turned all the devalued symbols of womanliness to her own ends."[56] Notably, Parton has continued to the present day to be claimed as a feminist icon by feminist magazines, even though she herself does not claim the title of feminist, which is a measure of the impact of her advocacy for women and gender equity.[57]

Musicologist Mitchell Morris has argued rightly that Parton was positioned as a kitsch "bad" object in the 1970s in the sense that she was targeting crossover pop and such subgenres as disco, but that her appeal in part had to do with her abject class positioning, meaning her self-presentation as a poor, rural, white southerner. In his view, Parton became a symbol for some audiences to draw an analogy with other marginalities, such as women in the women's movement, based on Parton's gender address, and gay and lesbian fans, particularly gay male fans, who read a story of triumph over marginalization in Parton's country diva persona. Morris suggests that Parton has had diminishing returns on her Daisy Mae persona because she has to keep the origin story present.[58] However, I read her life story as precisely the cornerstone for her ongoing mass appeal, one that affords Parton flexibility in her storytelling. Parton has turned her life story into a supple mythology she can take in different directions, across a range of various media platforms. It is important to keep in mind that there is continuing booming market for that very life story, as evidenced by the recent TV film deal with NBC for movies based on her life and the high ratings for those movies about her origin story. Morris's reading of Parton's camp effect is that it is largely based on her appearance, not on her music itself. It is worth noting, however, that Parton's song "Just a Wee Bit Gay" and forthcoming dance album do explicitly engage with gay camp performance, and some of her other songs could be interpreted as feminist camp rather than gay camp, such as "PMS Blues."

Rhinestones, Steel Magnolias, and *Straight Talking*

Also contributing to Parton's evolving image, her other three major film roles during this period continued the "strong woman" gender themes of *9 to 5* and *The Best Little Whorehouse in Texas*. In *Rhinestone*, Parton struggles to make it as a country singer in New York City and succeeds by drawing on her Smoky Mountain roots. The film's gender politics emerge because she has to face down a boss who is sexually harassing her. While the film critiques the boss's behavior and is entirely sympathetic to the Parton character, it nonetheless uses the sexual threat storyline as titillation in a problematic way. While *9 to 5* to a certain extent did so as well, the latter film does so much more. Parton's character, Jake Farris, must win a bet with her exploitative boss at a nightclub in New York City that she can turn cabbie Nick Martinelli (Sylvester Stallone) into a successful country singer. Trying to cash in on the urban cowboy demographic, owner Freddie Ugo (Ron Leibman) has signed Farris to an unfair long-term contract. If she wins, she is freed from the bad contract, while if he wins, he will add another five years to her contract and she must also sleep with him. The film thus narratively depends on placing Parton under a sexual threat, which positions her as a potential victim, just as her earlier character had been exploited by her male boss in unfair labor conditions.

The film thematizes different southern versus northern, country versus city, and femininity versus masculinity stereotypes in the storyline about Parton's character trying to turn a New Yorker into a country singer. Because Stallone's character declares that he hates country music ("it's like, worse than liver"), Parton's character takes him home to Tennessee for two weeks to immerse him in the music and culture. The film juxtaposes her fish-out-of-water story in New York City with his in Tennessee. Both characters appear as caricatures of the stars' personas. In her Tennessee scenes, some of Parton's family members appear and perform music; those sequences read like light references to her autobiographical contexts. Parton's character offers homespun jokes and spitfire remarks, telling her boss: "There are two kinds of people in this world, and you aren't one of them." The film's screenplay, loosely inspired by Glenn Campbell's "Rhinestone Cowboy," makes broad and reductive cultural distinctions, as when Parton's character teaches Stallone's how to "walk country" by pretending he has jock itch. After the two fall in love, the film's plot is resolved by Stallone successfully performing a country song, his fringed cowboy suit matching Parton's silver sequined fringe gown as she joins him onstage. While the film did not achieve critical or box office success, Parton had two songs on her soundtrack, "Tennessee Homesick Blues" and "God Won't Get You," reach the top ten on the country charts.

In a TV film that Parton appeared in after *Rhinestone*, *Smoky Mountain Christmas* (1986), she makes even more filmic references to her autobiography and personal mythologies. While it features the "strong woman" character striving to fulfill her career dreams and deter sleazy suitors and men who would exploit her, it ultimately offers a conservative romance plotline that reframes the character in terms of a marriage and domestic resolution. Parton stars as a lonely country star, Lorna Davis, frustrated with the materialism of Hollywood, including exploitative producers and stalker paparazzi, who goes home to the Smoky Mountains to retreat at a friend's cabin and ends up helping a group of orphaned children squatting there. In an odd plotline that seems designed to reference folktales as well as mountain folk culture, a mountain "witch woman" named Jezebel is jealous of the Parton character (who has caught the eye of the sheriff that Jezebel loves) and makes unsuccessful attempts on her life. A mountain man, Mountain Dan (Lee Majors), saves Davis, and they fall in love; he later frees her from imprisonment, and they are granted custody of the children. The film thus asserts a positive reading of mountain folk culture as the heroic male character uses his knowledge of the Great Smokies and common sense, as well as rugged survival skills, to save other characters. The film suggests that the country star must return to her folk roots to maintain her values, just as it places her in a romance narrative plotline that turns her into a wife and mother in the domestic sphere.

While Parton's film *Steel Magnolias*, based on Robert Harling's play (1987), is more explicitly another "strong woman" film, focusing on communities of women, it does draw on a small-town southern setting that jibes with Parton's persona. Harling based his play on events in his own life. It follows a group of southern women in Natchitoches, Louisiana, who provide support for each other as one dies from diabetes. Shelby Eatenton-Latcherie (Julia Roberts), a young married woman, dies after giving birth and having a kidney transplant from her mother, Mary Lynn "M'Lynn" Eatenton (Sally Field), that her body ultimately rejected. Parton plays hairdresser Truvy Jones as a warm, welcoming presence who jokes in her home-based salon and takes in and employs a young woman whose criminal husband is running from the police. Her salon becomes a space for the women to bond and provide emotional empathy and problem solving, forming an important source of support. Parton again plays a version of herself as a homespun, comedic personality, although her character is dressed and wigged more conventionally, in keeping with the other women. In this film, Parton is part of an ensemble cast rather than the headlining star, and her character serves a role by fitting into a community of women.

Finally, Parton's other major film during this era, *Straight Talk*, draws closely on her star persona and also imagines her overcoming gendered politics. Parton's character mistakenly fills in for a radio psychologist in Chicago and is so popular with her homespun wisdom that she is hired to masquerade as a radio personality with PhD credentials. She is impoverished because she has moved alone to the city from Arkansas, fired from her dance instructor job for dispensing advice but not teaching, and she has left her common-law husband, who refused to move. When James Woods's newspaper reporter character tries to expose her lie, he instead falls in love with her and helps her stay on the air due to listener demand, even after she has revealed publicly that she is an imposter. She faces manipulative gender politics, because Woods's character initially tries to date her in order to expose her true identity in the press. When confronted with a lack of career opportunities and financial insecurity, Parton's character falls back on her personality and homespun wisdom. The film associates the character's pithy maxims closely with Parton's star persona.

This link is germane to Parton's ongoing persona even after that film, as Parton herself has made a long career of being immensely quotable for her advice. For example, she published her own book of advice, *Dream More: Celebrate the Dreamer in You* (2013), which elaborates on a University of Tennessee commencement speech she gave highlighting her personal philosophy. Likewise, she has circulated digital versions of her pithy sayings and advice, as with her Twitter feed of "Dollyisms." The portrayal of Parton as a fount of wisdom is another layer of her elaborate star image. In chapter 4, I trace how Parton's star persona in the next stage of her career took another turn, as she began to reemphasize a more country inflection to her star image as she tried to garner more success with bluegrass albums. Again, she returned to her life story, with her autobiography becoming her fullest depiction of her "Dolly image."

Notes

1. Dickinson, "Hello Dolly."

2. Robertson, *Guilty Pleasures*, 28.

3. Parton, *Dolly*, 186.

4. Dyer, *Stars*.

5. *The Tonight Show Starring Johnny Carson*, 19 January 1977; *The Tonight Show Starring Johnny Carson*, 17 February 1977; *Barbara Walters Special*.

6. Edwards, *Triumph of Reality TV*.

7. *The Tonight Show Starring Jimmy Fallon*, 14 May 2014; *The Tonight Show Starring Jimmy Fallon*, 24 August 2016.

8. Nash, *Dolly*.

9. Chet Flippo, "Interview: Dolly Parton," *Rolling Stone*, 25 August 1977, 32–38.

10. Nash, *Dolly*, 257.

11. Ibid., 220.

12. Ibid., 229–245.

13. Ibid., 217–229.

14. *Dolly Parton*, 28 April 2006.

15. Miller, *Smart Blonde*, 4–5.

16. Ibid., 149.

17. Ibid.

18. *Kenny and Dolly: Real Love*.

19. Rogers, *Luck*, 176.

20. Neal, *Country Music*, 338–341. Eric Weisbard's book chapter on Parton avers that Parton was always both pop and country, like the country genre itself, and her use of the format middle of the road/adult contemporary for her crossover was part of

her claiming a centrist space in country music, mirroring trends in the genre. Weisbard, *Top 40*, 70–111.

21. Curtis W. Ellison argues Parton uses the evangelical tradition in songs like "Appalachian Memories," merging sacred and secular to assuage the loneliness of migration with gospel salvation. Ellison, *Country Music Culture*, 118.

22. Nash, *Dolly*, 217–229.

23. Cardwell, *Words and Music*, 16.

24. The Rogers song reached ninth on country singles and forty-fourth on the *Billboard* Hot 100.

25. Morris, *Persistence of Sentiment*, 196–197.

26. *The Best Little Whorehouse in Texas* soundtrack reached fifth on country, sixty-third on pop, with charting singles: "Hard Candy Christmas" (5th on country) and "I Will Always Love You" (1st on country, 53rd on pop). Less successful were the *Rhinestone* soundtrack (32th on country, 135th pop) and *Straight Talk* (22nd on country and 138th on pop).

27. See Joli Jensen on the problems of claiming purity by proxy. Jensen, *Nashville Sound*.

28. "Nashville Memories."

29. Nash, *Dolly*, 217–218.

30. Dyer, *Stars*; deCordova, *Personalities*.

31. Dyer, "Four Films," 228.

32. Ibid.

33. Ellis, "Stars," 302.

34. I agree with critics who argue, contra Ellis, that his extraordinary/ordinary model is applicable to TV as well, even though the constant exposure to the star could somewhat undermine the extraordinary side of the binary. Ibid.

35. Ibid. Ellis argues that the fragmented tabloid coverage makes fans want to see the stars in movies even more; the film unifies the star into a more coherent narrative persona.

36. Parton, *Dream More*, 57.

37. *Larry King Live*, 3 July 2003.

38. On how the film's female solidarity message reflected the era's feminist films, see Barger, "Backlash."

39. *9 to 5*.

40. Nash, *Dolly*, 222.

41. *Larry King Live*, 27 July 2011.

42. *The Best Little Whorehouse in Texas*.

43. Dickinson, "Hello Dolly."

44. Pamela Robertson cites Allen, *Horrible Prettiness*. Robertson, *Guilty Pleasures*, 28.

45. Robertson, *Guilty Pleasures*, 28.

46. Ibid.

47. Mulvey, "Visual Pleasure."

48. *The Best Little Whorehouse in Texas*.

49. Ibid.

50. Relevant references include Robertson, *Guilty Pleasures*; Bergman, *Camp Grounds*; Tyler, "Boys"; Ross, *No Respect*; Sontag "Notes"; Meyer, *Politics*; and Newton, *Mother Camp*.

51. Tyler, "Boys," 32. Rosi Braidotti reads Parton briefly as an example of posthuman, postmodern simulation. Braidotti, "Cyberfeminism," 643–645. Elizabeth Grosz has passing references to Parton as an example of her theories of embodiment. For her more general theories, see Grosz, *Volatile Bodies*.

52. Tyler, "Boys," 32.

53. Bergman, *Camp Grounds*, 14.

54. Robertson, *Guilty Pleasures*, 142.

55. Butler, *Gender Trouble*. See also Newton, *Mother Camp*. Pamela Fox has demonstrated how Judith Butler's theory of gender performativity is applicable to country music history, with the genre's intersecting performances of gender, race, and class. Fox, *Natural Acts*. See also Hubbs, "'Jolene.'"

56. Steinem, "Dolly Parton."

57. Butterworth, "All Dolled Up."

58. Morris, *Persistence of Sentiment*, 196–197.

Hungry Again
Reclaiming Country Authenticity Narratives

So, here in one place was God, music,
and sex. My fascination was complete.

—Dolly Parton

In the 1990s, Parton faced a career crisis and turned to folk authenticity to solve it. She found her career at a crossroads in her fifties, staring down the prospect of diminishing returns in the pop arena and becoming irrelevant on country radio. In response, she used a passel of "blue mountain" albums to salvage her career. Not only did she turn to making albums that could be embraced by the emergent Americana roots music movement but she also published her autobiography as a way to promote her music and to turn her persona into its most coherent version to date. In that memoir, she scandalously explains how when she was growing up, she found religion, music, and sex to be her foundational desires, and furthermore, felt that God wanted her to have musical fame and to be a sexual being. In effect, Parton claimed that God wanted her to be sex positive and to sing about it. Since she made this claim in a country music star memoir, her commentary was nothing short of incendiary, replete with a complex and subversive gender critique.

We could say that Parton's career crisis here was her second authenticity gut check, much like her crossover moment earlier when she had to prove why a country pop Parton was still genuine and believable. Here, she survived by adapting her gender performance to new contexts. While this phase of her career is often characterized as a return to country music, during the period of 1994–2002, it would be more accurate to see her as changing the ongoing balance of country and pop crossover at different stages of her career. Nevertheless, within that shifting balance, the country and emerging niche folk markets took center stage more forcefully during this epoch. Just as she altered musical directions, so did she modify her gender performance elements. She amplified her "mountain girl" components quite strongly to legitimate her new focus on her "blue mountain" music, including folk, old-time music, Appalachian ballads, and bluegrass.

Famously in 1997, Parton described herself as having a "crisis" and fled to her hometown, returning to the "Tennessee Mountain Home" cabin of her youth to write her *Hungry Again* (1998) album, in an effort to succeed again on country radio. While she had done country albums earlier, such as *White Limozeen* (1989), she was at this point finding less success with either pop or country releases. Country radio's targeted shift to a younger demographic of female listeners squeezed older stars like Parton out of radio play in the 1990s, as did higher commercial expectations for the genre. When Parton engaged the Americana roots music movement with her critically acclaimed albums *The Grass Is Blue* (1999), *Little Sparrow* (2001), and *Halos & Horns* (2002), she trumpeted for her own East Tennessee roots and "natural" familiarity with bluegrass and folk as part of her authenticity claims for these albums.

In this chapter, I trace Parton's authenticity narratives in this period beginning with her *Heartsongs: Live from Home* (1994) album, and her autobiography, *Dolly: My Life and Other Unfinished Business* (1994), which she used to promote the album. I undertake an extensive reading of gender construction in her autobiography. I see those texts as a precursor to her "return to country" narrative with *Hungry Again* and the "blue mountain" albums. I also attend to the Lifetime TV movie she produced and starred in, *Blue Valley Songbird* (1999), based on her song from *Hungry Again*.

Her autobiography is the most sustained articulation of how she integrates the mountain girl and the country tramp components of her persona. While parts of her life story were familiar before, appearing in everything from interviews to lyrics, the autobiography in book form hugely ratcheted up her truth claims. In it, she turns that life story into a distinctive narrative and cements her persona more fully. She looks back on her Appalachian childhood and reframes it as a full story, replete with personal philosophies and morals that she imparts to the reader. She polishes her pitch for how her life story could legitimate her albums.

In my discussion of her autobiography, I analyze her own self-contextualizing in terms of southern, white, working-class femininity, and more specifically gender codes in Appalachia. I trace how she at once romanticizes her impoverished rural background but also critiques that nostalgia. As in her other work, she uses her Appalachian narratives to buffer her potentially incendiary social critiques, especially around gender or class; she justifies her relationship to popular feminism as organic and reclaims a hillbilly identity in ways both ironic and earnest. Joking about her "early Appalachian feminist tactics," she records her resistant response to some restrictive gender role expectations and male chauvinism in midcentury Appalachia.[1]

Most striking in her autobiography is how she uses religion to justify her music as well as her model for her country tramp look. Through some astonishing rhetorical leaps, she seizes on a religious justification for her expression of female sexuality and links that expression to her musical career. As I discuss more fully below, in an infamous passage, shocking in the country memoir context, she links sex and religion in her description of how she claims she "found God" at age twelve. Surprisingly, she writes that she felt his message to her was to validate her own sense of herself as a "sexual being" and to pursue her dream of a musical career as her calling. In effect, Parton also cites personally revealed divine justification for female sexuality more generally. In terms of her own musical dreams and the gender discrimination she faced, given that she was already singing professionally at age ten, Parton retroactively expresses her staunch religious justification for her own ambitions.[2]

However, since it is the adult Parton writing later about her childhood, from the vantage point of country music and pop superstardom, she makes her own past a space where she can seize control of how she appears in relation to sexuality. She tries to take ownership of what she symbolizes. Countering the ever-present sexual objectification of female singers, Parton here uses music to express her own sexuality rather than letting the music industry frame her as merely a sexualized image to be sold as a commodity. Her rather ingenious gambit is to trump any negative positioning of her by invoking divine will. Meanwhile, her rejoinder to the objectification problem, with its intractable historical link to female stage performance being associated with prostitution, is to choose self-objectification, exaggeration, and camp. Those strategies generate ironic distancing and some degree of female agency for her, but her autobiography shows how fully she anchors that move back to her folk authenticity narratives. It is her "sincerity contract" piece, in terms of country music performance history, that holds her entire persona together. Her artifice is ultimately fully grounded by her autobiographical claims. As I have been arguing, the mass culture piece is shown to originate from the folk culture source, just as she transgresses the distinction between the two.

Biographical Contexts

The contours of Parton's career crisis included flagging solo album sales and uncomfortable moves to different record labels. Her solo albums during this period, including *Heartsongs: Live from Home* (1994), *Something Special* (1995), and *Treasures* (1997), did not achieve her customary chart success. One exception to this downward trend was her duet of "I Will Always Love You" with Vince Gill (1995), which enjoyed commercial (fifteenth on the country charts) and critical recognition (a CMA vocal collaboration award). The last solo platinum album she had had, *Slow Dancing with the Moon* (1993), had not produced any hit singles. In her movement among record labels, she had signed with Columbia in 1987 after RCA dropped her, then moved to MCA/Universal (Rising Tide in 1997 and Decca in 1998) until 1999, when Decca closed and MCA did not keep her. Parton then released *The Grass Is Blue* with her Blue Eye Records label and independent label Sugar Hill Records, as she began collaborating with smaller independent labels for distribution.

For Parton, *Hungry Again* was an attempt at a career reset, and she mounted an extremely elaborate press campaign to promote it. While it did not achieve the wished-for chart success, it did secure critical approval and gave her a path forward. In interviews, she stressed her homecoming story, returning to her "Tennessee Mountain Home" in the summer of 1997 because she wanted to go back to her roots in the face of a career crisis, not knowing which direction to take for her music and career. She described how she went on a three-week fast and wrote dozens of songs, including those on the *Hungry Again* album. Her rhetoric on this album draws on her familiar Appalachian authenticity narratives but also a "returning home" shift in her multimedia superstar image. She drives home her organic mountain identity claims with gusto. After the *Hungry Again* album failed to top the charts, she did have collaborative success again with the long-delayed release of *Trio II* (1999), with Linda Ronstadt and Emmylou Harris. It enjoyed critical and commercial success (fourth on the country chart). However, Parton's former solo success eluded her.

It is in that context that she turned to her bluegrass and folk albums as part of an Americana roots music revival, starting with *The Grass Is Blue*. For *Halos & Horns*, she went on tour again for the first time in ten years. She turned to a more niche market for her bluegrass and folk albums, addressing a smaller, more targeted audience. At the same time, she moved to protect her legacy, retrenching her position in terms of country music's hagiographies and a traditional country base of support. For example, in 1999, she promoted the opening of the Southern Gospel Music Hall of Fame at Dollywood with a Dollywood-exclusive gospel album and a TNN television special, and she was inducted into the Country Music Hall of Fame (and later the Gospel Music Hall of Fame in 2009).

During this time, Parton worked to find new ways to address different fan bases. She disbanded her fan club in 1997, citing her lack of radio play (just as fan club pioneer Loretta Lynn had disbanded hers in 1996). Parton said she wanted fans to focus their energies on Dollywood instead. Fan clubs have a long history of coalescing audiences in the country music industry, so the shuttering of a fan club was a noteworthy event. In Parton's case, she was in part responding to tensions within her fan club. The Dollywood Foundation had taken over an existing amateur fan club, leading to some conflicts (some fans did not want to pay membership dues to fund Dollywood Foundation projects, and some protested when she did not play a full concert for a Dollywood benefit). Such a story was common in country music history, as many amateur fan practices were replaced by professional fan clubs and monetized, thereby changing the fandom culture.[3] Within the official fan club, the Dollywood Ambassadors club handled mail-order merchandise and advance tickets to concerts; it used the annual dues to fund projects such as a buddy program and a library program in Parton's home region in Sevier County, Tennessee. In a letter to fans about the disbanding, Parton wrote, "It has always bothered me to profit from your devotion. . . . Many of you are donating your hard-earned money because you care for me, not because you believed in the programs of my foundation." Parton asked them to send their money to charities instead.[4]

Meanwhile, Parton expanded her TV work, extending her appeal to her fan base in a medium where she still had higher levels of access to them. In a forwarding-thinking media strategy, Parton generated a TV movie, Lifetime's *Blue Valley Songbird*, also based on the *Hungry Again* album, and targeted it to the niche market of female Lifetime viewers. She explicitly insisted the film was not based on her life. In the movie, she carefully presents her character as different from the Dolly Parton mythology. The woman escapes the mountains and an abusive father to pursue fitfully country music stardom. Parton wears a red wig, disrupting the regular "Dolly Parton" visual iconography. Parton's distancing move departs significantly from her earlier films and highlights the degree to which her film characters are usually framed as iterations of her personality and iconography. This movie thus insists on more figurative and metaphorical, rather than autobiographical, meanings. Some observers nevertheless assumed the story was from her life; biographer Alanna Nash notes Parton's denials but replies by saying Parton has admitted that all of her music is related to her life.[5] In contrast, I read the film as one of Parton's few efforts to depart from literal interpretations of her life story. Parton offers some metaphorical analogies to her own persona but largely presents the characterization as distinct from her own.

Parton's cross-platform strategy, as well as her amping up of her Appalachian roots to claim folk bona fides, had one crucial precursor during this period of her career. While Parton's earlier *Heartsongs* album did reach the *Billboard* country charts (rising to number sixteen) and the *Billboard* 200 (number eighty-seven), the album is more significant for how Parton combines different musical influences and legacies than for any critical or audience response to it. It also lives on as a themed show attraction at Dollywood, with a short film narrated by Parton and an integrated live musical theater performance, in which actors come out to play the roles of her characters and to sing live.

Narratives of Authenticity: *Heartsongs* and *Dolly*

Parton's autobiography and her *Heartsongs* album are linked texts, and it is crucial to unravel how each formulate her authenticity claims for her "blue mountain" turn. She explicitly published her autobiography as part of her publicity for the album. *Heartsongs*, recorded at a Dollywood concert, reads like a primer of Parton's musical influences. It features traditional songs and folk ballads, gospel, early country music, and many of Parton's earlier classic songs that exhibit her folk and traditional influences. Many of her own songs on the album focus on autobiographical material related to her Appalachian childhood, including "Applejack," "Coat of Many Colors," "My Tennessee Mountain Home," "Smoky Mountain Memories," "To Daddy," "Cas Walker Theme," and a new composition for the album, "Heartsong." She layers in gospel songs, such as "What a Friend We Have in Jesus," as well as traditional songs like "In the Pines," "Barbara Allen," and "Wayfaring Stranger."

It is particularly noteworthy that she includes the Carter Family song "I'm Thinking Tonight of My Blue Eyes," which has an infamous history in country music annals. That song illuminates how country music authenticity narratives are carefully fashioned performances, a point relevant to Parton because she places the song in her pantheon of music that is meant to legitimate her. The Carter Family's authenticity story is important to country music history because historians count them as the "first family of country music" in the sense that they were one of two acts coming out of the "big bang" of the 1927 Bristol sessions that established an ongoing organizing paradigm for country music. If Jimmie Rodgers was the rambler and genre-crosser, the Carter Family was the purveyor of domestic, home, and family-centered traditional music, with their family image being central to how they marketed their music. Yet their authenticity story is equally as distinctive for how fabricated it was.

The original trio of A. P. Carter, wife Sara, and his sister-in-law Maybelle skillfully sold an image of familial bliss, using their life stories as part of their public personae, becoming a symbol of the American family and domesticity. However, they were keeping up a "brave face" in public. In private, the married couple was estranged for most of their career. Sara broke gender taboos by leaving her husband and children and going to live with her family in 1933, and then divorcing him in 1936. However, they kept recording and performing together, maintaining a carefully curated public image until 1943. Her children described her as a forward-thinking proto-feminist known to break gender taboos of the time by wearing pants and smoking; granddaughter Rita says, "My grandmother was probably liberated before people knew the term, certainly for women in this area."[6] Sara fell in love with A. P.'s cousin Coy Bays, and while their families kept them apart and exiled Bays to California, she ultimately reunited with him via a Carter Family performance, throwing the artificiality of the act's familial image into stark relief. In a 1938 radio performance of "I'm Thinking Tonight of My Blue Eyes" on powerful border radio station XERA, Sara dedicated the song to Bays. He heard her on the radio, drove all night from California to Texas to reach her, and they were married three weeks later. Even given the strains underneath their public image of domestic harmony, the Carter Family group managed to project an image of home-centered bliss and lend it staying power, achieving a definitive influence on country music notions of purity.

Thus, when Parton includes that particular song, one could read the ways in which she is invoking their home-centered authenticity tale, particularly on her album of "home songs" meant to anchor Parton to Appalachia. Yet more importantly, on a deeper level, the parallel here involves how both the Carters and Parton had elaborately constructed images. While Parton's presentation of her public image may be "truer" in some sense than the Carter Family's, the fact that they are each ultimately carefully fashioned images meant to convey certain values is underscored by this analogy.

The album also features a song that is important to how her camp image functions. "PMS Blues," which first appeared on this album, has become a concert favorite. The song is campy, purposefully tacky, and in "poor taste." In it, Parton sings that premenstrual syndrome makes her "awful" and "lowdown" to be around, invoking stereotypical language in her descriptions. She suggests that a man could not write this song because he would be called a "chauvinist." Parton plays around with gender bending, singing, "It's the only time in my life I ever think about wishing I'd been a man." She concludes that even if she had been a man, her male version would then be stuck dealing with a "cranky, naggin', raggin' hateful woman" suffering from PMS and taking it out on him. Parton purposeful uses shock value in her discussion of menstruation, as her lyrics reinforce stereotypes about women and PMS. As she plays around with gender ideas, she implies on the one hand that there is gender essentialism, presenting a caricature of the offensive stereotype that all women would be hardwired to behave irrationally due to premenstrual syndrome. However, on the other hand, she does include hints of a more subversive undercurrent to gender themes in the song, because she slightly disrupts the essentialism when her lyrics imagine her being a man. Nevertheless, she returns to essentialism in that thought experiment when she says if she were a man, she would have to deal with a woman suffering from PMS. The song stands out as a camp performance amid other songs on the album that are much more focused on home and tradition.

Meanwhile, Parton's autobiography finds the roots of the superstar in a much earlier era, in her Appalachian childhood. Writing as Parton the adult superstar, she turns her critical gaze back on some key gender themes in midcentury Appalachian contexts, including gender socialization in her Pentecostal church, her parents' interactions in light of gender role expectations, her response to her brothers' roughhousing, and her quest for props of different versions of femininity such as makeup and stylish clothes. She describes her childhood and teen years as the foundation for her later image and persona. For the autobiography to have a legitimating function for her *Heartsongs* album, Parton uses it to crystallize stories she had been telling her entire career, but she also carefully situates the text in terms of how she is trying to claim her "down home" roots in order to play up her folk and country recording efforts.

Dolly Finds God

The most conspicuous passage in her autobiography establishes her complex version of gender identity and authenticity, in which she brings together the "fake" and "real" and merges a culturally legitimated version of femininity with a marginalized version. As I noted earlier, in her provocative account of "finding God," she argues that her three linked passions are God, music, and sex, and she maintains that she learned from God that it was "all right for [her] to be a sexual being."[7] Just as when Parton talks about a local woman who was seen as the "town tramp" being her inspiration for her signature look because the woman represented female beauty to a young Parton, Parton here uplifts negative stereotypes about women by tying them to a positive cultural idea. As part of her ongoing gender model, she links a culturally validated version of femininity (involving religion and piety) with an incendiary version of femininity (female sexuality). Instead of being a space of sinfulness and immorality, sexuality becomes part of her calling, religiously justified, which is a transgressive gender stance in the context of the country star memoir. Thus, when she uses spirituality to legitimate her expression of female sexuality, she implicitly attacks any cultural condemnation of women, particularly female singers, for being associated with sex.

In the chapter of her autobiography in which she writes about "God, music, and sex," she explains these drives in her life as a critique of her Pentecostal church upbringing. She observes that she objected to fundamentalist interpretations of the Bible, especially those she felt were imposed on illiterate parishioners, as well as to fire and brimstone preaching; she preferred an approach that embraced respect rather than fear for God. She writes that she was resistant to some fundamentalist teachings because she had her own opinions. Noting her support for others in their own beliefs, such as her maternal grandfather, the preacher Jake Owens, Parton nevertheless insists that she can determine her own beliefs. For example, she prefers her version of God, which is not the fire-and-brimstone God she learned about in her Pentecostal church but rather what she describes as a "friendly God"—one that she felt she could address personally, as you would a friend.[8]

As part of her critique of church practices she saw around her while growing up, she satirizes the gendered split in church-going behaviors, writing that men would often take their families to church but then exit the building to drink under the trees while the women and children attended the services and received religious instruction. She writes, "After all, they were men and needed nothing but their own wits and muscles." She implies that male avoidance of church services was hypocritical, as if their view of the "weaker" sex was that women needed the religious instruction while they themselves only needed to engage in male bonding and to embody masculinity. She suggests that it was common for a man from time to time to go through an intense but yet often brief period of conversion in which he cried and begged Jesus—and his wife—for forgiveness. Her final assessment of the gendered dynamic of church attendance is sharply critical: "I guess it wasn't unmasculine for the men to get their religion in these short, intense doses." In contrast, women, she writes, had relationships with God that they were more committed to, in a similar way to how each was committed to her relationship with her husband, implying that the men were not as committed to either.[9] Analogizing church truancy to infidelity, Parton ties a strict adherence to gender role stereotypes and double standards to religious hypocrisy, suggesting that if men avoided church because they were invested in a construction of masculinity that saw religious instruction as a sign of weakness, they were fleeing from their responsibilities when women did not. She challenges the construction of masculinity that put some men beyond the church walls.

Parton's autobiography further underscores her critiques of the gender socialization she experienced at her Pentecostal church, because she recounts her own everyday rebellions against its "training" in gender etiquette. While Parton recalls her irritation that her adolescent male peers were given more freedom at church than she was, as they joined the men outside because they were "training to be men," she further critiques gender role expectations in that context by underscoring her own sexual desire. She writes about watching boys watch her and being aware of the socializing and flirting that was going on after church. She notes how when girls and boys would flirt at church, and the boy would try to get the girl to go walk in the woods with him, the onus fell on the girl to set the boundaries of sexual behavior.[10]

Parton powerfully expresses her own rebellion against a double standard in which girls, but not boys, were judged for their sexual virtue and chasteness, and in which the church teachings linked female virtue to proper practice of religion. She writes that she would sit in church and pray for forgiveness for sins that "I couldn't put my finger on, repenting for things I had put my finger on," while she noticed the boys looking at her or thought about what happened in the woods behind the church. Parton jokingly refers to her developmental process of becoming aware of human sexuality and desire, and she frames her anecdote in humorous terms. However, her resistance to the idea that she was sinning by feeling sexual desire is a serious critique. She concludes that passage with a rhetorical flourish by satirically rebelling against the idea that she would be a fallen women if she felt sexual desire: "The devil and I certainly had one thing in common: We were both horny."[11] Her rejection of blind adherence to a fundamentalist tradition here comes into focus most strongly in reference to her pro–female sexuality arguments.

In the textual crux in question, as Parton articulates her own model for thinking about God, sex, and music together, she recounts that as she was about to enter her teenage years, she was thinking about finding her own relationship with God. She wanted to have an "authentic" connection like she saw in some devoted churchgoers. As part of her religious seeking, she kept going to an abandoned church in Caton's Chapel. Remarking that it had become a sinful space for all kinds of vices, including gambling, drinking, fights, and sex, Parton observes the irony of her having her own religious conversion there. But she writes that it was precisely the place she went to find her own religious revelation, and that at age twelve she "found God" there and subsequently asked to be baptized.[12] The setting of the scene itself matches her common practice of linking ideas of the pure and fallen in order to elevate the latter, because she describes having her religious conversion in that old abandoned church, with condom wrappers strewn about and pornographic graffiti on the walls. In a later passage in her autobiography, she launches into a disquisition on her spiritual beliefs, including her understanding of miracles, and those descriptions are in keeping with this account of her childhood religious conversion narrative.[13]

She draws more direct links among God, sex, and music when she describes her conversion moment. Parton recounts playing in the chapel in the midst of the sexualized imagery on the walls, making music using the old piano that stood in the church, and thinking about God. She took the tops of the piano keys from the old piano and used some strings from its soprano section for an old mandolin she found in her family's barn. As quoted earlier, she writes, "So, here in one place was God, music, and sex. My fascination was complete." She goes on to describe how she suddenly felt a spiritual revelation of a personal relationship with God and a divine support for her sense of both a musical calling and sexuality. She writes that she would routinely pray, sing hymns, or look at the pornographic graffiti, noting the irony of finding "real truth" in this particular place; one day while praying, she "broke though some sort of spirit wall" and "found God." She concludes, "I had come to know that it was all right for me to be a sexual being. I knew that was one of the things God meant for me to be."[14] Amid the contradictory images and environment, Parton found that the negative, fallen, stereotyped elements are actually part of the spiritual truth she sought. In addition to believing that her expression of sexuality was supported by her spiritual beliefs and divinely ordained, Parton goes on to link her revelatory moment to her dreams for a musical career. She writes that she felt validated for her dreams of a greater purpose of leaving Appalachia and becoming a musician, seeing them as "ordained and cocreated by my newfound heavenly father." She writes of feeling sanctified and reborn: "The joy of the truth I found there is with me to this day. I had found God. I had found Dolly Parton. And I loved them both."[15] In Parton's understanding, her musical dreams are also ordained, and she is following a divine will by pursuing her career. She claims a higher validation for her musical expression and her "greater purpose" in being a singer-songwriter. She draws her sense of identity from this spiritual basis, finding God and "Dolly Parton."

In some of Parton's later songs, such as "Seeker," she writes about searching for her religious and spiritual beliefs and expresses a wish for God to "show me the way." However, it is this earlier passage in her autobiography where she describes this childhood revelation that still forms the foundation for her spiritual beliefs later in life.

While Parton also notes that she would not identify as a Christian but rather as someone with spiritual beliefs in God, Parton nevertheless was baptized in the Pentecostal church as a result of this moment of religious conversion. When she asked her mother to be baptized, some in their church did not think she should be because they questioned whether a young girl could have "found God" on her own. However, her mother assented, and Parton was baptized by Brother L. D. Smith in the Little Pigeon River. When Parton describes her baptism, she brings her expression of sexuality back into the description, making a joke about the boys watching her in her white cotton dress in the water. She writes that already at age twelve, "those body parts" that were later "destined" to become her "calling card in life" and the topic of numerous jokes by many late-night talk-show hosts were "well in evidence." She claims the boys shouted "Hallelujah!" at the sight. When Parton noticed how others respond to her as if she was inappropriate, judging her with a double standard, she rejected their judgment and created her own meaning. She writes that some church women noticed the boys ogling her and looked on disapprovingly, but that she instead interpreted the scene in terms of her earlier revelation about her understanding of God, saying that he would not have "given them to me if he hadn't wanted people to notice them."[16] Significantly, when she is writing about these events as an adult many years later, she uses the moment of her baptism in the river to think about her fully realized media image from later in her career, as when late-night hosts like Johnny Carson stared at her breasts and responded to her as a sex symbol.

In what is a transgressive rhetorical turn, Parton insouciantly fashions her religious conversion narrative into a justification for her expression of her own sexuality, ending the passage with one of her well-known "boob jokes." By using humor, she reframes images of her and insists on her own agency and ironic distance from that embodiment, implying that she is not trapped by that exaggerated, sexualized image but rather she uses it to express herself. Of course, she cannot control how different audiences view her or how they narrate her identity. Nevertheless, in one of the crucial moments in her autobiography in which she establishes her religious beliefs, a moment that would traditionally be treated with great reverence in country music autobiographies, Parton links her sexuality, her embodiment, and her God, and she turns those links into the foundation and justification for her identity.

It is important to underscore how Parton is writing this passage in hindsight, from the point of view of her later fully elaborated town tramp image. Her recounting of her youth here sheds light on how Parton developed her "trash" image as a rhetorical style, combining it with other gender performance codes to develop a flexible repertoire. It speaks to how she developed her persona as a stage strategy (read as figurative, not as realism), as performance codes that signify in terms of country music history. Again, Parton brings together not only a gendered hillbilly trope from country music but also another key discourse of the "tramp" image from a burlesque tradition of female performers like her idol Mae West. As I discussed in chapter 3, West used a feminist camp tradition to comment knowingly on the history of female performers on stage being framed as prostitutes and to critique dominant gender codes. Parton's star image and gender performance pick up on these significations. As I make my case for Parton as transgressive, I contribute here to an ongoing scholarly conversation about her that has focused particular attention on her autobiography. Again, in Pamela Wilson's important reading of Parton's memoir, she believes that Parton uses parody to challenge patriarchal codes that view women as sexual objects, but she concludes that Parton remains trapped by those codes, at best making the possibility of subversive dynamics available for the audience by making them aware of their own social positioning.[17] Pamela Fox, meanwhile, reads Parton as reinforcing the power of religion in this passage; while she concurs that Parton bucks gender conventions and rehabilitates the hillbilly trash stereotype in country music, she avers that Parton ultimately becomes trapped in gender objectification.[18] While we agree that Parton uses parody to challenge gender and class stereotypes, I differ in my reading of the cultural work Parton's gender performance does, because I read a stronger subversive, transgressive element, especially in Parton's specific use of feminist camp and gay camp. I see Parton as camping her way, at least in some contexts, into a critique of that gender objectification, rather than being trapped by it.

Childhood Gender Socialization

It is worth examining in more depth how Parton's autobiography is also vital for its elucidation of her sense of gender role expectations and relations in her childhood context, in the local context of growing up in the Sevierville area near Gatlinburg—specifically Locust Ridge and later Caton's Chapel. Her memoir is also framed by her distinctive bridging of the folk culture–mass culture tension in country music performance history. Indeed, her book emphasizes the links back to a folk source for her gender practices, but her account of that folk source is always already impacted by mass culture, because her mass-produced autobiography is but one of her many public, mass culture performances of selfhood.

In her text, she walks a tightrope of gender and class because she recuperates a trashy, sexualized working-class stereotype in her look while refusing either to romanticize the working class or to advocate middle-class domesticity. The model of femininity she describes is a working-class femininity of dual laboring households, not the passive, emphasized femininity of the middle class. While her quest for makeup and "pretty" clothes in opposition to a mountain femininity that was about hardscrabble hard work might imply an aspirational desire for a white, middle-class norm or beauty ideal, the fact that she keeps claiming that she was drawn to a trashy look rejects those middle-class ideals. Parton, the fourth child but the second of six girls among her twelve siblings, critiques the gendered behavior of straying and alcoholic husbands while she registers the expectations for masculinity and her brothers' rough and tumble treatment as the kind of gender role expectations in which she knew how to fend for herself.

In her writing, Parton self-consciously presents her early childhood as one of poverty that was a fact of life, something she was "neither proud nor ashamed of." She describes herself and her family as "poor white trash" in terms of social positioning.[19]

Parton depicts how her mother clearly had to respond to the harsh labor conditions of the mountain women of that time, contending with poverty, isolation, and illness, and juggling a constant cycle of pregnancy, childbirth, and childcare for a large number of children. Yet Parton also implies that her mother found moments of resistance to some imposed gender role expectations, often by resorting to her motherhood role to claim the cultural authority to critique conditions. She notes that her father, a hard-working farmer who began as a sharecropper and later farmed their own small piece of land, would often be gone for days at a time, drinking heavily, having extramarital affairs. Parton describes this dynamic as a common one in their community and sociohistorical context. In one recounted joke, Parton details how her mother used her own cultural role as matriarch to challenge circumstances. Parton's father used to arrive home drunk and urinate off of the front porch. Her mother appealed to his sense of fatherhood, asking him not to be a negative example to his children. Parton joked that her father responded by standing in the yard and urinating up onto the porch instead. On a more serious note, Parton writes that from the point of view of gender roles in that context, it would have been taboo for her mother to criticize her father's drinking directly; thus, her mother found a different way of critiquing his behavior, by invoking his investment in being a respected father.[20]

The labor conditions Parton describes for her mother were stringent. Her mother was fifteen and her father seventeen when they married; her mother gave birth to all twelve children by age thirty-five. Parton details her mother's perseverance and "iron will" in managing the children, keeping them fed and clothed under impoverished conditions. She outlines how her mother sewed, quilted, and used mountain knowledge, which Parton characterizes as being passed down through families, in order to deal with emergencies or find creative responses to conditions of scarcity.

As part of this context, Parton connects her autobiography to folk culture practices of mountain survival, claiming authenticity through that connection. In one instance, when Parton accidentally cut her foot as a child, her mother used kerosene for a disinfectant, cornmeal to staunch the wound, and her quilting needle and thread to sew up the wound. Describing precious folk knowledge sources, Parton writes of it as a legacy bequeathed and passed down through generations for hundreds of years from each earlier "mountain dweller" who had learned survival skills, "starting with the Native Americans."[21]

Here, Parton pictures an American Indian source for her mountain folk culture knowledge, a kind of cross-cultural imagining that is a nostalgic projection, thinking of an indigenous source for folk wisdom.[22] However, in her larger oeuvre, her practice of claiming an American Indian folk culture as part of mountain folk culture does speak to a complex history of American Indian and Anglo-American relations, specifically involving the Cherokee in that area. Her cultural expression is complicated in this regard because she has also generated musical output that attempts a cross-cultural model of exchange, as on her *Sha-Kon-O-Hey! Land of Blue Smoke* (2009) album, where she tries to present Cherokee folk culture as well. Parton's framing of American Indian folk culture is also impacted by her own identity positioning. Nash states that Parton's mother was one quarter Cherokee, although Parton does not address that claim in her autobiography and some biographers have questioned that claim, thus the status of her possible American Indian heritage is unclear.[23] Johnny Cash is another country singer whose work attempts a cross-cultural model of exchange, as in his collaborative American Indian concept album, *Bitter Tears* (1964).[24] Cash at one point claimed to have American Indian ancestry but later admitted that he did not; he had made the claim because he wanted it to be true. Vine Deloria Jr. calls that dynamic the "Indian grandmother complex," where some Anglo-Americans claim an American Indian heritage that has more truth in fantasy than in fact, in stories passed down in their families, a way to romanticize American Indians and perhaps also assuage white guilt.[25] However, Parton's case is complex and differs from Cash's, and the identity positioning of her mother may not be an example of that trope, particularly since there is uncertainty in the biographical literature about her mother's positioning. Parton has not used such identity positioning in the marketing of music in the way that Cash at one point did.[26] Ultimately, Parton's work itself includes complex attempts to create models of cross-cultural exchange, particularly in her discussion of various folk cultures.

Of course, perhaps the most famous example of her mother's folk resourcefulness is sewing the famous patchwork jacket that Parton sings about in "Coat of Many Colors." Biographers have noted that Parton left out part of the story when she retold the tale. As the NBC film adaptation of the story later suggested, Parton would not take off the jacket at school because she did not have a shirt on underneath, due to their impoverished conditions, and her classmates taunted her about it.

Regarding mountain gender politics, Parton catalogues her "tomboy" behaviors and resistance to a male-dominated dynamic, but she also details how her mountain context made her value femininity and seek out elements such as makeup and female beauty standards. She and her sister Stella, she writes, wanted to wear makeup in order to distinguish their own femininity.[27] Noting that her father did not want them to wear makeup because he thought it would make them look "trashy," Parton references the clear gender stereotype of makeup signifying promiscuity, which plays into the "fallen woman" trope. By recalling her own desire for makeup, Parton is uplifting that "fallen woman" trope, or insisting on the validity of a marginalized version of femininity. Parton also discusses how her recourse to makeup made her think about the issue of sex appeal to male audiences, thus implicitly linking her search for cosmetics to the kind of public appearance her father was worried about, in this case, the female singer looking promiscuous onstage.

However, Parton nonetheless recounts using mountain techniques to express her sense of femininity, employing berries and household items as her beauty products. She put into action her mother's same kind of creative problem-solving and Appalachian perseverance to tackle the problem. Thus, in her autobiography she domesticates that process and describes it in terms of the mountain values and upbringing that she retains, making it part of her Appalachian genuineness claims because it seems to have a so-called natural, inherited source. Parton shows the harsh, gendered labor conditions and refuses to romanticize it, yet she also details the creative perseverance that allowed her family and others to survive; she outlines her own sense of their values, motivations, and cultural content, from songs to stories her mother used to tell them to the creative play of the children in the woods. Thus, when she invokes elements of the commodified mountain girl image that circulates in country music later as a justifying folk culture image, she has a different relationship to these images than some other singers might have, just as she claims an "authentic" source when she brings in the "hillbilly tramp" imagery.

As part of that gender socialization, she also describes specific gendered customs and practices, often tied to class stereotypes. For example, she recounts the rural custom of pie suppers, where each boy would buy a pie and share it with the girl who made it. At one supper, a male teacher told Parton not to chew with her mouth open, because that was not the correct etiquette for young ladies. He linked those culinary manners to a gender role expectation, and Parton likewise connects her attempt to follow those rules to her desire to act like a grown-up "lady." She quickly, however, turned that gendered rule into a carnivalesque rebellion. She recalls how she then went home to instruct her siblings on table manners, because they would normally all "smack" their food while eating, like "possums in a mulberry bush." When she attempted to impart her newfound knowledge of a different kind of social etiquette, she misquoted the instructions, telling her siblings never to "chew with food in your mouth," resulting in them still being "smacking possums."[28] While Parton is recalling rustic jokes in which she analogizes her family's behaviors to animal behavior in the woods, she is also describing a class and gender dynamic in which she feels ashamed of the table manners of her working-class family when a middle-class teacher insists she follow different class and gender etiquette. Her story effectively critiques the middle-class manners the teacher tried to impose on her, however. She says she misunderstood him and repeated his instructions incorrectly. Yet, on another level, she and her siblings translated his ideas in their own way and ended up retaining their own customs of eating.

Once Parton began performing professionally, her unusual role complicated her relationship to gender and class status. As a teen earning money and interacting with audiences and media images, she faced stigmas about female singers and promiscuity, as when her preacher grandfather objected to any makeup onstage. Fellow high school students circulated rumors of her being promiscuous, even claiming she had been raped. Such responses stemmed from the familiar policing rhetoric about women onstage being associated historically with prostitution or promiscuity. From a young age, Parton experienced Appalachian gender role expectations but also gender ideas in a larger performance world, as she performed locally, regionally, and eventually nationally.

Parton's dual roles as both "mountain girl" and professional performer also changed her relationship to the particular mixture of folk and mass culture around her. Her autobiography emphasizes her childhood pastoral, folk culture setting, full of mountain arts and crafts, stories and quilting and music passed down through generations. However, since she had begun appearing on radio and television at age ten, she was already part of a mass culture performance world from a very young age. In 1956, Parton bought her family their first television set so that they could see her televised performances and even the wider world, which meant more exposure to mass culture.[29] While they already consumed some mass media, including newspaper, magazines, and radio (such as the Grand Ole Opry), Parton's TV brought another dimension to their mass culture consumption. It also sparked cultural tensions. The nineteen-inch black-and-white set picked up eight hours of daily programming from the Knoxville station, and Parton and her sibling eagerly watched shows like *Gunsmoke*. When over two dozen neighbors began coming to watch *Gunsmoke* too, and then lingered until the station signoff, Parton's father sold the TV in irritation, saying it was interfering with his farm work. Parton's father rejected the social behaviors around TV viewing, tossing out the mass culture element, since he was not used to droves coming to watch television regularly. The anecdote also illustrates tensions around different kind of mass culture consumption, as families might have been used to rituals around listening to radio broadcasts, but the novelty of television viewing in that context introduced a new and, to some, disconcerting element of obsessive viewing into their daily domestic lives. Nevertheless, Parton's own appearances on TV raised multivalent ideas about how to perform one's identity through the mass media.

Distinguishing between public (mass culture) versus private versions of herself in her construction of identity in her autobiography, Parton is careful to note the difference between her own personal identity and her "Dolly Parton" persona, saying they are two different people. She talks about "playing Dolly Parton." She notes that her family members, particularly her younger brothers and sisters, whom she helped raise, as well as their children, see her as "Aunt Granny"; they know the difference between her stardom and their relative, seeing her without the trappings of stardom or her star persona, like her makeup. She writes that her younger relatives can distinguish between "Aunt Granny" and "Dolly Parton," seeing them as "two separate people"; they are proud that their Aunt Granny gets to don makeup and "play Dolly Parton."[30] Parton here speaks to how she negotiates her stage persona, and how her family members are aware of her identity projections. As she takes up the props of stardom, like elaborate makeup and costumes, she can eschew that celebrity in favor of other roles, such as familial roles as a sister and aunt. Even this discussion of her familial role is one that rejects gender role expectations however, because she invokes her relationship with her family to explain why she never wanted to have her own children. She admits that she even used to lie and say she was unable to have children in order to avoid people's judgments of her decision to remain childless. She bucks the maternal role imperative by insisting on the value of her contributions to her family, although she does claim she did maternal labor by helping to raise her younger siblings.

Parton's construction of her own gender performance in her autobiography thus draws together her folk sources, replete with her authenticity claims. However, it also speaks to her mass culture practices, from the mass-produced memoir itself to the events she describes in it, like becoming a local TV star in the 1950s in the context of her family not even owning a television. Her autobiography records how she created her town tramp persona as well as how she later framed it with camp and sophisticated irony.

1990s Context

After *Heartsongs* lagged in sales, even though her promotional autobiography was a bestseller, Parton eventually made her turn back to "blue mountain" music in *Hungry Again* and then more successfully, in her bluegrass and folk albums *The Grass Is Blue, Little Sparrow,* and *Halos & Horns.*[31] It is worth detailing how Parton's neotraditionalist turn illuminates the political economy of the country music industry in the 1990s and the Nashville establishment. Parton's earlier crossover success contributed to the broadening of country music, alongside the work of other stars who were gaining mainstream success, such as Johnny Cash, whose own career trajectory provides a telling comparison with Parton's. That appeal to a larger mainstream audience altered sales practices and amplified financial expectations. Parton later suffered as a result of these very dynamics she helped create. Parton engaged in obvious struggles against Nashville customs for creative control; during her 1970s crossover period, she was castigated as much for using non-Nashville musicians as she was for doing country pop. After her successful crossover album *Here You Come Again,* Parton was critically rewarded for the broadening of her appeal, winning a Grammy and a CMA, yet she still faced significant resentment from the country music industry. Parton had a history of finding audiences outside of the Nashville establishment, since in her earlier recordings, the folk music influences in her own singing and songwriting appealed to the urban folk music revival that had gained significant attention in the 1960s.

But since the full roots of the 1990s context Parton faced are found in her notable country-pop success in the 1970s, it is important to note how that success not only raised financial expectations for country music but also affirmed a greater nationalization of the market. Noting that southern culture more generally enjoyed greater relevance and respectability during this era, scholar James C. Cobb cites this epoch of country music's expansion as an instance of what historians have dubbed the "Southernization of America."[32] If the Nashville Sound had success in the 1960s in responding to the challenges of rockabilly and rock in the 1950s, in the 1970s, crossover country pop was taking that pop impetus out of the Nashville Sound context, eschewing the Nashville formula and moving some artists more fully into pop, to an extreme that some thought eroded the core influence of country music. Meanwhile, some other country artists in the 1970s were finding greater mainstream appeal, such as Johnny Cash as well as the Outlaw Country movement of Waylon Jennings and Willie Nelson. In one significant example, Cash's successes in the late 1960s and early 1970s, especially in 1969 when he was the bestselling act in the world with his prison albums, *Johnny Cash at Folsom Prison* (1968) and *Johnny Cash at San Quentin* (1969), did much to bring country music to a broader audience. Biographer Michael Streissguth notes that with the success of Cash's network TV show in 1969 (which ran on ABC from 1969–1971), he suddenly became "the ambassador of country music."[33] Likewise, the 1970s Outlaw Country movement broadened country's appeal; founding figures Jennings and Nelson bucked the Nashville system and produced records themselves, backed by their touring bands rather than studio musicians. Succeeding on both country and pop charts, their album *Wanted: The Outlaws* (1976) (also featuring Jennings's wife, Jessi Colter, and Tompall Glaser) rebelled against the Nashville formula because it used more rock influences, a driving beat, edgy lyrics, and a more iconoclastic sensibility.

While Parton was not associated with the Outlaw Country movement, she did open for Nelson on a tour during that time. She was also marketed alongside him in one high-profile instance. In 1982, Monument released *The Winning Hand*, a compilation double album, with Parton, Nelson, Kris Kristofferson, and Brenda Lee, featuring each's unreleased tracks recorded for Monument in the mid- to late 1960s. Seemingly designed to capitalize on Nelson's Outlaw and Parton's crossover successes, the album was also promoted by a syndicated TV concert special (1983), hosted by Johnny Cash, where the four singers performed together.

In the 1980s, country's broadening appeal led the industry to focus on younger artists and commercial formulas, targeting a younger demographic (twenty-five to fifty-four year olds). The country industry tried to capitalize on the urban cowboy craze sparked by the John Travolta film (*Urban Cowboy*, 1980). Older artists were getting pushed out and not receiving country radio airplay. In 1986, Cash was dropped by Columbia when he was averaging sales of only fifty thousand records a year. Meanwhile, the industry was looking for acts that could sell in the millions, like Alabama, who sold over 2 million records a year then.[34] As Rick Blackburn, former CEO of CBS Records Nashville and Atlantic Records Nashville, says of the industry formula at the time, "It was just new faces, who's new."[35] By the late 1980s, a new generation of young artists with higher sales emerged, like Garth Brooks, Clint Black, Travis Tritt, and Alan Jackson. In the 1990s, some of the emergent female artists who had financial success with crossover styles included Shania Twain, Martina McBride, and Faith Hill. Parton herself has commented on her falling country radio airplay. Notably, in a famous tag line she often repeats, she satirizes some of the gender stereotypes involved in that dynamic: "I think of country radio like a great lover. You were great to me, you bought me a lot of nice things and then you dumped my ass for younger women."[36]

As part of a larger shift that prompted a crisis rhetoric in country music at that time, the industry's political economy also changed after the 1996 Telecommunications Act, which allowed corporations to own up to eight stations in a single market, prompting severe narrowing of playlists. The industry also began efforts to target a female demographic. Thus, as country music radio began focusing on niche markets, it followed a pattern common in the mass media after the federal regulatory change, resulting in the conditions we see today, notably the dominance of huge companies like Clear Channel and techniques like narrowcasting, where companies target a smaller, more narrowly defined demographic. As some older artists struggled to find a new way to fit into such country music industry models, some turned to the Americana roots music trend as a viable audience base for their music.

Parton's efforts to recapture a country base with her album *Hungry Again* and especially her three subsequent bluegrass and folk albums can be interpreted as part of that Americana trend. Many of the artists involved in the Americana roots music revival shared similar frustrations with the country music industry just as their fans sought out a fresh revival of critical-minded, folk-based music, again in some ways similar to the 1960s folk revival. Parton's neotraditionalist turn also coincided with the 1990s alternative country movement of acts that mixed country and punk sensibilities and influences to update the genre, such as Wilco, Ryan Adams, and Hank Williams III. In a similar vein, Johnny Cash likewise staged his own career resurgence, signing with producer Rick Rubin in 1993 to generate his critically and commercially successful American Recordings albums, which banked on the Americana roots music trend. When his album *Unchained* won the 1997 Grammy for Country Album of the Year, Cash expressed his industry defiance in a full-page ad in music industry magazines. It pictured Cash's famous flip off of the cameras from his San Quentin live prison concert, and the text sarcastically read, "American Recordings and Johnny Cash would like to acknowledge the Nashville music establishment and country radio for your support."[37] The ad became a banner for other artists similarly frustrated with industry practices.

While Cash hewed to the Americana model in his later work and stayed there, Parton engaged strongly with Americana in her work during her "return to country" 1994–2002 epoch, but since that period, she has returned to recording albums targeting a mainstream appeal as well as continuing with albums directed to more niche audiences. Parton's case is different because she was explicitly refocusing on country music after her pop crossover efforts became less successful, but her response to industry practices was in some sense similar. Her bluegrass albums targeted a niche audience that was mobilized by a rejection of mainstream country industry practices, and the Americana movement's embrace of her generated resurgent critical and commercial successes. Parton's checkered history with the Nashville music industry reflects how she resisted the Nashville system in a gendered way, refusing to "stay in her place." She strove for her own creative expression and acceptance from the country music industry for cross-genre work, and she tried to mainstream country music as a larger force in US popular culture.

Her music videos from her 1994–2002 Americana era capture her shift from targeting mainstream commercial country hits on country radio (as with some of the songs on *Hungry Again*), to much more folk-oriented, bare production for bluegrass songs on albums like *Little Sparrow*. In the video for the country pop song "The Salt in My Tears" from *Hungry Again*, Parton sings about striving to please a man and only getting heartbreak in return. Meanwhile, actors dramatize the lyrics—a beefcake man in jeans and a tank top works in a salt mine then collapses to the ground, exhausted from his toil. A young woman brings him water. But as Parton sings about the man making the woman suffer in their relationship, the woman pours the water over the man lying on the ground, with the sexualized cheesiness played for full effect, then she leaves him. The analogy is that the husband ignores his wife for work, and she has decided not to take it anymore. Although the single received little airplay on country radio, the video was popular on CMT.

In contrast, the video for Parton's bluegrass Collective Soul cover "Shine" from *Little Sparrow* is largely in black and white and focuses on the music itself by picturing the musicians playing onscreen, including young bluegrass band Nickel Creek, with respected mandolin player Chris Thile, Sara Watkins on fiddle, and Sean Watkins on guitar. Parton, clad in a more simple denim dress, walks down a country road while singing, the camera focusing on pastoral images of trees, a bridge, and natural scenery. The video mimics the song's tempo changes by speeding up or slowing down the visual images along with the music. When Parton sings, "Heaven let your light shine down," the video intercuts a montage of scenes in color with the musicians playing outside in the pastoral setting. The video continues with intercut scenes in black and white and color. In up-tempo sections toward the end of the song, Parton walks through the streets of Nashville, with the visual effect of the background sped up behind her. Parton appears in a more natural-looking wig, with less exaggeration. By juxtaposing the pastoral scenes with the high-speed urban scenes, the video visually connects her pastoral folk culture's rural roots with her urban mass culture context. What makes those two disparate elements cohere is the emphasis on her sincerity address and projections of genuineness throughout the video.

In the next chapter, I examine how Parton continues her gender performance in very different contexts in her most recent career epoch. As she has taken her identity performance into cyberspace, she has found new ways to combine folk and mass culture. With her new iterations of her "real" and "fake" persona comes an even higher degree of complexity in her gender performance.

Notes

1. Parton, *Dolly*, 56–57.
2. Ibid., 77.
3. Pecknold, *Selling Sound*.
4. "Dolly Parton: Singer Disbanding." Biographer Stephen Miller claims Parton was disheartened that the club's independent magazine, *Paper Dolly*, authorized by the Dollywood Foundation, ceased publication amid accusations of possible financial impropriety. Miller, *Smart Blonde*, 301.
5. Nash, *Dolly*, 285.
6. *Lost Highway*, part 1.
7. Parton, *Dolly*, 77.
8. Ibid., 72, 69–70, 77.
9. Ibid., 73.
10. Ibid., 74–75.
11. Ibid., 75.
12. Ibid., 76–79.
13. Ibid., 297–299.
14. Ibid., 77.
15. Ibid., 77–78.
16. Ibid., 78–79.
17. Wilson, "Mountains."

18. Fox, *Natural Acts*, 138–142.

19. Parton, *Dolly*, 3.

20. Ibid., 31–32.

21. Ibid., 26, 24.

22. I use "American Indian" as the most commonly used term in current academic discussions, while noting that the issue of naming for indigenous groups is a contested one, fraught with the power dynamics of colonialism and imperialism.

23. Nash, *Dolly*, 9, 13; Miller, *Smart Blonde*, 18.

24. Edwards, *Johnny Cash and the Paradox of American Identity*, 108.

25. Deloria, *Custer*, 11–12.

26. In his liner notes for *Bitter Tears*, Cash avers that he is justified in singing about American Indian-white relations from "the Indian's viewpoint," because he has "Cherokee blood." Edwards, *Johnny Cash and the Paradox of American Identity*, 108.

27. Parton, *Dolly*, 58–59.

28. Ibid., 31.

29. Ibid., 102.

30. Ibid., 220.

31. In Cecelia Tichi's review of *The Grass Is Blue*, she notes the roots music revival context and analogizes the lyrics to poetry and short stories. Tichi, "Consider."

32. Cobb, "Country Music," 75.

33. Streissguth, *Johnny Cash*, 165.

34. *Controversy*.

35. Ibid.

36. Parton, *Dream More*, 105.

37. Edwards, *Johnny Cash and the Paradox of American Identity*, 42.

"Digital Dolly" and New Media Fandoms

In the current era, from the early 2000s to the present, as Parton has incorporated higher levels of camp and fluidity into her image, she has fit her combination of "pure" mountain girl and country tramp to new contexts, including digital culture. Her evolving media image questions gender, performance, and authenticity in a new media environment. In this chapter, I assess Parton's career output in this recent period, including her ongoing and more active relationship with her fan community in the age of Web 2.0 and social media. I address fan documentaries, Parton's tours and albums, and key music videos. Likewise, I analyze how her staging of her persona on reality television is a development that rehearses her "fake" and "real" debate in new contexts.

In this chapter, I link her gender performance to several other key related theoretical questions, including how Parton's work uses recent media developments, such as transmedia storytelling, participatory fan culture, and media convergence, in which old media and interactive new media are combining across media platforms. In a discussion of Parton fandoms, I argue that some of the online fan website communities can be seen as examples of digital folk culture, in that they take Parton as a marker for a new way of expressing folk culture online. The ways in which those websites combine mass culture and folk culture elements are entirely in keeping with how Parton balances her fake versus real persona and her own intervention in the mass-folk tension in country music. In my discussion of her fandoms, I explore the fan reception of Dolly Parton through fan documentaries, such as *For the Love of Dolly* (2006), *Jake's Adventures in Dollyworld* (2007), and *Hollywood to Dollywood* (2011), all of which discuss Parton as a fetishized gay icon like Liza Minnelli or Cher. Likewise, I examine fan websites, fan postings, and Parton's efforts to engage her fans through new media.

Also in this chapter, I assess how her gendered star image in this era fits into newer paradigms of stardom, such as a focus on performing multiple versions of the self in knowingly manipulated settings. In discussing recent models of stardom in the age of reality television, I analyze how Parton in this period makes her star image more fluid and yet emphasizes the emotional realism of her sincerity address, which is in keeping with these emergent models of stardom in the digital era. I assess Parton's interactions with reality TV, which includes her appearance on *American Idol* for "Dolly Parton Songs" week (2008). In particular, I undertake a case study discussion of her appearance on *The Bachelorette* (2012), because it epitomizes how Parton is fitting into a new media marketing setting. Likewise, in her film career during this era, she makes her star image more campy, as in *Joyful Noise* (2012). Meanwhile, her cameo appearances in feature films similarly reinforce her media iconicity but amplify her camp content (*The Beverly Hillbillies, Miss Congeniality 2: Armed and Fabulous*). In contrast, in some lesser-known films, Parton tweaks her own celebrity image, parodying and even satirizing herself at times, most notably in the scathing, campy satire *Frank McKluskey, C.I.*, where her satirical character dismantles middle-class domesticity and has Parton explicitly send up her own persona as overdone camp. Elsewhere, some of her television roles feature parodies of Parton that reinforce her persona (*Designing Women, Reba*, Aunt Dolly on *Hannah Montana*).

Finally, I address how Parton signifies in terms of her larger cultural politics, from her increasingly camp image and her relationship to gay rights advocacy to how her gender performance signifies as compared to other relevant female performers, such as Madonna and Lady Gaga. In addition, I analyze her complex interactions with discourses of race and authenticity, such as ongoing debates about how the "hillbilly" or the "redneck" stereotypes signify in the media. I conclude with a discussion of her relationship to debates about the politics of country music itself.

Biographical Contexts

In the period since her 2002 bluegrass album, as Parton has generated albums that are stylistically varied, she has targeted her mainstream audience but also different niche markets, a common approach in our current era of narrowcasting, where producers target smaller and smaller niche audiences for media texts. Her two cover albums included patriotic and spiritual songs (*For God and Country* [2003]), and, in a narrower focus, her 1960s and 1970s folk music covers (*Those Were the Days* [2005]). Her four mainstream country albums maintained a broader audience focus (*Backwoods Barbie* [2008], *Better Day* [2011], *Blue Smoke* [2014], and *Pure & Simple* [2016]). Her genre work during this epoch also includes gospel, on the soundtrack for her return to Hollywood film, starring in *Joyful Noise* with Queen Latifah (2012). She sang on several gospel choir songs on the album, in addition to adding her country ballad duet with Kris Kristofferson, "From Here to the Moon and Back." Some significant compilation albums have appeared during this time period, including the Parton-supervised *Ultimate Dolly Parton* (2003), with songs from RCA, Warner Brothers, and Columbia Records. The boxed set *The Acoustic Collection: 1999–2002* (2006) from her own label Blue Eye Records and Sugar Hill, quickly moved to enshrine her bluegrass and traditional recordings from that period of her career. The tribute album *Just Because I'm a Woman: Songs of Dolly Parton* (2003) features a range of country, pop, and alternative artists, including Emmylou Harris, Melissa Etheridge, Shania Twain, Alison Krauss, Shelby Lynne, Norah Jones, Sinéad O'Connor, and Me'Shell NdegéOchello.

Parton's gender performance for her albums and tours remains consistent with her mountain girl–camp tramp persona, although she nuances the campy elements in different surroundings. Since she did 1960s and 1970s pop and folk covers on *Those Were the Days*, she was recycling styles of an earlier time, and she collaborated with musicians from that period, such as Judy Collins and Roger McGuinn. For her tour, in her gender performance she used stage costumes like a 1960s flower child, a campy reference to outmoded styles that also mark the earlier context for this music.

However, she continues to include her mountain girl elements of her persona, most significantly in her trademark "down home" music medley segment of her concerts. On her *Those Were the Days* tour, she performed her multi-instrumentalist take on her mountain songs, such as "My Tennessee Mountain

Home," "Jolene," and "Coat of Many Colors," playing multiple instruments, each briefly, during the medley. She has continued to use that "blue mountain" music medley, replete with her multi-instrumentalist display, on her tours. For example, they were a featured part of her *Better Day* tour in support of that album.

Her most recent tour to date, in support of *Pure & Simple*, placed an even greater emphasis on her "blue mountain" music, with a much more elemental and straightforward presentation rather than a big production show, with few backing musicians and a focus on her singing and songwriting as well as audience interaction. She included full versions of songs she used to play as part of a medley. Her set list included "My Tennessee Mountain Home," "Jolene," and "Coat of Many Colors, " as well as other songs in that vein, including "Precious Memories," "Smoky Mountain Memories," and "Applejack." She also featured religious songs such as "The Seeker" and "He's Alive." It was her most extensive tour in twenty-five years, including over sixty show dates in the United States and Canada. Parton noted that she had not undertaken such a vast tour in that time because she did not have hit songs on the radio and worried that audiences would not materialize, but the tour was successful, with strong sales. Parton said she was inspired to do the tour by her two sold-out shows at Nashville's Ryman Auditorium in 2015 that were minimalist and much more intimate.[1] For those two Ryman shows, benefits for the Opry Trust fund, Parton was largely backed only by guitar, bass, piano, and three singers. She played full versions of "Tennessee Mountain Home" (accompanying herself on dulcimer), "Coat of Many Colors" (accompanying herself on autoharp), and "The Grass Is Blue" (accompanying herself on piano), and sang her Appalachian-style ballad "Little Sparrow" mostly a cappella. She only used a fuller band for several concluding country-pop hits, including "Here You Come Again," "Two Doors Down," and "Islands in the Stream."[2]

Parton's work during this period also reflects the larger gender politics of today's country music industry and radio programming, as well as the new context for her as an older musician. She still does not receive country radio airplay today, a situation that she has often attributed to an age bias, although the gendered programming in country radio is also an obvious factor. Many observers have critiqued the male-dominated programming on country radio stations today. That dynamic seemingly stems in part from ongoing demographic targeting of a female audience and the industry assumption that women want to hear male singers; only one or two female artists are getting consistent country radio airplay (singers such as Carrie Underwood or Miranda Lambert). Female artists are currently 15 percent of the radio airplay. A recent controversy, dubbed "Tomato-gate," involved a radio consultant's comments that women should not be played on country radio back to back. Speaking to the country radio trade publication *Country Radio Aircheck*, consultant Keith Hill said, "If you want to make ratings in country radio, take females out. Trust me, I play great female records, and we've got some right now; they're just not the lettuce in our salad. The lettuce is Luke Bryan and Blake Shelton, Keith Urban and artists like that. The tomatoes of our salad are the females." A press controversy ensued, and the debate has galvanized efforts by the industry advocacy group Change the Conversation to gain greater representation in radio airplay, publishing deals, contracts, awards, and performances for female artists.[3] A number of younger female country singers, like Kacey Musgraves, Cam, Maren Morris, Margo Price, Mickey Guyton, and Aubrie Sellers have slammed the "Tomato-gate" discrimination and have cited Parton as a role model for gaining greater representation for women.[4]

In addition to radio airplay discrimination, Parton has also responded to more general negative stereotypes about female celebrities and aging. In one of the most significant changes she has made to her gender performance and media image during this era, Parton has made adjustments due to age as a performer in a youth-focused industry. That dynamic is evident in Parton's CMT *Crossroads* episode with Etheridge (2003), where she promoted the Parton tribute album. There, Parton jokes about her age and frames herself as an "elder stateswoman." Parton belts out Etheridge's rock songs, like "Come through My Window," while Etheridge covers Parton hits like "Jolene," interpreted in a similar folk-rock vein. Parton uses her familiar country sexpot stage banter; when a male fan yells out to her, she delivers the playful rejoinder: "I thought I told you to wait in the truck!" In a joint interview, Etheridge seems taken aback by the power of Parton's mythology, her own forceful personality largely contained by the Parton framework. Etheridge listens reverentially as Parton trots out familiar autobiographical stories, such as composing her first song as a child about her doll, "Little Tiny Tasseltop." Parton goes one step further and sings the song. Etheridge responds to her as if Parton embodies folk authenticity. While Parton does not show the same familiarity with Etheridge's life and work, she easily moves into the folk rock genre to cover Etheridge's songs, and she expresses her support of Etheridge's gay rights advocacy. In their banter, Parton also jokes about being much older than Etheridge.[5]

Likewise, Parton has elsewhere used more ironic humor and parody to respond to aging, which adds to her camp effect. For example, instead of making talk show jokes about her sex life as in the past, she now kids that no one wants to hear about such things because she is old. However, she updates her campy tramp persona in new age-related jokes; while she jests that her anniversaries are less eventful now because she and her husband are "old people," she jokes that he still will never need Viagra. That evolving dynamic is evident on her 2003 *Tonight Show* appearance to promote the Parton tribute album. In her interview with then-host Jay Leno, Parton maintains her standard sexualized banter with him, yet she also deflects some repartee onto the past or domesticates it by referencing her husband.[6] When Leno asks her to describe her type, she replies with her standard line: "I like all men. I never met a man I didn't like." She recounts her story of streaking through Tom Jones's yard when she was young. She does a risqué "pec dance" (as a joke about Chippendales dancers flexing their pectoral muscles), but she frames it in reference to her husband. She laughs, "My husband's going to kick my ass!" because she "saves the pec dance just for him." She then makes "boob jokes," showing onscreen a picture of her 1977 *Rolling Stone* photos with Schwarzenegger. Leno's standard leering jokes about her breasts culminate with her going outside to do a running comedy bit with him; she hits the button on a catapult machine that tosses melons across a parking lot.

On that *Tonight Show* appearance, Parton combines elements of the barn dance country rube with her sexualized burlesque humor. Again, she defuses the potential threat of her sexualized jokes by re-containing her banter with nonthreatening references to her husband or to the domestic sphere. When Leno says she should run for governor, she demurs by referencing the domestic: "I can't even balance the budget of my own house," much less for a whole state. Her refutation is obviously belied by her vast financial holdings. While she recounts standard autobiographical stories, proving her connection to her music as she sings "Jolene" with Mindy Smith later in the episode, she nevertheless underscores a different age context for herself, saying the tribute album is a way for her to "make way" for a new generation of singers.

Related to her changing gender performance over time, her ongoing plastic surgery has received increased public scrutiny as Parton has aged. As I detail below, one *Joyful Noise* scene has Queen Latifah's character castigate Parton, harshly joking that no one recognizes her anymore because of the cosmetic procedures to her face. In the scene, Parton responds with irony, making her own aging jokes; she also insists that she looks how she wants to look, and that her "heart" is still the same underneath. More generally in this career epoch, Parton turns her age into a joke; entering her seventies, she is the wisecracking

"Aunt Granny" figure (as her family calls her) who makes dirty jokes or wears sexy clothes and thus bucks gender stereotypes and norms for women of her age group.

Building on such new inflections of age and camp, Parton includes a different range of gendered images on her album covers during this period, with varying levels of camp in different contexts. Some reiterate her familiar camp tramp imagery, while others emphasize a more subdued performance persona. On the cover of *For God and Country*, Parton is styled like a campy version of 1940s singers such as the Andrews Sisters, known for their patriotic repertoire for the troops. In a campy effect, her mini-dress looks like an American flag. She is posed with one leg kicked up behind her, singing into her vintage-style microphone, standing in front of a graphic of an American flag. Meanwhile, her album covers for *Live and Well* (2004) and *Better Day* emphasize Parton in performance. The former includes her overdone makeup and a sequined white dress. The latter offers a more glamorous image, with a natural-looking wig, sequined blue mini-dress, and Parton singing into the vintage microphone. While some album covers from this period position Parton with more natural, less exaggerated wigs, *Backwoods Barbie* insists on elaborate camp. There, Parton looks like a Barbie doll. She wears her outfit from the music video, including her pink dressing gown, leopard-print mini-dress, and platinum wig piled high. In a staging that somewhat echoes her Daisy Mae poster from the 1970s, Parton reclines on hay bales. She sits in the back of a garish yellow vintage pickup truck with "Backwoods Barbie" painted in pink underneath the back window. Her signature "Dolly" symbol appears as a pink logo. In contrast, the *Sha-Kon-O-Hey!* (2009) cover amplifies her authenticity claims, picturing her with her guitar, long wig in a side ponytail, dressed more demurely in a blue denim outfit, with a graphic of the Smoky Mountains as a backdrop. Similarly, the *Pure & Simple* cover has Parton dressed in a more subdued blonde wig, demure white long pants, and long-sleeved shirt, holding her acoustic guitar, sitting in front of the backdrop of a mountain stream.

Her album *Blue Smoke* offers a typical case of marketing that encapsulates her approach during this era. On the album's cover, she has been turned into a graphic, with an image of her in blue denim and more contemporary wig. She is pictured in front of the graphic of a Smoky Mountain backdrop, illustrating the album's name, which comes from the mist over those mountains. Released in a partnership between Dolly Records and Sony Masterworks, the album enjoyed strong sales, reaching number two on the country chart, and it went platinum in the United Kingdom, her bestselling album there over the course of her career. On it, she showcases her eclecticism, with a cover of Bob Dylan's "Don't Think Twice" as well as songs in a traditional country style, like "Blue Smoke." Notably, she also includes a cover of Bon Jovi's "Lay Your Hands on Me," which turns the rock song about sex into a religious revival song. When asked about her decision to cover that song, Parton has contextualized it in terms of her Pentecostal upbringing: "I love Bon Jovi, first of all. So when I got ready to record this album, I thought, well, which song am I going to choose to Dolly-ize? And that one popped into my mind. I thought, wow, now that sounds like it would make a great gospel song. 'Cause I grew up where we believed in laying hands on people, prayin' for em."[7] Guitarist Richie Sambora performed that song onstage with her at the Glastonbury Music Festival, his aggressive rock posturing making for a sharp contrast with Parton's country sincerity stage persona. For example, when he tried to approach her onstage for some standard rock interplay, like him thrusting with his guitar, she backed away from him, maintaining her own stage persona. The album also includes "From Here to the Moon and Back" with Willie Nelson rather than Kris Kristofferson (who sang the original duet with her for their roles in *Joyful Noise*), and a new duet with Kenny Rogers, "You Can't Make Old Friends," originally released on his album of the same name (2013). In further branded marketing, a version of the album sold exclusively at Walmart stores had four bonus tracks, including a rerecording of "Early Morning Breeze," a song from her *Coat of Many Colors* (1971) album.

The album is typical of her output during this period because of its genre mix and re-recordings of earlier material. Likewise, it makes use of transmedia marketing such as film tie-ins as well as duets. The album is significant for how it includes religious themes that also contain her own signature addition of sexual themes, as in how she frames her cover of "Lay Your Hands on Me" as both a religious and a sexual song.

In addition to her recurring religious themes, Parton's work has taken on another distinctive trend in this era with more frequent references to her fans and inclusion of them in a more interactive way. Significantly, for the music video for "Together You and I" from *Better Day*, Parton had fans join her on a bridge going into Nashville, staging a spectacle and modelling that fandom for viewers, who could join that imagined community by watching. She used social media to invite fans to participate in the video as extras. In the video, Parton walks across the bridge with fans, singing as the camera focuses on a chain of fans stretching across the bridge with hands linked, purposefully focusing on people of different races, ethnicities, and nationalities. The lyrics discuss her devotion to fans, suggesting that "we'll always be together," and that in solidarity they can overcome hardships through communal support. Based on an earlier song Parton repurposed to address fans, the song repeats her familiar mythology. The video imagines a global, multicultural Parton fandom as well as one with religious diversity (as in one of Parton's tag lines: "God and I have a great relationship, but we both see other people").[8]

In another example of how Parton increasingly incorporates references to her fandom into her oeuvre, Parton's music video for "Better Get to Livin'," from *Backwoods Barbie*, pictures a mountain carnival sideshow, entitled "Dolly's Circus of Human Emotions." The video emphasizes Parton's familiar autobiographical elements. Filmed at a farm in Pigeon Forge, it echoes Parton's childhood glee over mountain carnivals in her autobiography. With the "freak show" sideshow theme, the video also references her frequent analogies between her exaggerated appearance and circus freaks; she highlights the genuine emotion of both underneath the outsized appearance, plus a critique of stereotypes in favor of a universal appeal to underlying shared humanity. In keeping with the album, the country pop song's instrumentation emphasizes country genre references, with fiddle, pedal steel guitar, and mandolin featured prominently. Gospel singers Sonya Isaacs and Rebecca Isaacs Bowman sing background vocals.

The video's themes also emphasize Parton's sincerity mode of address and her self-positioning as someone audiences look to for advice. In the opening sequence, comedian Amy Sedaris, appearing as a sideshow barker, tries to get audiences to come in to see the circus "freaks" embodying a range of human emotions, like the woman who is literally "green with envy." The video cuts to Parton backstage in her makeup chair, dressed as the ringmaster. Sedaris, humorously dressed all in green as the envious woman, in ludicrous green taffeta and bows and a blonde wig full of ringlets, intones in an absurdly exaggerated voice: "You know Dolly, I wish I could be a positive as you are!" Parton replies, "Aw, it's simple!" She explains (in one of her oft-repeated maxims), "Don't think I don't see what you see and feel what you feel. But I've got a little voice down right inside me, keeps me on track." As the scene shifts, the camera pans over the faces of women in the audience, and Parton targets her message to women specifically. The camera pans to her singing in front of the crowd under the circus big top. In intercut scenes, she also runs the projector to play a silent movie of women complaining of their problems. As the ringmaster, she is dressed in a red and black satin mini-dress with a long train and black fishnet stockings, wearing a jaunty, tiny black top hat perched on the side of her head, a piece of trendy camp.

In her lyrics, she sings about people asking her what her secret is, and she gives the chorus advice of "better get to livin'," by which she means making one's dreams come true rather than wallowing in defeating emotions. She stands in front of a purposefully tacky backdrop of a painting of zebras running around a circus ring. She demurs, "I'm not the Dalai Lama, but I'll try." She describes a scene of a girlfriend coming to see her and crying over her problems, and the video pictures Parton in red gingham on a house set comforting the upset woman, staged as if it is a sideshow scene. She advises the woman to forgive and heal, to avoid negativity, and to pray. Her message to the other women in the carnival audience is the same.

The song and video emphasize her common pro-woman themes, but here she also underscores her own autobiographical position and role as advisor to her fans. Parton implies that since they keep scripting her into that role, she will reluctantly fill it. However, she makes her frequent move of directing them to their own spiritual beliefs, rather than focusing onto her all of their quest for meaning and seeking energy. In this video and in the "Together You and I" video that literally puts fans in the scenes, Parton marks an increased level of media interaction with fans, which is part of how she is capitalizing on larger new media trends.

Transmedia Storytelling

In recent years, Parton's savvy use of social media, from her Twitter feed to her Facebook page to her iPhone Dolly application, reveals how Parton has adjusted her persona to a new media context. She uses digital media to reach her active fan base on spaces like her current official website DollyParton.com (which has been combined with her previous website, DollyPartonEntertainment.com, that was run by her management, CTK Management; an earlier, now-defunct website, DollyPartonMusic.Net, performed similar outreach functions). Parton calls herself "Digital Dolly." She even employs what she calls an "image manager," an employee charged with overseeing all aspects of her media image and sparking further fan engagement with it, from internet sites to mobile phone apps. Parton's persona has become a flexible marker of kitsch cool in the digital era, as new generations of fans "play Dolly."

Successfully drawing on active audiences, Parton and her team make use of some key features of what scholar Henry Jenkins terms "convergence culture," or the coming together of formerly separate old and new media on media platforms, the rise of participatory fan culture, and "transmedia storytelling," which is coordinated storytelling across multiple media platforms, such as TV, film, music albums, and interactive digital texts like smart phone apps, mobisodes (short television episodes made for mobile phone viewing), and webisodes (television episodes made for online viewing). Parton has proven herself to be adept in what Jenkins terms "affective economics," or marketing strategies trying to get audiences so emotionally invested in a star or text that they will move across different media platforms to consume products.[9] Her skill at navigating these new kinds of media investments by audiences is evident in her extensive new media presence on Twitter. She has over 4.5 million followers, and her Dolly-isms have proven popular, often going viral. Her Facebook page has approximately 4 million followers. Her ALS Ice Bucket Challenge video also went viral, getting over 2 million hits on YouTube in 2014. That popular social media campaign raised awareness and money for ALS research (Lou Gehrig's disease); people "challenged" others to donate money or to dump a bucket of ice water on their heads. In her video, Parton talks about why the challenge matters to her. She skillfully combines her sincerity projection and her camp persona; she makes fun of her appearance, wears a wig that gets wet when the ice water hits it, and squeals with laughter.

Her engagement with fandom in particular is multifaceted, as she both banks on and critiques idolatry. In a savvy formulation of the dynamics of identification in fandom, Parton has said she knows that her fans do not want to see her on the stage; they want to see her being a version of themselves that they wish they could be. Further, she frames her career as a "ministry" to fans, whom she says should be finding their devotion in religion instead of fixating on her.[10] Again, she contends that she started Dollywood in part to give fans another site other than Parton herself on which to focus.[11]

Parton's use of transmedia storytelling is significant, as epitomized by her theme park, where she takes narratives and content from her songs and autobiography and tells those stories in other formats, whether as park attractions, museum displays, or musical theater performances and concerts inside the park. *Heartsongs* (1994) would be an example of Parton's own transmedia storytelling. She did a live concert at Dollywood, recorded and released it as an album, developed a film production for an attraction at Dollywood out of it—a short film called *Heartsong*—and turned it into an ongoing theater attraction at her theme park. During that park show, the film is screened while actors come out to enact some of the stories and interact with the audience in a special theater. For example, she talks about Applejack in the film, at which point an actor walks out as Applejack and plays the banjo in the theater. Foliage and shrubberies decorate the inside of the theater, with water sprayed out at various points in the presentation, lending a fantasy of a pastoral material experience for the audience. Again, the fact that she has used her autobiography to promote that album is also a piece of transmedia storytelling.

In reference to the economic conditions of her ability to engage in transmedia storytelling, it is important to note how her own business holdings echo the kinds of media and entertainment industry developments that have led to the dominance of transmedia as a business model in the industry today. At various times, she has had her own song publishing companies (OwePar and Velvet Apple Music), record labels (Blue Eye Records and Dolly Records), and a television and film production company (Sandollar Productions with then-manager Sandy Gallin).[12] Parton's properties also include the Dollywood theme park and related attractions, like Splash Country and the Dixie Stampede, as well as her newest residential holdings in conjunction with Dollywood, such as the DreamMore suites. Notably, Dollywood continually wins top awards worldwide for theme parks of that size, and it draws almost 3 million visitors to East Tennessee annually. While she shelved plans to build a water and snow park in Nashville with Opryland and Gaylord Entertainment (2012), she has announced that she still wants to build a theme park in the Nashville area.[13]

Parton's use of transmedia storytelling fits into recent larger media trends. It is not a new innovation to tell a story in a coordinated way across different media forms. Witness earlier formats that combined different media to tell a tale, like medieval illuminated manuscripts that used the written word alongside elaborate illustrations, or graphic novels doing something similar today. What is new, however, is the degree to which that model has become foregrounded in recent media culture, the extensiveness and complexity of the storytelling across platforms, and how it keys into media convergence developments in the digital era. The industry structure for multiplatform storytelling stems from how media conglomerates in the 1980s responded to deregulation by buying up interests across the industry, including in film, television, popular music, computer games, websites, toys, amusement parks, books, newspapers, magazines, and comics.

As Henry Jenkins notes, in our media convergence era, various media systems coexist and content flows across multiple media platforms. Old media (like television, film, and books) interacts in novel ways with new media (defined as media that uses interactive digital technology, sending information to and from digital networks, such as the internet or "smart" mobile phones). An obvious example of media convergence would be how a company like Amazon takes books online with electronic readers like Kindle. Other key features of convergence culture include a rise in participatory fan culture, where consumers become more active. In that model, audiences seek out the entertainment they want across different media platforms and interact with those texts, often adding their own fan content to them as, for example, they comment on an image or add to it and then share it with their social networks online. This new media sharing is highly contextual and specific to digital networks, because fans are motivated to spread content to others in their social network who would appreciate it because of shared values.[14] Also witness increased cooperation between various media industries, emerging financing formats, and new, unpredictable interactions between grassroots and corporate media, where consumers are starting to gain more power and access on the one hand, but media consolidation and centralization are happening on the other.[15] Media companies have developed multiplatform models in part by monetizing preexisting fandom practices, like fan websites, and mainstreaming them.[16]

Parton's personal mythology offers apt content for transmedia storytelling, because it functions so effectively as a multiplatform text, as we have seen with NBC's recent TV films drawn from her songs and autobiography. Elsewhere, Parton can use her website to promote her autobiographical narrative, her albums, her concert tours, her merchandise, her Dolly smart phone app, her Twitter feed, her Facebook page, and her other ventures, like her casino games. For transmedia storytelling to work, it must attract active fans who will become brand advocates and nurture fan networks, reposting content and links to their social networking sites (such as Twitter, Facebook, YouTube, Tumblr, Snapchat, Instagram, and Pinterest). Parton's longtime active fandom is particularly adept at increasing her circulation, as evidenced by the numerous fan websites devoted to her. While Parton does not have an official fan club after she disbanded hers in 1997, there are fan features on her succession of official websites. There was a fan section and street team (local promotional team) area on one of her earliest websites (DollyPartonMusic.net for Dolly Records), a streaming "Dolly radio" feed on her penultimate website (DollyPartonEntertainment.com), and a fan mailing list on her current site (DollyParton.com).

Parton's retelling of her life story as a transmedia franchise has features in common with other successful transmedia stories, such as theme park tie-ins, like the *Harry Potter* and *Star Wars* franchises, and fans "playing at" being part of those storyworlds, from costumes to conventions to video games. Parton's participatory fan culture ranges from Parton drag queen shows to Halloween costumes to her annual parade at Dollywood. Multiplatform storytelling creates an immersive world, one with an entire encyclopedic mythology that prompts fan interaction.[17] At the same time, the media companies involved profit from corporate synergy, since they own different kinds of media production and distribution platforms. Jenkins avers that in successful transmedia storytelling, each additional piece of planned content needs to contribute to the larger transmedia text but also exist on its own, so that audiences can consume it as a freestanding text or in relationship to the larger whole. Each piece of media content also needs to draw on the strengths and resources of each medium.[18] Those media elements could range from TV's skill at telling stories in ongoing episodes and narrative arcs, to film's immersive potential, to music's embodied affects and emotional appeal.

Other specific examples of Parton's transmedia storytelling include how she took the material from the 9 to 5 film in 1980 and made her concept album at the time, then in 2008 wrote seventeen new songs for the Broadway musical version (2009), adding her own autobiographical material to the Doralee character, using some of those songs for her *Backwoods Barbie* album. Her *My Tennessee Mountain Home* album (1973) included the concept album and song, but she has used themes from it in her replica of her family's Locust Ridge cabin at Dollywood as a theme park attraction and at her museum in Dollywood. Additionally, her autobiography could be seen as transmedia storytelling in conjunction with Parton's oft-announced future plans for a Broadway musical and a Hollywood film based on her life, while her NBC TV movies based on her life would at least fulfill the promise of her autobiography.

Dolly Fandoms

The degree to which her fans do fulfill this model of active fandom and participatory fan culture is evident in several fan documentaries, all of which convey her supporters' devotion both to Parton's sincerity projection and to her campiness. In addition to the fan documentaries I discuss below, a mainstream film in this period is based on the idea of a fictional character pursuing her Parton fandom. Set in 1976, *The Year Dolly Parton Was My Mom* (2011) is a Bildungsroman coming-of-age story. When an eleven-year-old girl discovers she was adopted, she runs away to a Parton concert, convinced that Parton is her real mother, while her adoptive mother chases her to be reunited with her there. The young girl projects her quest for identity and belonging onto Parton in a way that is similar to fan responses in the extant fan documentaries.

The most substantial fan documentary, *For the Love of Dolly* (2006), follows several longtime, die-hard Parton fans as they discuss their fandom practices, why they became Dolly supporters, and how their fandom generates cultural meaning for them. A gay male couple in Texas, Harrell Gabehart and Patric Parker, who collect Dolly memorabilia, talk about how important she is to their sense of social activism, interpreting her as a gay camp icon who advocates for gay, lesbian, bisexual, and transgender rights. They use their home as a Dolly shrine of sorts, and the sense they make from their relics and rituals is reverential. Their articulation of their fandom and how it has personal meaning for them is akin to the kinds of practices scholars have found in Elvis fans, who create shrines for him and whose fandom involves a high degree of religious-type rhetoric, directed at a secular source.[19] Other fans pictured in the documentary make Dolly art objects, like porcelain dolls one man hopes to have sold at Dollywood, while some perform in Parton tribute shows. One interviewee, David Schmidli, a young man challenged by cerebral palsy, says he has been able to function in the world more as a result of the positive effects of his Dolly fandom. His family explains that after he met Parton in 1990, he gained motivation and confidence as a result of identifying with his fandom; they say that it "changed his life."

The meaning that fans attribute to their objects of fandom is varied and extremely nuanced, just as many theorists would argue that popular culture meaning is generated by a complicated combination of factors of textual production and consumption.[20] Again, a full discussion of all of those interrelated issues is beyond the scope of this study, since I have primarily focused on a text and context literary studies model, with some discussion of production and consumption where possible. However, in terms of the multifarious nature of reception, through studies of fandom, we can get a hint of the unexpected range of meanings that consumers can create, meanings that far exceed the logic of the marketplace.

One particularly storyline in the documentary *For the Love of Dolly*, for example, indicates the idiosyncratic and communal meanings some fan communities can make. The ritualistic and relic-oriented fandom practices are much more amplified in this storyline, which follows two young women, Jeannette Williams and Melisa Rastellini. Explaining that they became close friends because of their shared Parton fandom, they recount the lengths to which they will go to express their fandom. In one storyline, they explain how they followed Parton's best friend and assistant Judy Ogle in order to locate the car she traded in at a Nashville dealership. The documentary pictures the young women searching the car, where they find strands of Parton's hair, as if searching for relics. One of them licks the passenger side seatbelt in the car, where Parton presumably rode with Ogle driving her. They even find old car insurance papers in the car, belonging to Parton. They recount other examples of their fan obsession, such as moving to Nashville and unsuccessfully trying to get a job working for Parton. One of the young women built a replica of Parton's "Tennessee Mountain Home" in her own backyard. Footage shows her sitting on the front porch, imagining herself reenacting scenes from Parton's autobiography, a practice that she says is calming to her. Both recount following Parton around to concerts and appearances and looking for her in Nashville. They specify that they wish to interact with the star and gain her acknowledgment. One of the young women says, "I wish she knew seriously how much she means to all of us or how much we go through to get close to her." For both young women, the tone of their discussion is one of an almost religious devotion, just as they admit that they are willing to go to extreme lengths to express their fandom.

In the documentary, Parton herself observes that she feels ethically troubled by the degree to which some of her fans are directing their obsession at her when she feels they could be spending their time and energy on their own lives. She also avers that for some who might be all consumed by their fandom, she wishes they would find something else to follow, like religion. Parton thus deflects the idol worship, aware that she has become a mythology for some fans to live by. When the two young women continue to follow her, even camping out on the set of a film Parton was acting in, Parton is worried about them and feels compelled to sing to them each night as they camp outside. Parton says they seem to have turned to her for the comfort and support they felt was missing in their own lives or childhoods. Both young women talk on camera about life difficulties, whether troubled childhoods or even abuse, and how Parton became a source of inspiration and strength for them, through her uplifting music, positive attitude, and motivational messages. One explains, "When I was a little girl, I would pray Dolly would tuck me in so I would be safe." The women try to get Parton's attention at her yearly Dollywood parade every year, and Williams explains in direct address to the camera: "It's like a drug, you need your Dolly fix," and "we go everywhere you think she might be, you go there." She expresses a need to Parton to validate her, saying, "She has to see I was there, you know, acknowledge me."

For both young women, the music appears to function as a source of comfort, as does Parton's elaborate mythology and star image. They make their own meaning out of the products of the culture industry, further building their own sense of community around their identification with this fandom. They acknowledge that the lengths of their fandom are particularly elaborate. Indeed, the film's tag line is, "Dolly Parton is more than a country singer. She is a way of life."

Ultimately, all of the expressions of fandom in the documentary illustrate the very individualized meanings fans make of popular culture, with a wide range of understandings and fandom practices. As devoted audiences use their expression of fandom to build community and fashion identity, some treat their fandom like a job or a religion. Parton's fandom here is not dissimilar from others, but it is distinctive for the length of her career, the vast output of popular culture materials, and the degree to which many of her fans identify with her sincerity address, folk culture message, and particularly elaborate authenticity narrative.

In another documentary, this one made for television, *Jake's Adventures in Dollyworld* (2007), the gay male lead singer of the Scissor Sisters, Jake Shears, discusses his fandom and visits with Parton while she is in London to perform. He wants to fulfill his lifelong dream of meeting his idol. When Parton invites him to come visit her, he is ecstatic, particularly when she invites him to sing her song "Calm on the Water" with her. He tours her wardrobe area, which he admires for the camp effect. The enthusiastic young singer clearly fetishizes her as if she is a folk culture icon, responding both to her camp appeal and to her sincerity contract address, genuflecting to her. In direct address interviews to the camera, he rhapsodizes about how charming and genuine she was with him.

Likewise, in the documentary film *Hollywood to Dollywood* (2011), twins Gary and Larry Lane travel to Dollywood in an attempt to give Parton a copy of their screenplay, *Full Circle*, pitching her a part they wrote for her. The film focuses on their experiences of traveling cross-country in their RV, nicknamed Jolene, and their discussion of how their Parton fandom was helpful to them in their experiences of growing up as gay men in a Southern Baptist family in North Carolina. Parton later gave them rights to use her songs in the soundtrack, and she supported the film in interviews, just as they contributed a small percentage of the film's earnings to her Imagination Library. For the Lane brothers, Parton is a symbol of acceptance and gay rights activism, just as her gay camp significations were a significant source of identification for them as they were growing up and facing a hostile mainstream culture.

It is also important to note how other country singers express their Parton fandom, as when they imitate Parton, attempting to embody Parton's persona as kitsch cool. In one typical example, Carrie Underwood and Broadway star Kristin Chenoweth both do Dolly impersonations on Underwood's holiday television special, *Carrie Underwood: An All-Star Holiday Special* (2009). Each wants to "play Dolly" in what Underwood dubs a female country singer's rite of passage. Parton herself performs "Here You Come Again" onstage, and then Underwood comes out dressed as her, replete with massive wig, thick makeup, long nails, stuffed bra, and a campy gold lamé outfit. Parton expresses amusement at such homages. After Parton exits, Chenoweth enters, pretending to mistake Underwood for Parton, and gushes about wanting to sing a duet with Parton (an honor Underwood was reserving for herself). When Underwood then announces the obvious, that she is in Dolly disguise, Chenoweth cannot resist trying on the wig herself, and they both happily indulge their dreams of being Dolly. Indeed, Chenoweth herself has often been discussed as an actor who might be able to play Parton in a biopic, and those moments of enacting Parton become part of her own fandom expression.[21]

Similarly, stars in other genres express Dolly fandom; actor Rebecca Romijn named her daughter Dolly after her idol (with Parton's blessing), while movie star Reese Witherspoon has a "What Would Dolly Do" tote bag in her clothing and accessories line. Pop star Katy Perry, meanwhile, spoke of her love of Dolly as she sang with Parton at the Academy of Country Music (ACM) Awards show in 2016, including a duet of "Jolene," "Coat of Many Colors," and "9 to 5." While Perry played up her own version of ironic camp, dressed in glittery pink and an outlandish cowgirl costume, her camp was noticeably different from Parton's. While Perry's camp was only ironic, Parton still references her mountain girl imagery and her autobiographical links to her Appalachian working-class background, giving her camp a different, more multilayered resonance than Perry's.

Digital Dolly

Amid all these expressions of fandom, the online, interactive component of Parton's media image is particularly important to her address to audiences. In terms of her digital presence, Parton's techniques for engaging with fans online are varied. Her most extensive online presence is on her websites, including her official site, DollyParton.com, and her Dollywood site, as well as her Twitter feed and Tumblr blog. Her sites have included interactive features such as her blog, her parodic Dolly wall art, and Dollyite fan center postings. (This last was an online fan club via subscription that ran from 2007–2013 on Dolly Records' Dolly PartonMusic.Net website; it was disbanded when Dolly Records stated that the company wanted to focus on other social media efforts.) Her online enterprises have also included Dolly "Big Wig" volunteers who previously helped promote her, and her current Twitter joke feed of Dollyisms and various online stores.

Parton's current main website, DollyParton.com, has been combined with her previous website, DollyPartonEntertainment.com. When it functioned as Parton's main official website, DollyPartonEntertainment.com provided a particularly illuminating snapshot of her gender performance in this epoch as well as her address to her fans. As a text (that still appears in online caches), it includes older images from different stages of her career, but the more recent pictures carefully combine the mountain girl pastoral references with the campy tramp aspect. For fans, the site provides an encyclopedic coverage of her as an artist, emphasizing her life story and a timeline of her career highlights. The site foregrounds her camp image, with Parton pictured at the top as a gaudy butterfly, dressed in a blue, low-cut dress with flowing sleeves, huge butterfly wings added behind her as if she is the living embodiment of her butterfly spirit animal and symbol. She is surrounded by graphic images of butterflies flying all around her, some pictured in the foreground and blurry, as if they are close to the camera, that is, the subject position of the viewer's gaze, mimicking a three-dimensional effect. In front of a deeply textured sky-blue backdrop, Parton stands flanked by graphics of trees, as if she is posed in nature, surrounded by leaves, communing with the butterflies. She peers skyward, suggesting looking to the heavens for spiritual inspiration. She is framed by her familiar "Dolly" graphic symbol logo (the one that began on her crossover album *Here You Come Again*); that animated symbol brightens and sparkles, drawing the eye. Her image is exaggerated and sexualized in her signature hillbilly tramp look, while it is carefully framed by the pastoral and the references to her childhood innocence and butterflies, symbols of Appalachian nature.

Likewise, the website image from the tour section of the site has Parton dressed in the black leather mini-dress from her Graham Norton appearance, with her white shirt and tie and black leather gloves. There, she is pictured in front of an old gas station and barn, with a sign indicating that it is an historic site in Tennessee, although the sign is not pictured clearly enough to discern what that place is. The fact that the picture has an historically significant yet anonymous site makes it both grounded in a specific historical reality, with particular material conditions, and yet generic. The gas station features a Pure sign, the wooden barn a Gulf gas sign. While that part of the scene signifies an actual place, the sky overhead has elaborate graphic embellishments that make the visuals hyperreal, with an impossibly pink sky. Thus, the visual image grounds Parton in historical conditions in Tennessee but quickly makes her part of a digital, hyperreal image, floating online, unmoored from the original source. That dynamic of an online image that ultimately circulates separate from its source is a common one on social media today (particularly sites that easily obscure the source of images and often render them anonymous, like Instagram).

Here, Parton is sexualized, fully the campy tramp in her exaggerated makeup and ironic gender-bending leather mini-dress with tie. Yet she is also ensconced in a pastoral setting that directly references her Tennessee authenticity narratives—and shows how those narratives have become a digitalized mythology for her fans. That image sits right next to the neighboring section of the site, a timeline picture of her as a child in black and white, again referencing her folk authenticity life story. The juxtaposition of the two, the folk pastoral Tennessee element versus the mass digital media component that mainly refers back to itself, encapsulates Parton's star persona.

In terms of fan address and prompting active fandoms, the site encourages immediate social media sharing (with buttons for Facebook, Twitter, YouTube, Google Plus, Tumblr, and Instagram). It also highlights Parton's own Twitter feed, running her latest tweet near the top of the page. The site encourages users to sign up for a mailing list. The menu buttons for site navigation demarcate the site's sections, including the store, her life story, information on her tour, media, music, gaming, and news, as well as on her multimedia efforts in the categories of theater, movies, and TV. The site emphasizes visual images, such as pictures of her to trace her life story, which is in keeping with the increasingly visual storytelling of social media and particularly images that go viral and that users share across social media platforms.

The website, curated by her Dolly Parton Productions, includes similar biographical material that emphasizes her authenticity narratives in a section entitled "The Front Porch: Precious Memories from the Heart." It also adds more promotional material for her other commercial ventures, such as her "family destinations" attractions, including the Dixie Stampede dinner theater; Dollywood; DreamMore Resort at Dollywood; Dollywood's Smoky Mountain Cabins (where a fan can stay at a mountain cabin, as if living out Parton's history); Splash

Country; Pirates Voyage Dinner and Show at Myrtle Beach, South Carolina; and her Imagination Library book gifting program.

Her current website, DollyParton.com, similarly mixes images of her Appalachian childhood and her campy tramp image, which is a highly mass mediated one. The site emphasizes her Instagram feed by posting images from it in a prominent section on the homepage. It also organizes recent news about Parton at the top of the homepage by using photographs and graphic images readers can click on to read the stories, a technique that again speaks to the prominence of images over text on social media platforms like Instagram. The website retains her childhood stories with the "Front Porch: Precious Memories from the Heart" section. In addition to marketing her albums and theme park and resorts, the site encourages readers to sign up for a fan newsletter. Indeed, while her websites, past and present, all serve a marketing function, they also prompt fan interactions. Meanwhile, Parton fan websites themselves offer a robust case of online community-building.

Digital Folk Culture

In addition to Parton's extensive digital presence in this commercial promotional material, there are other Parton digital texts and fan sites that create a different dynamic, one that can be interpreted in terms of digital folk culture.[22] The crowdsourced webfilm *The Summer Adventures of Travelin' Dolly* (2010), for example, was made from fan submissions, where they took a paper cutout image of Dolly, printed it, and took it with them to places they traveled around the world. When fans submitted photographic footage via Parton's earlier website, her producers compiled a web video, with the conceit of "Travelin' Dolly," for her song "Travelin' Thru," from the *Transamerica* (2005) soundtrack. That web video can be interpreted as a crowdsourced webfilm or collective digital music video, one that is interactive and depends directly on fan contributions. The video was a summer promotional contest in which fans sent in images to be featured on her website at the time, DollyPartonMusic.Net. They were then compiled into this video. The video has the "Travelin' Thru" Parton song playing over fan-submitted images, such as cut-out Dolly sitting at the edge of the iconic "Welcome to Fabulous Las Vegas" sign or "sitting" next to Vegas showgirls. The cartoon drawing cut-out Dolly is a particularly exaggerated caricature of her Daisy Mae country sexpot image. She is drawn in a low-cut, cleavage-baring red gingham mini-dress with a white fringe around the sleeves and hem, seated with her legs crossed, an extremely short skirt, red high heels, a long platinum blonde wig, excessive makeup, and holding a rather phallic microphone, a caricature of one of her signature retro microphones that she often uses in her promotional imagery.

The video imagery frames Parton as a campy folk spectacle by placing her in Americana sites, her own historical sites, pastoral scenes, and kitsch settings. She is positioned next to a series of Americana sites, like Weeki Watchee Springs in Florida. She appears in front of the W. C. Handy Museum, with him marketed as the "Father of the Blues," an historic blues site in Florence, Alabama. Elsewhere, she incongruously pops up in front of a NASA rocket and in front of a little league team in Mooresville, North Carolina. Some of the images function as visual jokes, with her placed nonsensically in front of images that seem to have no relationship to her or with juxtapositions that are comical. In contrast, some sites are from her own history, such as the Sevierville hometown statue of her. Others place her in nature settings, such as numerous mountain views. She is pictured next to purposefully kitsch references, such as in front of the Pez building headquarters, or in front of a large moonshine jug and sign. Some pictures are in international contexts, like tourist locations in Australia, New Zealand, and England. The video ends with the graphic message, "Thank you, Dollyites . . . for sharing a little piece of your world . . . with us!" The tag line is directed at her online fan club members of that time, with a graphic quotation of lines from the song: "Oh sometimes the road is rugged, and it's hard to travel on / But holdin' on to each other, we don't have to walk alone." Finally, it wishes them all good luck on their own travels. From these juxtaposed images, the video takes the message of solidarity from the song, directed at transgender acceptance in the movie, and reframes it in terms of fan community in this context.[23]

In addition to this crowdsourced webfilm example, Parton's fan hosted websites are also particularly numerous and extensive, evidencing a high degree of fan labor. Fan Duane Gordon created an extensive website entitled first "Duane's Dolly Pages," in 1996, renaming it Dollymania in 1998 (www.dollymania.net). He presents it as an online Dolly Parton newsmagazine. In explaining the fan site, he claims it as "the oldest continually operating internet site dedicated to Dolly Parton and the only regularly-updated resource about her available anywhere in the world." Gordon, who also appears in the DVD featurette accompanying the documentary *For the Love of Dolly*, includes extensive original content that he updates daily. In addition to frequent news updates, he includes links to all Parton-related information; full discographies; a "year in review" feature; photos, including "Fan Antics" submitted by fellow fans, which sometimes consist of pictures of them with Parton; digital wallpaper; links to where fans can purchase Parton goods; his own frequently asked questions (FAQ) giving detailed answers to common fan questions; and tour information. An interactive feature provides opportunities for fan contributions, including letters to the webmaster and replies, a space for collectors to find memorabilia, and contests. He features an especially interactive fan section entitled Pen Pals Page, where fans can send in a letter about themselves, have it posted to the page, and then start chatting with other fans. The site offers a thorough collation of a large amount of Parton information. In addition to investing his own extensive labor in the website, Gordon models his approach to fandom by including detailed answers to fan questions and explicitly attempting to promote a sense of community and camaraderie among digital consumers who visit his site, as in features that prompt fan interaction.

Such digital fan spaces can create a sense of community, where users conceive of themselves as part of a larger whole via the media text with which they interact. A site like that one can function somewhat like a small version of an "imagined community," a term critic Benedict Anderson coined to refer to how people use media to conceive of themselves as part of a larger group.[24] Some of the Parton websites are certainly extensive enough for fans to use them for community building.

Likewise, her U.K. fan community has a website, called Dolly Part'ners, at dolly partonfans.co.uk, which includes similar information categories as well as a fan forum and over 32,000 visitors, and a space for fan contests. Founder Joe Skelly shares memorabilia information with other collectors on the site and includes videos of him appearing on shows about Parton. In his rationale for the fan site, he references how this site functions almost like a shrine to Parton, helping to ensure her legacy: "We set up this website as a way to share with other fans around the world a collection, news and other interesting facts and fun things about the Queen of Country music. Dolly is always young and vibrant in our hearts and she will be a well remembered icon from now until perhaps the end of time." Skelly also includes pictures of himself with Parton, an authenticating move. Many other Parton websites echo similar content, including various fan interaction spaces, such as Dolly On-Line.net, Dolly On-Line, Rare Dolly, The Dolly-Blog, Dolly Parton Archive UK, Dolly Pins, Dolly Freaks, I Just Love Dolly, Night of 1,000 Dollies, Dolly Forever, MySpace Big Wigs, We Love Dolly, Our Queen Dolly Parton, The Ultimate Dolly Parton Fan Website, and Dolly Life and Song.

I contend that the Parton fan websites are examples of "digital folk culture," meaning online folk culture texts that are passed around, shared, and created through a collective interaction by a group, even though that interaction is now happening on the internet.[25] Critics have long debated how to define folk versus mass culture and how to explicate their intersection and arbitrary distinction, since the category of folk culture was an industrial-era concept defined in opposition to emerging mass culture. According to folklorist Dan Ben-Amos's oft-cited formulation, folk culture refers to "artistic communication in small groups."[26] More recent definitions in folklore studies emphasize folk culture's performative aspects; critic Kiri Miller defines it as "a form of expressive culture transmitted through intersubjective performance."[27] Scholars have queried whether folk culture applies to digital environments, since the internet is construed as mass culture. I side with those who argue that digital networks can be a conduit for folk culture, seeing the internet as both mass culture and a storehouse for folklore, because the person-to-person interaction of folk culture can now happen through digital networks.[28] In this line of thinking, digital folk culture underscores the imbrication of folk and mass culture categories, and can even further blur the distinction between folk and mass media.[29]

The Parton music video for "Travelin' Thru" that employed fan content would be an example of crowdsourcing, used in the general sense of labor performed by fans for free, which makes the video an example of user-generated content. Critic Ioana Literat has mapped "online crowdsourced art" into levels of audience participation, from lower levels in which users perform small tasks with no sense of the larger project, to higher levels of full co-creation. In Literat's model, Parton's video would fit the category of "crowdsourced art," because the fans contributed their content; it would not count in one of Literat's higher categories of more substantial fan interaction because when fans uploaded their content online, the process did not let them see how their piece would fit into the whole.[30] Thus, their level of interaction is slightly more limited. Nevertheless, the video would be an example of the growing trend of online interactive music videos, one that popular music studies must continue to assess in order to account for how popular music and fandom are evolving in a Web 2.0 context that emphasizes user-generated content and digital interactivity. Building on the long-running scholarly discussion of music videos in popular music studies, critics have been addressing newer developments as music videos are increasingly platformed online and viewed on a variety of screens, ranging from computers to smart phones.[31] More broadly, media scholars have been debating if such interactive media are merely instances of companies turning the democratic promise of the internet into profit; as they find more ways to monetize fan culture, corporations might simply invite superficial audience participation for free labor, making users advertising targets but not cultural producers themselves. The unpaid digital labor boom has critics like Robert McChesney raising serious concerns about exploitation, suggesting that trends like contingent underpaid labor and unpaid volunteer labor are undermining democratic institutions.[32]

Nevertheless, more audience-centered uses of this media technology exist that allow consumers to contribute substantially and to gain greater access to media production themselves.[33] The cultural politics of these interactive texts often depend on the context. Some scholars optimistically hope these trends can help consumers, since the rise of participatory fan culture and the user content–driven Web 2.0 (since the early 2000s) has prompted unpredictable power shifts between grassroots and corporate media and a greater interdependence between corporations and consumers. Even given the corporate synergy impetus, Henry Jenkins, for example, still upholds the possibility of consumers having meaningful impact on mass media, perhaps achieving equal input with producers.[34] Even though the Parton video does not give fans as much control, and it does raise the issue of who is profiting from unpaid user generated content, it nevertheless offers an example of what Pierre Lévy terms "collective intelligence," where digital networks allow each person to contribute to a larger pool of knowledge.[35] I would suggest that such fandom websites attempt to create collective digital folk culture and that they make their own range of meanings from it, exceeding the logic of the marketplace.

Drunk History and Glastonbury: Nostalgia for Early Dolly

Another instance of professionally made fan culture about Parton that has gone viral, a Comedy Central *Drunk History* (2013–) television episode, is worth discussing at more length here for how it explicates the content of some of the ironic hipster fan culture love of Parton.[36] (I use the term "hipster" here to refer to a progressive youthful audience that identifies itself as au courant about fashionable recent media trends.) Parton has been embraced in such popular culture contexts, as in the *Drunk History* episode and at her headlining performance of the Glastonbury Festival (2014). Festival organizers originally feared Parton would be too "old" or irrelevant to teen and twenty-something audiences targeted by the festival. Instead, she drew the highest attendance and TV viewership.[37] Both examples show how Parton functions as a marker for a certain kind of youthful, savvy fandom in these recent contexts.

One aspect of the *Drunk History* episode that is important to address is how it focuses on her crossover moment. It is significant that Parton's crossover moment is highly fetishized in her subsequent media image, particularly the life story of her break from Wagoner and her subsequent effort to chart her own course. It is a truism that Parton's classic songs from the early 1970s, like "Jolene," "Coat of Many Colors," and "I Will Always Love You," are the ones that her mass audience most associate with her and that form the foundation for her appeal. Some critics have argued that her songwriting at that time has garnered the most attention because she was devoting more time to it, while her work since then has been split between multiple media endeavors, such as film, television, touring, her theme park, and other business and philanthropic efforts. However, I would also argue that the moment of her break and crossover is fetishized in part because her pre-crossover star image functions like a prehistory for Parton—it is after her crossover that she most successfully combines the elements of her star persona into a marketable commodity, and she does so by repackaging the country elements into a more mass appeal, crossover image. It is the fully evolved Parton crossover star image that is most easily recognizable to today's audiences, since she has maintained it since that time. Parton includes those classic songs from the early 1970s in her tour shows to this date, and she showcases her multi-instrumentalist talents during that section of her concerts, but she often frames that throwback section with more crossover material as well as more country pop material. The effect here is that Parton becomes fully Parton after her crossover, and what people identify with is the crossover Parton singing her earlier music, as if looking back to an earlier self. That kind of recycling of her own past also has an added camp effect.

Indeed, the 2013 *Drunk History* episode fetishizes Parton's crossover moment, depicting Parton's 1976 split from Wagoner and her telling RCA executives that she was going to be a crossover star. It is that moment that this hipster series lionizes. The fact that the break with Wagoner has continued to get such media attention is perhaps in part because "I Will Always Love You" symbolically marks that break, and because that song became such a pop phenomenon when Whitney Houston covered it for *The Bodyguard* soundtrack. However, again, I contend that the continued attention to this Wagoner break and crossover moment is also about how audiences are nostalgic for early Parton, but from the point of view of later Parton singing earlier Parton (with the earlier and later images all being constructed sets of media images, of course).

Based on a previous *Funny or Die* web series created by Derek Waters and Jeremy Konner, *Drunk History* involves two comedians discussing a key moment in American history. In each episode, one comedian gets drunk on camera and tells the other their version of the historical events. While the drunk comedian begins making elaborate commentary on the events, often to humorous effects, the series intercuts comedic reenactment scenes in which other famous comedians play out the story just as the drunk comedian has told it. We hear the soundtrack of the drunk comedian telling the story, but we see the actors mouthing those words as they reenact what the comedian is describing. Thus, the series emphasizes the often amusing way that the drunk person is telling the story. It is significant that the series chose Parton's break with Wagoner and pop crossover as a key historical moment, on the level of other historical events the series has depicted, such as the American Revolution. In the Parton episode, "Nashville," which aired on August 20, 2013, other segments retold stories about the Lewis and Clark Expedition and the Scopes Monkey Trial. This mix encapsulates how the series collapses "high" and "low" culture stories, just as many pop culture theorists, following sociologist Pierre Bourdieu, would insist that any distinction between and high and low culture is merely arbitrary and an attempt to reinforce a class hierarchy via a subjective taste hierarchy.[38]

As the narrator for the Parton segment, comedian Seth Weitberg, sits down to tell his friend the Parton story, he gets progressively more inebriated and garbled as he drinks whisky from a Mason jar. He emphasizes how he sees Parton's act of leaving Wagoner as a feminist rebellion. His tale focuses on Parton deciding to leave, writing the song, and starting her solo career. His story scenes are shot in direct address to the camera, with Weitberg speaking as if directly to the audience, inviting them to enjoy his tale. The episode intercuts reenactment scenes with Weitberg continuing to tell his story in voiceover, then it cuts back to scenes of him telling his account as he visibly gets drunker. In the reenactment scenes, again, the actors mouth the exact words Weitberg is saying in his story voiceover, lip syncing to his lines. Comedian Casey Wilson plays Parton, bedecked in a huge blond platinum wig, a stuffed bra to signify fake breasts, flashy rhinestoned dresses, and elaborate makeup, including blue eyeshadow, false eyelashes, ample rouge, and bright lipstick. She looks at herself in a mirror backstage and wonders how to tell Wagoner she has to leave him, mouthing the words as we hear Weitberg say in voiceover: "I've gotta write a song because that's how when you're

Dolly Parton, that's how you express yourself." Weitberg explains that Parton sings "I Will Always Love You" to Wagoner, and the episode pictures Wilson in a long-sleeved, pink frilly dress singing to Wagoner, played by Rich Fulcher, who is dressed in a purple, rhinestoned Nudie-style suit. As the episode cuts back to the scene of Weitberg telling the story, he drunkenly shouts, "Fact, it's probably the most beautiful song that's ever been written."

Weitberg goes on to imagine their communication and the gender politics of their interaction. He claims Parton uses the song to convince Wagoner to free her: "She makes this promise to Porter Wagoner: 'I will always love you,'" and Wagoner replies, "That is the most beautiful song I've ever heard in my life, that is the best song you've ever written, of course you can go." Weitberg describes how Parton then marched right off to the RCA offices in New York and says, "Yeah, it's me, Dolly Parton, here's what's about to happen, I'm leaving the Porter Wagoner Show, I'm gettin' brand new producers, I will be bridging country music and pop, I'ma be in movies. Are ya in, or are ya out, back me or back the f---off!" He describes their response as: "They're all like 'Cool, we're in, yeah, absolutely, we're in, yeah, you're f-ing Dolly Parton, yeah, great, let's do this s---!'" Weitberg then recounts that she fulfilled her promise to succeed in her crossover, recording pop music and making movies. The episode intercuts images of Wilson as Parton vamping in mockups of movie posters for *9 to 5* and *The Best Little Whorehouse in Texas*.

Weitberg describes how Wagoner sued Parton for 15 percent of her past, present, and future earnings, while the episode pictures a split-screen of Wagoner and Parton fighting on the phone. Post-crossover, Wilson as Parton now has a more glamorous platinum blonde wig, a more contemporary pink jumpsuit with rhinestones, more blue eyeshadow, and long dangling pearl earrings. She tells Wagoner, "Porter Wagoner just chill, chill out, man." In this scene, Wilson plays Parton as earnest yet ironic while Fulcher plays Wagoner as both over the top and deadpan. Weitberg recounts how Parton paid him $1 million and goes on about her successes ("she is killing it"), while Wagoner falls into debt, makes bad decisions like buying an orange grove, and owes the IRS $500,000. The comedian finishes his story by explaining how Parton later bought Wagoner's song catalogue and gave it back to him in order to help him when he was in dire financial straits. Weitberg explains, slamming his fist on the table for emphasis: "Dolly Parton made a promise to Porter Wagoner that she would always love him and she did!"

During his retelling, Weitberg emphasizes the interactive, participatory fan culture elements of this series and of how fans retell Parton stories. He takes out his phone to Instagram what he is doing, sharing it on social media while he is taping the scene. The TV episode itself is specifically designed to go viral in online clips. He explains his need to post to social media while taping his part by saying, "This is the most fun I've ever had!"

Thus, this hipster retelling of her story, which was popular enough to receive almost 500,000 YouTube views, imagines her break with Wagoner and her declaration of independence in a way that further fetishizes Parton as a feminist icon. It frames her as someone who can be impersonated so easily because of the drag queen exaggeration of her immediately recognizable signature look. The comedic episode also illustrates how actively fans rehearse and retell elements of her life story, precisely because she has created and continually repeated a mythology around it. The entire episode signifies kitsch, via poor wigs and costumes and drunken slurring, but it also foregrounds fans' earnest love of popular culture and of Parton. The comic retelling emphasizes Parton's ongoing camp appeal, with key elements of that parodic appeal including her well-known look, feminist icon message, and famously covered song combining to encapsulate her star image quickly and effectively. Since she is already campy, this campy retelling of her is easily done. The video speaks to how fans incorporate their own interpretation of the star's life story in this kind of interactive digital culture.

The video also makes mention of rumors about Parton, from whether she has tattoos to whether or not she has had affairs. It thus speaks to how Parton also functions in a new media fandom context in the sense that a higher premium is placed on gossip about celebrities. Rumors about media celebrities become a new way of building community at a new media moment where people are more mobile, spreading out geographically, often not as connected to their home communities or institutions, and instead identifying with media communities.[39] Sometimes, for example, pop culture figures might be the only people some individuals would have in common to discuss. Parton skillfully navigates that kind of media terrain. She deflects rumors about affairs but also keeps engaging with them, using the media and fan fascination with her personal life as a way to circulate further her public persona.

Other fan culture responses to Parton during this era likewise indicate how much fans have a particular kind of nostalgia for early Parton—and how vociferous their fandom of her can be. During her triumphant headlining performance at the Glastonbury Music Festival, for example, it was that classic section of her set, with "Jolene" and "Coat of Many Colors," which had the hipster teens and twenty-somethings crying and singing along to every word. Again, the festival had been criticized for signing Parton to headline, with some arguing that she was too old (sixty-eight at the time) and out of date for a young, more alternative rock, folk-rock, and even EDM (electronic dance music) audience at that festival. However, Parton's set ended up garnering the highest television ratings on the BBC for the festival (2.6 million, 13.4 percent share). Press pundits hailed her performance as a triumph and noted that her set drew the largest live attendance at the festival with over 200,000 attendees.[40] The press coverage also commented on the marked devotion to Parton from a younger generation of fans, as well as the other artists on the bill, all of whom were eager to see Parton. Lars Ulrich, lead singer of Metallica, characterized his own Parton fandom: "I'm a big fan. We all bow to the altar of Dolly."[41] The young festival audiences responded to her with both reverence and cheerful camp, with some in the audience dressed up as her and their response peaking during her "down home" songs.

The affective investment in Parton became even clearer after a media controversy erupted about her performance at Glastonbury, with some journalists claiming she was lip syncing instead of singing live. Celebrity fans from Elton John to Boy George to Stephen Fry quickly chimed in to defend her, asserting that she sang live and chastising her detractors. Many Parton loyalists argued that when the show was broadcast live on the BBC, there was a slight delay caused by the camera technology, thus some viewers could have become confused. Parton's team noted that she sings live in concert and that while she has a very small number of added vocal effects in her shows, they are miniscule, and her performance is live. The official Parton team response also cheekily noted that perhaps some audiences were not used to performers singing live, so perhaps they were not used to what it looks and sounds like.[42]

Star Discourse and Reality TV

In chapter 3, I discussed how Parton's model of stardom fits an older Hollywood stardom model. When she appears in a reality TV setting, however, she interacts with a newer model of stardom that has become prevalent with the advent of the reality TV genre since the late 1980s, one that incorporates a performance of the self as knowingly staged. Parton is suited to that model, with her insistence that she plays herself as a persona 24–7, which shares some similarities with people playing "themselves" as characters on reality TV. The reality TV trend is also relevant to Parton because that model of stardom creates more ironic distance in someone's performance of the self, since audiences are aware of how reality

TV is staged. Thus, a reality TV context allows Parton to incorporate even more complex irony into her persona.

If an older model of stardom has it that a film would seem to reveal something about a star's personality, the star discourse then banks off of the interaction between public and private, extraordinary and ordinary, with each side of the binary informing the other. Reality television offers a complex twist on this formula. Celebrity reality programs in particular invite audiences to see the star's "authentic" personality coming out even in the midst of a mediated show where a star can perhaps best be understood as playing a role as oneself. Annette Hill observes that reality audiences know people act differently when a camera is watching, yet they still look for authentic moments of self beneath the performance.[43] Likewise, in society more broadly, we still search for some version of an authentic self even while knowing identity is constant performance.

As more and more people appear on reality TV as themselves, they can become stars just for being themselves, and that dynamic creates a new model for fame and selfhood in society more generally. Again, scholar Richard Dyer, in his classic argument, asserts that Hollywood film stars function to articulate a discourse of individualism in capitalist society—the unique, exceptional individual who becomes famous for some quality or talent, and who has an authentic self behind the star image.[44] Reality TV channels new versions of fame in a culture increasingly obsessed with celebrity. As critic Su Holmes notes, media critics have described our new culture of stardom as one in which everyone can get their Warholian fifteen minutes, but that fame is understood to be based not on merit but on the creation of media selves—people famous for "playing" themselves on camera, manufactured fame. For Holmes, the new anxiety this model of celebrity speaks to is how to have an authentic selfhood in the context of the mass mediation of identity.[45] She reads reality TV as negotiating this dilemma, capturing a fluctuation between a newer postmodern understanding of identity as a constantly changing performance (a model in which someone could be a star for "being themselves," or performing as oneself on TV) and a complex investment in an older, premodern conception of stable identity (a model in which people become stars for their unique talents).[46]

In this larger process, reality TV in general speaks to new models of celebrity and consequently new models of identity. Most relevant to Parton, shows that focus on preexisting celebrities provide an opportunity for the star to perform a version of their star persona in a knowingly constructed environment, and indeed to perform multiple versions of their identity. Audiences perceive reality

TV to be only "moderately real" and know it is loosely scripted and prompted.[47] I argue that the effect of celebrities appearing on reality TV is to create more ironic distance for their personas. Reality TV's use of documentary techniques, combined with fictional genres, emphasizes this idea of having more "direct" access to the celebrities pictured, with direct address interviews to the camera. However, reality TV speaks to the ways in which documentary is always already mediated as a form, even though documentary as a genre has historically tried to insist on higher truth claims. The problematic status of documentary here is further complicated because reality TV combines documentary with fictional TV genres such as soap opera, drama, and the sitcom, again creating more ironic distancing. On reality programs about celebrities, we see multiple layers of performance, as the stars navigate their public persona, their private persona, and different kinds of selfhood. Viewers are encouraged to parse out which moments are "authentic," even in the midst of obvious manipulation and fakery.

Parton's sincerity contract mode of address works particularly well in that context. Indeed, as I have argued in previous work, country music stars more generally have been successful in the reality genre, precisely because the county genre's sincerity contract matches up well with the reality genre's emotional realism performance of believable selfhood.[48] Both formulations involve nostalgic reactions to mass media and modernity, looking for an "authenticity" anchor in the midst of mass mediation. For example, in a common reality TV subgenre known as "hicksploitation" (with shows ranging from *Buckwild* to *Big Smo*) the South is framed as a site of rural folk exceptionalism, which such series reaffirm through exaggerated "rube" humor and slapstick. However, just as Barbara Ching has shown with "hard country" artists, reality performers often use burlesque to critique the outsider tourist gaze that would frame southerners as abject stereotypes of "white trash."[49]

Meanwhile, when reality singing competitions like *American Idol* during their Dolly tribute week invoke country music, such series also call on country music's authenticity rhetoric of the premodern pastoral as somehow uncorrupted by modernity and the music industry, alongside a symbolic association of country music with southern, white, working-class culture. Such series incorporate reality TV's discourses of authenticity, where "being yourself" on reality TV involves performances of the self as multiple and as seemingly genuine, even in the midst of the obvious mediation. The genre reflects anxieties about how digital culture is changing our understanding of "truth," since any digital image can be manipulated.[50] Again, as Annette Hill has shown, reality TV audiences acknowledge that reality TV is "fake" in the sense of often being loosely scripted and manipulated,[51] but they nevertheless look for moments of what theorists Stuart Hall and Paddy Whannel call "emotional realism" or psychological believability.[52] On reality TV, those moments are ones in which audiences believe cast members' psychological reactions, even when events are staged. The emotional realism becomes what audiences can believe in, even when they cannot trust the veracity of the reality genre itself (or of digital media more generally).

Thus, I argue for a larger trend in which reality TV often turns to southern subcultures to look for emotional realism precisely because of pastoral nostalgia and southern exceptionalism stereotypes. There, the South still appears as a quaint imagined community that embodies a nostalgia for a supposedly "simpler" time and the pastoral rural folk. Reality series refract a particular idealized vision of the South in order to convey a version of "authenticity."

Parton's appearances on reality television fit in with this larger trend, where the southerner symbolizes quaint authenticity. Significantly, Parton performs herself as a character on reality TV in an amplified way, because she not only uses her stage persona in song performances but also in her reality scenes of talking with contestants, which involve her performance of her "sincere self" for the camera. For example, on her The Voice appearances, in addition to having Parton perform live and give advice to contestants, the show has Parton make jokes with country star and coach Blake Shelton. The segment focuses on their cornpone humor and projections of sincerity. She tells his team of contestants that it is all about "heart" and sincerity in their performances, and being themselves. The program also mines Parton's and Shelton's personae for humor, with a prefilmed comedy segment in which they claim there is a "country mafia" and they both know the secret password. Likewise, Shelton observes that since Parton is such a huge star, he is not sure if she is even real.

Parton's performance of "Jolene" on The Voice offers a key case study of how she performs her gendered persona in a reality TV context. During Miley Cyrus's first season as a coach (2016), Parton makes taped appeals for contestants to pick her goddaughter, underlining her sincerity address. Later during that season, Parton sings "Circle of Love" onstage in an episode with Jennifer Nettles and the top ten contestants, promoting her Christmas of Many Colors (2016) movie. Later during that episode, Parton also sings "Jolene" with Miley Cyrus and a cappella vocal quintet Pentatonix. There, just as in her taped comic bits, Parton presents herself as a persona with her sincerity projection, which plays perfectly in a reality TV context in which people must appear to be their "authentic" selves.

Parton trades riffs with Cyrus and plays her fake nails as percussion. Meanwhile, Pentatonix provides elaborate harmonies and male and female solos, with all the performers dressed in rhinestoned black and silver wardrobes. The high-profile rendition garnered press attention and online views in addition to being watched by the millions of Voice viewers. Prior to her collaboration with Pentatonix on The Voice, Parton's earlier rendition of "Jolene" with Pentatonix went viral online (2016) with over 20 million views.

The song's potential gender play was amplified in the reality TV setting because Cyrus had been using "Jolene" as a touchstone throughout the season. During auditions, Cyrus campily sang it with a contestant to convince her to join her team, doing an ironic country jig. Later, with her team, Cyrus also performed a stylized, campy version of the Parton–Porter Wagoner duet "There'll Always Be Music"; Cyrus wore a rhinestoned, tasseled Parton-style miniskirt, while a male team member did a Hank Williams Sr. homage in a music note suit. As Cyrus brings her own connotations to the stage, her media image includes gender fluidity and gender play, as she has become well known for not identifying with a gender category and for popularizing the term pansexual to describe her sexuality.[33] Cyrus is also well known for performing "Jolene" specifically (her acoustic Backyard Sessions version has 97 million YouTube views). An earlier Parton-Cyrus duet version at Dollywood (2010) garnered 17 million views.

Parton's reality TV performance of "Jolene" on The Voice underscores in particular how some of her renditions of "Jolene" highlight the possibility of gender play, as when the male singer from Pentatonix sings to the female "Jolene" "please don't take my man" (other covers by male singers like Jack White likewise mirror that dynamic). Indeed, the significations of that song in particular can vary greatly based on the performance context, just as the cultural politics of the song are a matter of open debate. Parton creates subversion in the song when in concert she often sings "drag queens" instead of "Jolene." Lyrically, the speaker in the song has tended to be interpreted as passive and conforming to traditional gender stereotypes because she tries to place blame on her female rival rather than the cheating husband. However, Nadine Hubbs argues in her article on "Jolene" that the lyrics can be interpreted as having a homoerotic subtext because the female speaker focuses on how she admires her female rival's beauty. In contrast, Kate Heidemann reads the song's vocal approach and composition as aspiring to normative white, middle-class femininity.[54] Ultimately, Parton's complex collaborative performance of the song on The Voice amplifies the way the lyrics can be seen to play with and question gender in that particular reality TV performance context.

Given Parton's long history of reclaiming the hillbilly stereotype, her guest spots on reality TV also fit into another key trope, the "redneck" stereotype, which is often how the South appears on reality TV. In a hicksploitation context, country music signifies as a backward stereotype. The rhetoric implies a pastoral nostalgia for an idealized rural space, one that is at the same time seen as embarrassing by mainstream culture precisely because it is associated with the past and with rural, working-class stereotypes. The rural past is lauded as a simpler time and simultaneously disparaged as the low Other. In this kind of framing, country singers are seen as quaint country bumpkins of a bygone era, like the "contemporary ancestors" who are seen as throwbacks to an earlier time even as they still exist in the present. That the pastoral nostalgia is staged through a popular music genre only underscores how this stereotype is also about mass culture's nostalgia for the folk culture it has displaced and commodified.

The version of southern authenticity I am addressing refers specifically to country music as a discourse, but one can also see this rhetoric in larger cultural discourses about the South and authenticity. Scott Romine has argued that the South in a late capitalist context functions as a multivalent signifier; narratives try to claim different versions of the "authentic" South as commodity, but no one "real" South exists, merely simulacra formed through narratives.[55] That kind of dynamic could actually be seen as part of a larger cultural trend in the context of media studies, in which media in a digital era recurs to unstable concepts of what is real versus what is fake in order to make sense of a confusing digital landscape.[56] In the case of reality TV, that search for authenticity involves reality television's own particular codes of authenticity, that is, a projection of the self as genuine, thus merging a country music genre source with a reality TV convention to signify authenticity.

Ultimately, because the reality TV genre is so highly mediated and obviously various degrees of "faked," prompted, and scripted, the prevalence of hicksploitation shows points to how often reality TV uses the South as a shorthand for sincerity. In this formulation, the South is idealized as the premodern pastoral while reality TV responds to anxieties about what is real and what is fake in the context of easily manipulated digital images. The larger reality country trend speaks to how country music is a specific mixture of aesthetics and commodity, what Hall and Whannel call the mixture of the authentic and the manufactured in popular music more generally.[57] The projection of sincere selfhood on such reality TV narratives involves finding the self or the project of the self, which scholars have critiqued as a problematic rhetoric stemming from neoliberalism and the idea of self-fashioning as self-regulation.[58] However, here, the reality TV identity trope is secondary to the larger authenticity narrative that is about mass culture's nostalgia for folk culture and about cultural fears over the status of truth claims in our digital era of easily manipulated images.

Because of Parton's already convoluted and multifarious authenticity projection, when she appears on a reality show like *American Idol*, *Strictly Come Dancing* (where she guested in 2011), or *The Bachelorette* in order to promote her music, she nevertheless takes her persona and her gender performance into a new environment, one in which she interacts with reality TV codes and with reality TV cast members. Her reality show appearances speak to the layered ways in which all of these different authenticity narratives intersect. Parton as reality star illuminates how such tensions can play themselves out across different media platforms, here involving popular music, television, and new media in these retellings of familiar southern stereotypes.

Parton and *The Bachelorette:* Reality TV Marketing and Transmedia Storytelling

Parton's reality TV appearances encapsulate the new media practices involved in television marketing and advertising, including transmedia storytelling, corporate synergy (such as cross-marketing and corporate sponsorship), mass customization marketing, and monetizing fandom practices. Many reality shows incorporate repeated cross-promotion and advertising directly into plotlines, often advertising the TV network itself.[59] Such synergy epitomizes what media scholar Eileen Meehan terms "excessive branding," where a company floods the market with branded product to such an extent that it displaces nonbranded products.[60] For a "Dolly Parton week" on *American Idol* in 2008, Parton advised contestants and cross-promoted her *Backwoods Barbie* album. Well-known for branding deals, *American Idol* frequently integrates products into storylines, as when contestants make music videos to advertise Coke.

Likewise, when Parton appeared on the reality dating show *The Bachelorette* in 2012, it was in the context of "excessive branding" and cross-promotion of Dollywood and Parton's music. The season had crossover marketing of country music more generally, notably when Luke Bryan sang in an earlier episode to promote an album. It also promoted elements associated with a country fan base, such as NASCAR tie-ins. In other aggressive cross-promotion that season, ABC's parent company, Disney, integrated a storyline from their Pixar animated film *Brave* (2012), having *Bachelorette* suitors compete in Scottish highland games to win the maiden's hand, echoing the film's storyline. Meanwhile, the Dollywood episode provides a helpful case study for corporate synergy, as well as some unexpected transmedia storytelling.

In that episode, contestants go on a surprise trip to Dollywood and have the country doyenne serenade them.[61] The fact that viewers would certainly not expect Parton to come sauntering onto the set of *The Bachelorette*, and that the episode would be marketed as an incongruous "surprise trip," speaks to how the advertising drives the plotline. During the Dollywood segment, Parton promotes her theme park, sings one of her songs from the film soundtrack to *Joyful Noise* (2012), and sings a new song she wrote specifically for *Bachelorette* star Emily Maynard and her date.

Throughout the episode, Parton's sequences of cross-promotion are deeply integrated into the storyline, becoming key parts of Maynard's character development. The episode characterizes single mother Maynard by her Parton fandom, imaginatively linking her to Parton. Like other reality shows, the series turns cast members into characters with storylines, creating what I have elsewhere termed "character narratives"; reality shows then turn those characters into brands, often focusing on what they consume and their taste in everything from clothes to music.[62] Here, Maynard rhapsodizes about how Parton has always been her favorite singer, explaining to her male suitor why Parton is such an icon. When Parton later surprises the couple with a private concert, Maynard says she "could die" right there, because she has realized her lifelong dream of meeting the singer. In intercut interviews, she emphasizes Parton's importance to her and suggests that the experience of meeting her idol will help guide her. At season's end, when Maynard picks a winner and (temporarily) becomes engaged to him, she explains in voiceover narration that she and her fiancé (though he was not the one on the Dollywood date) used the code names "Dolly" and "Dean" (for Carl Dean) when they had to meet secretly until the results show had aired. The series continually links Maynard to Parton fandom, country music, and NASCAR (noting that Maynard had previously been engaged to the late NASCAR driver Ricky Hendrick, the father of her daughter). While furthering Maynard's characterization, each link also becomes a cross-promotion opportunity.

Meanwhile, Parton's participation helps further her own character projection. The episode uses the standard reality TV documentary technique of direct address interviews to the camera. In her intercut interviews, where Parton talks about being happy for the reality show contestants, she speaks directly to the camera as if talking right to the home audience; this confessional form scripts the audience into the confessor and encourages viewer sympathy and identification. The reality TV form presents direct address comments as if they are unscripted, spontaneous thoughts and feelings. Those interviews are in precisely the form that encourages identification, a bit of reality TV confessional marketing.

The episode functions as a transmedia text, going beyond simple cross-promotion into coordinated multiplatform storytelling, precisely because Parton actually wrote a new song specifically for the couple and sings it onscreen. After singing the song to Maynard and her suitor, with lyrics about finding "true love" and knowing it is the right person, Parton meets with Maynard, advising her about how Parton has kept her marriage to Carl Dean going for so long. Parton asks Maynard, "What are you really looking for in a guy?" Maynard replies, "That feeling that you just get when you know." As Parton empathizes with Maynard's quest, their exchange moves the storyline forward. Maynard, meanwhile, gushes, "Dolly Parton is unbelievable." Dollywood itself is integrated into the storyline further as the episode pictures Maynard and her date at park attractions, then the series sentimentalizes it as one of her "favorite places in the world," frequently using that footage in flashbacks later in the season.

During the Parton segments, Maynard continually remarks that most of the top songs on her iPod are Parton's. The implication here is that the episode is her iPod come to life, that is, her consumer tastes generate a reality TV story about herself. The show creates a profile for country music fans, who are also assumed to be NASCAR fans and Emily Maynard fans, or at least women who would want to buy the boots and dresses she wears.

This emphasis on popular culture taste and targeted audiences is an example of mass customization marketing, a prominent advertising trend where products are customized for audiences but on a mass scale (as when Amazon greets you with "customized" suggestions based on their market research of you and millions of other consumers). Media scholar Mark Andrejevic argues that the interactive nature of reality TV (which encourages audiences to go online to vote and express preferences about reality shows, or even to appear on shows themselves) becomes a way to get audiences to accept and even seek out greater surveillance of them in practices like mass customization marketing—and also to get fans to perform their own marketing research on themselves for free. For Andrejevic, the democratic promise of the internet becomes hijacked by corporate interests.[63] In addition to mass customization marketing, the Dollywood episode is also an instance of television's effort to monetize fandom practices like fan websites and blogs.

In *The Bachelorette* example, fans have opportunities to interact with their Parton fandom across different media platforms. They can watch the episode, listen to the new Parton song coordinated with the TV series, and read Maynard's online blog where she attests that Parton was sweet to her and down to earth. There, Maynard cites her favorite Parton songs on her iPod and reinforces how her love of Dolly and country music frames her as a character. The diaristic address to fans on the blog uses an "everywoman" style of address, encouraging viewers to feel they could experience such an adventure too, by watching the episode and listening to the Parton song.

As the episode demonstrates, Parton is perfectly suited to "play herself" as a character on reality TV, because she already performs her persona all the time. Parton finds new ways to commodify that persona and market it across new media platforms. She here participates in the world-building that the *Bachelorette* franchise is trying to create. She not only promotes Dollywood and her music but actually creates coordinated new content for the show with the song, an unexpected bit of transmedia storytelling. Because Parton also sings to the couple a song from the movie *Joyful Noise*, "From Here to the Moon and Back," she is simultaneously promoting both that album and the movie.

Notably, Parton has participated in earlier examples of transmedia storytelling with Disney. In the Disney channel's *Hannah Montana* television series, she appears as the character "Aunt Dolly."[64] Her television persona there is similar to her Dolly Parton public persona, and she builds on her autobiographical stories of being close friends with collaborator Billy Ray Cyrus and goddaughter Miley.[65] Earlier, Parton actually had a Disney studios CBS TV series that never aired, *Heavens to Betsy* (1994), slated to be the first Disney MGM Studios network prime-time series, produced by Parton's Sandollar Productions in association with Touchstone Television. Parton wrote the soundtrack, about a Las Vegas lounge singer who has a near-death experience and returns to make amends in her Tennessee hometown. Although the pilot never aired, Parton turned some of that material into her TV movie *Unlikely Angel* (1996).

In this transmedia storytelling model, advertisers enter into branded entertainment deals in order to capitalize on this new advertising model in which producers still address a large broadcast audience but also narrower, niche audiences.

That model requires engaged fans who will interact with their favorite series, joining the world-building by posting on social networks and building up fan communities.

Cultural Politics

Parton's identity performance thus reflects larger media trends, and her sincerity address and star persona intersect with newer developments in star discourse. Meanwhile, her cultural politics signify, particularly as relates to country music's cultural politics, in one other important context. I have been reading some aspects of Parton's transgressive potential in her use of feminist camp and gay camp, including her support for gay rights and marriage equality. On gay marriage, Parton has stated publicly: "I think gay people should be able to marry," and she critiques Christians who oppose gay marriage: "They've forgotten that the Bible preaches acceptance, tolerance and forgiveness."[66] It is important to note that her appeals to her Christian fan base and her religious themes are framed in terms of tolerance, acceptance, and anti-homophobia. I read Parton's use of gay camp not as a mainstream takeover of gay camp's potential for social critique but rather as part of her larger advocacy for gay rights and marriage equality, notable in her country music context, and also as related to how she uses feminist camp.

When queried about her own cultural politics, as noted earlier, Parton does not claim the feminist moniker but freely advocates for gender equity and female empowerment.[67] She links her criticism of female stereotypes to critiques of homophobia, explaining that it is her feeling of being different, misunderstood, and judged based on gender stereotypes that has in part contributed to her connection to her gay male fan base in particular.[68] My reading of her subversive elements fits into a larger context of some more progressive strains evident within the country music genre that scholars have been examining.

However, it is important to underline that Parton's cultural politics are themselves also multivalent, thus my reading of transgressive politics within her gender performance must also observe that she has a range of different significations on top of that. For example, her albums during this recent period take on multifarious political positions, from the conservatism and seeming nationalism of *For God and Country* to the progressive, pro-transgender song for *Transamerica*. On *For God and Country*, she includes songs linking nationalism and country music, such as "Red, White, and Bluegrass," and her seeming response to terrorists, "Go to Hell," in which she sings, "Get thee behind me Satan" and "take your weapons of mass destruction, terror and sleaze" and be "banished to hell for the corruption and evil." She argues in the lyrics that God will triumph and the speaker will go to heaven. The album also includes her music for religious scripture, such as "The Lord Is My Shepherd." Her religious songs include her music for "The Lord's Prayer." Her lyrics implicitly link Christianity, patriotism, and American nationalism, and the album seems designed to appeal to a particular conservative country music fan base. While Parton did not explicitly pitch the album as a response to 9/11, it did emerge and was received in the context of country music's numerous patriotic albums in response to the attacks. Meanwhile, she included a pro-peace song on the later album *Those Were the Days*, where she dueted with the former Cat Stevens on his song "Where Do the Children Play?" and earlier covered his "Peace Train" with a pro-peace video, for *Treasures* (1996).

Parton thus has multiple significations and can sometimes be a bit of an "omnipolitician," Chris Willman's term for how some country singers like Johnny Cash and Merle Haggard tried to appeal to both sides of the aisle to maintain a large and varied fan base. Willman maintains that country has its own internal political debates, in which "redneck" and "hippie" strains have always coexisted, with mainstream country dominated by conservative rhetoric but with "outsider" genres like "alternative country" and Americana evidencing progressive voices. He suggests that the country genre is characterized by a dialogue between mainstream and alternative.[69] The larger country genre's politics are variegated and contain both conservative and progressive strands. Historically associated with populism because of its bond with southern, rural folk cultures, country music fluctuates in its political affiliations and is sometimes read as apolitical. Often seen as conservative when it does include political content, the genre has been posed as a "medium for the transmission of rural conservatism" and, more recently, as a mouthpiece for angry, urban, NASCAR dads.[70] Since at least the time of Nixon's courting of country music's support in the 1970s, the genre has been stereotyped as a bastion for conservative, white, patriarchal family values. Bill C. Malone dates this trend to the Cold War 1950s, although he avers that country music's politics vary so much that they are neither right wing nor left wing, conservative nor liberal. However, he questions whether the genre merely engages in escapism or if it actually makes structural social critiques; for him, the genre focuses on individual rather than collective response, which he traces to union decline in the South and class anger being offset by working-class individualism and fatalism.[71] While registering more space for social critiques in country music,

Paul DiMaggio, Richard Peterson, and Jack Esco nevertheless see a combination of fatalism and "primitive rebellion," which reflects a "populism in retreat."[72] Meanwhile, Chris Willman maintains that the genre shifted to conservatism over the last two generations as part of a broader political transformation of the South, although he notes that the country music conservatism stereotype does not always hold true.[73]

Others read resistant strains in the country genre, as when scholar Nadine Hubbs avers that country music can make structural critiques.[74] Likewise, Aaron Fox suggests that country music in the age of globalization offers a space for the working class to grapple with dislocation and lower wages by identifying with communal and local cultural lineages (plus nostalgia for the postwar era of class compromise). In his view, the country genre also provides a site for other groups to find social identification as they are squeezed by globalization and neoliberalism (such as groups of Native North and South Americans, Aboriginal Australians, and black Africans who are country fans).[75] Jock Mackay reads a populist ideology in country music, what he calls the genre of the "classical industrial proletariat."[76] For him, with varied political messages reflecting the multiple tensions inherent in working-class life, the genre imagines thwarting authority or undermining the system, which he thinks moves beyond individual escapism. As examples, he points to local cultures that translate country songs into working-class anthems, moving across regional and ethnic barriers (like Quebecois translations of country songs, such as Willie Lamothe's "Le Mur d'Acier" [Steel Wall], an adaptation of Cash's "Folsom Prison Blues").[77]

Parton offers an example speaking to how the genre can frame multiple different political positions. As a case study, Parton also illuminates how greater critique is possible within the genre. She does make some structural social critiques of gender, as in her 9 to 5 album, and her enactment of her gender performance itself opens up a subversive space for identity construction. Parton also links her gender critique to a class critique, in her articulation of a southern, white, working-class femininity. While she does not make as extensive a class critique in her oeuvre, her multilayered portrayal of an Appalachian context does at times make relevant critiques.

Comparisons: Madonna and Lady Gaga

In terms of the larger cultural politics of Parton's gender performance, it is useful to compare Parton to two obvious case study examples from pop music,

Madonna and Lady Gaga. Both have been widely debated in scholarly circles for their attempts to control and commodify their own sexual objectification. The broader question is whether Parton (or other singers similarly engaged) is transgressive in controlling her own sexualized image when that image it-self reinforces capitalist patriarchy. I side with those many scholars, like Pamela Robertson, who contend that Madonna does not assert female agency but rather reinforces patriarchal capitalism.[78] In contrast, I see Parton as more transgressive, like Lady Gaga. In providing exaggerated parodies of emphasized femininity, Parton does not merely profit from those images. Instead, she questions the act of signification and, like Gaga, returns askew the objectifying "male gaze" of Western visual culture.

Indeed, I would argue that Parton is closer to Gaga's model (notably, Gaga cites Parton as an influence). My reading of Gaga is that she disrupts the male gaze of the camera, using disproportionate costumes (such as shoulders raised several feet, a simulated hunchback, or cat eyes) to frame her image as freakish and mis-shapen in order to trouble an objectifying gaze. Gaga's content messages include diversity, acceptance, polymorphous perversity, bisexuality, pro-LGBT rights, and anti-heteronormativity. Meanwhile, Parton departs drastically from Madon-na's model, in which Madonna simply profits off her own objectification and does not alter patriarchal capitalism. Madonna displays a superficial investment in queer advocacy as she objectifies herself for profit and commodifies gay camp (such as Vogueing) and empties it out of meaning. In contrast, theorist J. Jack Halberstam goes so far as to claim Lady Gaga as a new model of feminism and gender fluidity.[79]

Picking up on references to Madonna as "Mae West for yuppies," Robertson argues that Madonna commodifies gay camp as a privileged subcultural tourist, only paying lip service to gay rights advocacy and instead draining gay culture of meaning and turning it into empty, marketed style.[80] Disagreeing with crit-ics who have read a feminist gender parody in Madonna, Robertson insists the singer uses a privileged position to advocate for fluid identity and polymorphous perversity when those in a nonprivileged position would not have the freedom to leave identity and identity politics behind. Again, I would agree with this kind of critique of Madonna, and I would assert that Parton is more like West, not like Madonna—the "hillbilly Mae West" is different in kind from the "yup-pie Mae West." In her autobiography, Parton contrasts herself with Madonna, arguing that Madonna is trying to "shock" people while Parton attempts to "live and let live."[81]

Race Relations

In other important political significations, Parton's recent work has been address-ing race relations more directly, as she has long taken antiracist stances in country music. In one recent television film, Parton symbolically lends her support to the long-running history of African American artists and fans in country music. The film has Parton select the next big country artist, a young African American girl who wins a singing competition Parton judges. In the Lifetime original movie *A Country Christmas Story* (2013), which has a Christmas theme and religious overtones, Parton plays herself, presiding over several scenes in a singing competi-tion, for which the young girl, Grace Gibson (played by Desiree Ross), has been preparing and dreaming about, even as she deals with discrimination and ridicule for wanting to sing country music. The girl's father, played by R&B singer and producer Brian McKnight, loves country music just as she loves R&B. As the girl goes on to become the next future country star, the film references the ways in which race and popular music stereotypes still circulate. For example, there are currently no African American female country superstars, although there are re-cent emerging African American female country artists such as Mickey Guyton. The way the film imagines musical influences references the ways in which the country and R&B genres share musical roots and have impacted each other in popular music history, just as country music exhibits the influence of blues and gospel alongside what was earlier called "hillbilly" music. In the film, Parton, as herself, warmly praises the singer and encourages her in her career path, impart-ing words of inspiration as the girl faces down racial stereotypes.

In addressing these themes, the film joins a larger conversation about race, popular music, and scholarly efforts to recover the history of African Ameri-cans in country music. The movie's premise speaks to the historical stereo-types involving country music and race, in which the genre was associated with white, working-class southerners. Some of that association came about, as Diane Pecknold and others have shown, because as the genre was professionalizing in the mid-twentieth century, the country music industry attempted to create marketing categories and maintain segregation and racial boundaries between white and black artists, even though the roots of the music itself are in the combination of Anglo European and African American music that developed historically in the South.[82]

In contrast, Pecknold points to a transracial history of country music, in ne-glected histories of African American country artists and fans, as well as international music cultures that identify with country music beyond national borders.[83] Scholar Adam Gussow has argued that "hick hop" (a subgenre that mixes hip hop and country) singer Cowboy Troy imagines a transracial country music.[84] Gussow reads a transracial West in Cowboy Troy's work as an evolution of rap-country hybrids, arguing that Troy's hick hop performances court scandal, question the racial stereotyping of musical styles, and insist that the two forms are always already creolized and hybridized, from rap boasts to singing cowboys. Pecknold helpfully analyzes the paradox that country music has been stereotypically framed as "white music" but a long tradition of black performers and fans exists, uncovering the historical discourses that over time obscured country music's multiracial origins and history.[85] The hybridized music of hick hop thus speaks to a certain degree to the more complex multiracial origins of country music as a genre.[86]

Parton included a brief parody of a rap performance in her *Better Day* tour, referring to her collaboration with Queen Latifah on *Joyful Noise* (2012), in which they went on a promotional tour together and talked about their friendship and musical collaborations growing out of the film. Parton's collaborations with Queen Latifah also point to shared musical histories involving race relations. When Parton and Latifah starred together in the film, they played up a gospel singing rivalry and demonstrated how country and R&B draw from each other and from similar gospel sources. The film likewise follows a Romeo-and-Juliet-style love story between a young African American woman and her Anglo American boyfriend. The young woman is Latifah's character's niece, while the young man is Parton's character's grandson. Parton and Latifah famously had scripted scenes where they argued and satirized each other, as Latifah made fun of Parton's plastic surgery and Parton made fun of Latifah's weight. Parton was lauded in the press for being self-deprecating about her own well-known plastic surgery and jokes about her appearance. As Parton was touring while composing music for that film, she added a rap song into her act, one in which she talked about herself and Queen Latifah and joked that she was the queen of Hollywood but Parton is the queen of Dollywood. Parton's rap is a brief parody and is certainly not an example of hick hop as a substantive subgenre. Parton rapped, "She's the queen of her own hood . . . but I'm the queen of Dollywood! . . . I don't hip and I don't hop . . . I'd black both eyes with this big top. . . . I know the Queen has got 'em too . . . but she don't work 'em like I do!"[87]

With her parodic take on her own rapping ability, Parton makes fun of herself, turning a "hillbilly" stereotype into a parody, using cornpone humor tropes.

However, she does not of course control how she might signify in this context. For example, she went on Queen Latifah's talk show to promote her album. There, when she performed her rap routine, she donned her version of a stereotypical "rapper wardrobe" with gold chains and a blonde afro wig, though she would certainly not wish to be interpreted in terms of country music's highly problematic history of blackface minstrelsy. While Parton is seemingly trying to bring race into her camp aesthetic, questioning stereotypical categories of race and music, her rhetoric is not as nuanced there as her references to gender are. On one level, her performance of that routine on the Latifah show satirizes racial stereotypes in the sense that it sends up the stereotype that a white country singer would not be singing hip hop. On another level, however, her performance in that context risks reinforcing racial stereotypes that she is attempting to satirize. Meanwhile, more broadly, some of Parton's other artistic outputs about race and country music have a more successfully clear message of antiracism and prodiversity, such as her appearance in A *Country Christmas Story*.

Parton's "Home"

Within Parton's complicated and varied political significations, in the strain I have been tracing of her gender critique, Parton continues to tie her authenticity narrative to her gender performance in quite intricate ways. In Parton's recent video for the song "Home" from her *Blue Smoke* album, Parton sings about seeking the comforts of home in the midst of her busy life. She invokes explicitly autobiographical lyrics, talking about leaving home at age seventeen and having a "magic door" in her mind, where she can return whenever she wishes to those memories. She describes pastoral, idyllic views. Opening on a scene of Parton in her dressing room putting her makeup on in a mirror, the video purports to give the viewer a behind-the-scenes, backstage window into Parton's life. As she powders her nose, a banjo sitting next to her and pink neon lights spelling her name outside the window, the scene is not presented as realistic but rather has the feel of a set for a photo shoot. As Parton lyrically genuflects to country music history by quoting Hank Williams, singing about being "so lonesome I could cry" just like "old Hank," she goes on to sing that she needs to turn to a place "where I can be happy and just be me." As she pulls a white dress from the rack, the video cuts to the next scene, which is Parton in the white dress at a photo shoot, dancing and singing the chorus about wanting to go "home."

The song's lyrics focus on her wanting to return "home" to enjoy pastoral scenes of hills, rivers, fishing, front porch swings, fireflies, crickets and katydids, hills and whippoorwills, church bells and singing, and a place where she can lay down her "heavy load" and "always be welcome." The video cuts to multiple distinct photo shoots, with Parton in different outfits in front of various backdrops, one with her playing her banjo in front of a graphic image of an artificial mountain backdrop. As she collapses into her "Dolly" chair on set, tired from her exertions, the video suggests that her mental space of home memories is what fuels her to keep going with her daily toil, on one set after another, from posing to singing to picking photographs with the photographer. Her lyrics carefully state that she is not complaining about her work or the pressures of fame, because she is thankful for all that she has, but the "magic door" of memories is necessary for her to function.

The video is striking because on one level, it suggests that she is returning imaginatively to her memories of her Appalachian childhood when she is engaged in her daily labor in the country music industry, as when she sits for numerous photo shoots against fake backdrops of scenes of mountains or fields of sunflowers. However, on another level, it implies that this hybrid space, in which she is enacting her media persona in different multimedia spaces while recalling her folk culture mountain childhood, is actually her figurative "home" space. The "magic door" leads back to the media image, and she is comfortable creating identity and expression in that mediated space. In my conclusion, I discuss Dollywood as one of the best examples of Parton's synthesized "Dolly image," where she brings together the media image and performance elements of her persona in a theme park, itself a highly mediated space including everything from a replica that simulates her childhood home to her self-depiction in her museum.

Notes

1. Mansfield, "Dolly Parton Returns."
2. Ibid.
3. Peoples, "Are Women Finally Getting"; Keel, "Tomato-Gate."
4. Hight, "Female Country Stars."
5. "Melissa Etheridge and Dolly Parton."
6. *The Tonight Show with Jay Leno*, 9 October 2003.
7. Butterworth, "All Dolled Up."
8. Parton, *Dream More*, 106.
9. Jenkins, *Convergence Culture*, 2–3, 20.
10. *For the Love of Dolly.*

11. "Dolly Parton: Singer Disbanding."

12. Gallin stopped managing artists in 1998 to go into real estate development; he passed away in April 2017.

13. DollyParton.com.

14. Jenkins et al., *Spreadable Media*.

15. Jenkins, *Convergence Culture*, 4–16. Jenkins cites political scientist Ithiel de Sola Pool's book *Technologies of Freedom* (Cambridge, Mass.: MIT Press, 1984), originally published in 1983, as the first to discuss the media convergence concept.

16. Gillan, *Television*, 2.

17. I have argued elsewhere that such models can apply not just to fictional worlds and characters but also to real people as characters, from reality TV franchises to multimedia stars. Edwards, *The Triumph of Reality TV*, 24.

18. Jenkins, *Convergence Culture*, 4–16.

19. Doss, "Elvis Forever."

20. Witness models such as Stuart Hall's circuit theory model or Julie D'Acci's four spheres model of production, text, consumption, and sociohistorical context. Hall, "Notes on Deconstructing"; D'Acci, "Gender."

21. *Carrie Underwood: An All-Star Holiday Special*, 7 December 2009.

22. Edwards, "Johnny Cash's 'Ain't No Grave.'"

23. *The Summer Adventures of Travelin' Dolly*.

24. Anderson was referring specifically to citizens in the eighteenth century starting to conceive of themselves as part of nation-states through reading newspapers and literature, with political implications for the rise of nationalism. I am of course only loosely adapting his concept for digital fandoms. Anderson, *Imagined Communities*.

25. Jenkins, *Convergence Culture*, 136.

26. Ben-Amos, "Toward a Definition," 13.

27. Miller, "Grove Street Grimm," 280.

28. Blank, *Folk Culture in the Digital Age*, 4.

29. Blank, *Folklore and the Internet*, 20.

30. Literat, "Work of Art," 2977.

31. Beebe and Middleton, *Medium Cool*.

32. Terranova, "Free Labor"; Robert W. McChesney, *Digital Disconnect* (New York: The Free Press, 2013).

33. Edwards, "Transmedia Storytelling."

34. Jenkins et al., *Spreadable Media*.

35. Jenkins, *Convergence Culture*, 4.

36. "Nashville," *Drunk History*, 20 August 2013.

37. Szalai, "Glastonbury."

38. Bourdieu, *Distinction*.

39. Jenkins, *Convergence Culture*.

40. Szalai, "Glastonbury."

41. Savage, "Dolly Parton Draws Huge Crowd."

42. Szalai, "Glastonbury."

43. Hill, *Reality TV*; Hill, *Restyling Factual TV*.

44. Dyer, "Four Films."

45. Holmes, "'All You've Got'"; Gamson, *Claims to Fame*, 44.

46. Holmes, "'All You've Got,'" 128, 132.

47. Naby et al., "Reality Based Television Programming."

48. Edwards, *The Triumph of Reality TV*; Edwards, "*Big Smo.*"

49. Ching, *Wrong's What I Do Best*, 26, 139.

50. Fetveit, "Reality TV."

51. Hill, *Reality TV.*

52. Hall and Whannel, *Popular Arts*, 269–283.

53. Ramin Setoodeh, "Miley Cyrus on 'The Voice,'" *Variety*, 11 October 2016.

54. Hubbs avers that the song expresses homosocial or homoerotic themes common in country music lyrics. Hubbs, "'Jolene'"; Heidemann, "Remarkable Women."

55. Romine, *Real South.*

56. Fetveit, "Reality TV"; Dovey, *Freakshow.*

57. Hall and Whannel, *Popular Arts.*

58. Ouellette and Hay, *Better Living.*

59. Edwards, "Contemporary Television Advertising."

60. Meehan, *Why TV*, 111.

61. *The Bachelorette*, 28 May 2012.

62. Edwards, "'What a Girl Wants'"; Edwards, *The Triumph of Reality TV*; Edwards, "Transmedia Storytelling."

63. Andrejevic, *Reality TV.*

64. *Hannah Montana*, Disney, 2006–2011.

65. In the press, both women now identify Parton as Cyrus's godmother. However, in the past, Parton has said that when Billy Ray Cyrus asked her to be the godmother, she technically declined because she was gone on tour so much of the time.

66. Sterdan, "Dolly Parton." Parton made a similar, widely publicized critique of intolerance on *Larry King Now*, 24 August 2016.

67. In a 2014 cover story for feminist magazine *BUST*, when asked if she is a feminist, Parton does not identify with that label but explains, "I consider myself a female. I think of myself as somebody who's just as smart as any man I know. I don't think anybody should ever be judged by whether they're male or female, black, white, blue, or green. I think people should be allowed to be themselves and to show the gifts they have, and be able to be acknowledged for that and to be paid accordingly. You know, I love men, but I love women too and I'm proud to be a woman. I just really try to encourage women to be all that they can be and I try to encourage men to let us be that." Butterworth, "All Dolled Up."

68. Price, "Dolly Parton Q&A."

69. Willman, *Rednecks*, 248.

70. Buckley, "Country Music," 298; Kimmel, *Manhood*, 231; Thompson, "Forbidden Fruit," 260; Willman, *Rednecks*, 3, 7.

71. Malone, *Don't Get*, 211.

72. DiMaggio et al., "Country Music," 51.

73. Willman, *Rednecks*, 8, 16.

74. Hubbs, *Rednecks, Queers, and Country Music.*

75. Fox, *Real Country*, 320.

76. Mackay, "Populist Ideology," 289, 290, 298.

77. Ibid., 298–300.

78. Robertson, *Guilty Pleasures*, 119.

79. Halberstam, *Gaga Feminism*.

80. Pamela Robertson quotes Russell Baker: "Madonna isn't the cultural elite. . . . She's just Mae West for yuppies." Robertson, *Guilty Pleasures*, 119.

81. Parton, *Dolly*, 259.

82. Pecknold, *Selling Sound*.

83. Pecknold, *Hidden in the Mix*.

84. Gussow, "Playing Chicken with the Train."

85. Pecknold, *Hidden in the Mix*.

86. Gussow, "Playing Chicken with the Train."

87. "Parton Stuns Fans."

Conclusion
Brand Evolution and Dollywood

I have been arguing that Parton's gender performance is transgressive because she uses feminist camp to combine images of the pure mountain girl and the hillbilly tramp. As she plays a culturally validated version of femininity off of a vilified one, Parton in effect questions negative stereotypes and the social hierarchies that create them. Her media image critiques how gender gets stigmatized. She also slams stereotypes about southern, white, working-class femininity, specifically in an Appalachian context. Her hillbilly tramp element gives her an increasing level of camp in her stage persona and star image, which she uses to create ironic distance and to critique gender stereotypes rather than being trapped by them.

Her gender performance also maps onto tensions in country music rhetoric between ideas of the pure versus manufactured, which is, at its core, another way of saying folk versus mass culture. Parton's work and image question the distinction between those arbitrary categories. She resolves the binary tension by claiming both sides, a both/and status, saying she is both real and fake, folk and mass, pure and manufactured: both are true at once. The most fake—Parton's arbitrary, excessive, manufactured image—is the most real, because it is grounded in her "real" mountain folk culture. The one leads to the other. Her star image illuminates their imbrication and interdependence in country music history as well, as an art form that combines folk and mass culture in distinctive ways.

As a concluding case study, Dollywood offers a particularly good example of Parton's staging of the real and fake as conjoined and ultimately not distinct from each other. With nearly 3 million visitors annually, the park showcases Parton's iconography and mythology for a mass audience in an interactive format. It emphasizes her authenticity narrative, with features such as her replica of her "Tennessee Mountain Home"; tourists and fans can interact with a simulation of the material culture she draws on for her folk culture truth claims. Parton also lauds the park as a space that preserves mountain folk culture and crafts stretching back to earlier centuries. She continually refers to "authentic hillbillies" working there, whom she often renames "skillbillies," many of them members of her extended family. Dollywood houses a large number of artisans who make mountain crafts and demonstrate to visitors how to do so as well, passing on folk culture practices. There, for example, visitors can watch artisans make mountain dulcimers and learn how to play them or make them themselves. In addition to Parton's expressed desire to provide economic opportunities for people in her home region, with Dollywood the largest employer in Sevier County, she and the park management also attempt to expand on the range of cultures represented in the park. Parton invokes a rhetoric of multiculturalism to bring in performances from cultures around the world that residents of the area might not otherwise interact with directly. Dollywood has international musicians and street performers there for summer residencies, from Chinese acrobats to Irish singers of Celtic music, which places that Smoky Mountain region in a different relationship to other cultural traditions and a broader global context.

At the same time that Dollywood offers a space for Appalachian folk culture, it is also aggressively a piece of mass culture, a commodified tourist experience of that folk culture. Media studies scholar Melissa Jane Hardie argues that while the park presents mountain folk culture from a century ago, the images are more like a commodified simulation or hologram.[1] In that sense, walking through the park is like walking through a multimedia version of manufactured authenticity. However, Parton's theme park does offer examples of material culture, as with mountain crafts being made and taught to others, a preservation of folk culture. Both elements are true at once, the fake and the real.

Importantly, it is Parton's life story that offers the thread holding together the park's transmedia storytelling, as in her museum, home replica, and Parton-themed restaurants. A number of the park's musical shows and theater productions draw on Parton's own life story to anchor them. In addition to her *Heartsong* film and music show about her life and music, billed as "a multi-sensory music/ film experience narrated by Dolly Parton," she features a music venue for her relatives, dubbed "On the Back Porch with the Kinfolks," at one of her outdoor stages. There, her "kinfolk" tell stories, play music in tribute to Parton, and sell recordings, as her uncle Bill Owens used to do.

Other attractions target her experience of the Smoky Mountain context and history. Some of the different shows running at Dollywood at different times have included *Sha-Kon-A-Hey!* her version of Smoky Mountain history; *Back Where I Come From*, a multimedia show of Smoky Mountain film and images set to country music; and even mountain comedy sideshows. Drawing on Parton's multiple musical genres, the park's various musical shows range from contemporary to traditional country, gospel (as with the Kingdom Heirs, Dollywood's southern gospel quartet), bluegrass (for example, with Naomi and the Wood Brothers), mountain string bands, and pop music and rock music shows, including doo wop from the 1950s and 1960s.

Parton's own museum at Dollywood is the most elaborate instantiation of her autobiographical narrative there. Called Chasing Rainbows, the museum collects relics, staging a space for Parton's production of her mythology and for fans to participate in that mythology. It showcases her actual childhood coat of many colors in a glass case. Other items of memorabilia include her early musical instruments, pictures of her in school, her high school marching band outfit as a snare drummer, and pictures of her with friends and family, including husband Carl Dean and best friend Judy Ogle. A series of awards deck the walls, alongside her increasingly glamorous costumes over the years, and artifacts like her handwritten lyrics. Parton's handwritten lyrics are also a fetishized collection piece for her fans, and their display in museum settings is common, speaking to her self-presentation as a songwriter first. For example, her handwritten lyrics for "Jolene" are on prominent display at the Country Music Hall of Fame and Museum, with Parton noting that she wrote "Jolene" the same night she wrote "I Will Always Love You," in the same writing session.

Other park areas likewise follow her life story. The 1950s-themed Jukebox Junction section of the park (replete with Red's Drive-In, a rendition of a 1950s burger joint with doo-wop singers) includes Cas Walker tributes, memorializing her time as a singer on his show. A farm-themed area called Owens Farm honors her mother's side of the family. Dolly's old tour bus, dubbed "Dolly's Home-on-Wheels," is on display for fans to walk through and have their pictures taken, alongside some of her wigs. While the Robert F. Thomas Chapel preexisted her involvement with the park, it took on new meaning when the park became Dollywood, with a sign marker noting that he was the doctor who delivered her. Also housed at Dollywood is the Southern Gospel Music Hall of Fame, which inducted Parton in 2010, and its connected gospel museum.

The park's marketing aggressively foregrounds Parton's Appalachian childhood nostalgia, turning it into the big business of mass culture. In the Dollywood.com website description of the DreamMore family resort, the tagline references Parton's authenticity narrative: "Located next to Dollywood Theme Park and Dollywood's Splash Country, this resort is inspired by Dolly Parton's warm childhood memories of growing up on her family's front porch in the Tennessee mountains near the Great Smoky Mountains National Park." The three-hundred-room resort, which opened in the summer of 2015, also focuses on storytelling as a folk art. It has planned "story spots" included in the resort design. They try to achieve a nostalgic setting, "beckoning to a time when families and friends sipped iced tea, enjoyed homemade ice cream and socialized." The resort's physical layout is designed to encourage related family activities: "Centered on the rich traditions of storytelling, family and togetherness, the resort will feature many special touches including family sanctuaries like fire pits, swings and hammocks plus story spots scattered through the grounds." While that resort certainly does not memorialize Parton's working-class mountain childhood, instead gesturing to a gentrified, commodified vision of an upper-middle-class South, it nonetheless drapes the concept underneath Parton's mythology. Parton's mountain cabin housing at the park likewise gentrifies a version of Parton's Appalachian mountain background. As an aspect of the park's regular attractions, Dollywood trumpets Parton's attendance at the annual parade, with fans who want to see her in person making a pilgrimage.

Part of Dollywood's marketing is aggressively interactive as well, drawing on media convergence models in the sense that it incorporates interactive digital media in new ways. The Dollywood.com website includes Dollywood apps and games, links to top social media networks, and a mailing list with news and special offers. The advertising rhetoric pinpoints a familial, domestic rhetoric: "Known for its down-home charm, this world famous 150-acre theme park is as unique as its namesake and owner Dolly Parton. From award-winning shows to educational craft demonstrations and ground-breaking rides and attractions, Dollywood offers something for everyone and every interest, so the whole family can experience the park together as a unique bonding experience for families."

The park in effect claims to give visitors an approximation of the experience of Parton's Appalachian childhood context.

Taken together, such marketing and the Parton-themed Dollywood attractions imply that this piece of popular culture can convey to tourists what it felt like in that earlier time and place, and even what it felt like to grow up as Parton did. Thus, it attempts to convey a particular "structure of feeling," Raymond Williams's term for a particular group's shared perceptions and values at a particular time, as popular culture especially can express the group's members' lived experience of their ideological beliefs.[2] Here, Dollywood is an imagined community with familial bonds, all rooted in historical claims about the Smoky Mountains and Parton's personal mythology.

Parton, in fact, functions as a metonymy for the park in the website's verbiage, which hails the consumer and tries to interpellate them into this imagined community in ways both affective and commodified:

> Ask anyone who has visited Dollywood before, and they'll tell you this place is different. It's not a difference that you can touch or see. It's a difference you can feel. When you're at Dollywood, time slows down a bit and your troubles don't seem so troublesome. You could name a million things that make Dollywood so special, but we think it boils down to the simple things like the feeling you get when you're with the ones you care about most, or the warm, inviting smiles of the Dollywood Hosts who treat you more like family than a guest.

Such familial rhetoric is a map for business relations, all legitimated by the Dolly mythology. The park also draws on current media convergence models in their efforts at transmedia storytelling and their corporate sponsorships, with Coke and Humana, for example. Tag lines on the voluminous kitsch for sale at the vast number of stores in the park similarly emphasize a commodified familial space, including "Dollywood, it's homespun fun!" The park's trademarked tagline is "creating memories worth repeating," and it markets Parton's "own special brand of charm" alongside the rides and the Smoky Mountain culture.

When the park anchors itself to domestic imagery of family and home, particularly with the "kinfolks" musical performances, Dollywood does fit into a particular kind of country music celebration of the domestic, like the Carter Family's home, family, and domesticity-focused traditional music.[3] That kind of authenticity narrative takes on obvious gender stereotypes. Parton adeptly takes such stereotypes and uses them, incorporating them into her authenticity persona and marketing them. Thus, when she uses a familial home narrative in this way, she fits into country music history's iconography as the home-centered, domestic branch. This same tradition can be traced back in country music origin stories to the Carter Family, which is an equally artificially constructed authenticity narrative.[4]

Dollywood's Origin Story and Cultural Politics

Dollywood's history and how Parton went into partnership with the managers speaks to the park's multifaceted cultural politics.[5] While Dollywood opened in 1986, it was a revamping of an existing amusement park, Silver Dollar City, that had been purchased in 1977 and run by the Herschend Brothers, Jack and Pete. The Herschend family already owned another Silver Dollar City in Branson, Missouri, which opened in 1960 (and was previously known as Marvel Cave). There, they developed their theme park formula, one that they would later adapt for Silver Dollar City in Tennessee. The Branson site used an 1880s theme, replete with frontier-style buildings, including a general store, blacksmith shop, ice cream parlor, doll shop, church, homestead, and "Stage Coach Inn." Entertainment included hillbilly music and reenactments of the Hatfields and McCoys feud. Their conception used cultural preservation and historical tourism as the focus of the park. Similarly, for Silver Dollar City in Tennessee, they highlighted late nineteenth-century Appalachia, with the Craftsman's Valley area of the park showcasing Smoky Mountain crafts and folk arts, and local artisans selling their work and teaching tourists folk practices. The owners later added rides to the park. Crafts featured included leather smiths, blacksmiths, lye soap makers, and a working grist mill. After Parton partnered with the Herschends in 1986, they added Parton-specific attractions, such as a replica of her "Tennessee Mountain Home," themed restaurants, and theaters and musical performances. The park also added features such as the bald eagle sanctuary and an ever-increasing number of rides, including rollercoasters and water flumes, with new attractions added annually. The Craftsman's Valley area now also includes candle makers, glassblowers, wood carvers, and potters.

While the Parton partnership represents the park's modern incarnation, there were two earlier incarnations that form the prehistory of the property. These earlier versions are relevant because they included some features that still exist in the present theme park, such as the steam engine train. Prior to the Herschend purchase in 1977, NFL owner Art Modell owned the park as Goldrush Junction. In that earlier incarnation, the park had rides and attractions, including what they called pretend "Indian attacks," that is, an elaborate staging of an American frontier mythology fantasy that supported Manifest Destiny rhetoric. Prior to Modell's ownership, the park began in 1961 as Rebel Railroad, opened by the Robbins Brothers from North Carolina. In that original version, the park was a small attraction with children's rides and some Smoky Mountain cultural attractions, like the steam engine train that still runs at Dollywood.

It is important to note that Herschend Entertainment operates Dollywood, and their corporate difference in political views from Parton has sometimes become evident. The park's corporate mission statement includes a commitment to "Christian values and ethics." Parton's working relationship with them extends to her performances in yearly concerts at other Herschend Entertainment parks across the country as well, thus she does bring her performance context into their park properties on a national scale.

In contrast to the company's rhetoric, press coverage of the park has emphasized the progressive affiliations and gay camp Parton brings to Dollywood. In reporter Kim Severson's *New York Times* travel article, "Dollywood: A Little Bit Country, a Little Bit Gay," she describes the park as "the place on a Venn diagram where gay camp and Southern camp overlap." She characterizes the juxtaposed politics in the park as the "most culturally conservative amusement park in the country" but one with a "campy gay undercurrent," such that Parton's pro-gay stance is much different from the conservative stance of that area and that company. Observing the wealth of campy elements of the park and its performances, Severson points to the inclusiveness in some of the songs in theater performances, such as the "My People" personal narrative show from Parton, which includes the song "Family," with the line "some are gay." Severson interviewed a performer in that show, Parton's niece Jada Star Andersen, who states that Parton has close family and staff members who are gay and that Parton loves that "Dollywood is a mecca for gays." In an interview promoting DreamMore, Parton tells Severson that gay families are welcomed there: "We're in the business for all families." Parton goes on to reject Christian justifications for homophobia: "A family is a family whether you're a gay family or a straight family. If that's your family you should be treated with the utmost respect, and we do that no matter what. I say a good Christian wouldn't be judging anyway. We're supposed to love and accept each other." However, Parton's stance is at odds with the surrounding context, as Severson cites in two incidents: Dollywood lawyers required organizers to stop using the park name for a "gay day" event fans held, and park officials censored a tourist's pro-gay marriage shirt because they deemed it offensive.[6]

Authenticity and Multiple Meanings

Thus, the theme park itself stages a debate and cultural battle over Parton's image, with different sides claiming Parton as their own. Such a struggle over meaning speaks to how Parton's camp can have multiple significations in different contexts and to varying audiences. While Dollywood enshrines her mythology, it also marks the complex cultural politics Parton enters into with her media image, as it invokes complicated significations in terms of gender, race, class, and sexuality, particularly in a southern regional context.[7] Her oeuvre offers a telling perspective on country music history and the genre's authenticity debates. I maintain that her media image can signify as transgressive in some contexts, with her model of gender performance that critiques gender stereotypes and norms.

Dollywood stages Parton's evolving persona and specifically her gender performance over time, and it represents a prime example of how she navigates the folk-mass culture split. The mountain crafts section of the park highlights the preservation of folk culture, sitting right in the midst of mass culture tourism. The most fake, highly kitschy, manufactured, artificial, commodity-filled theme park is at the same time the most real. It is up front about being aggressively staged and marketed. It nevertheless does in fact help preserve mountain folk culture, supporting local artists who can teach parkgoers how to do some of these folk practices, showing them lifeways and vernacular culture, placing them in a context, conveying a structure of feeling. That structure of feeling is both mass and folk at the same time, and Parton's work is questioning the distinction between those arbitrary categories, the fake and the real. The one leads to the other, in Dollywood, in Parton, and in country music.

Again, Parton is not the only artist to question the folk-mass tension, but she does so in a distinctive way, precisely because she grounds it in her authenticity narrative of mid-twentieth-century Appalachia.[8] Over the course of her over sixty-year career in country music, Parton has contextualized her own gendered persona and authenticity claims first and foremost in terms of country music's gendered performance history. However, as she has expanded her star persona into multimedia contexts, ranging from popular music to television, Hollywood film, and her theme park, she has added more complex layers to her media image. Throughout, she has balanced her mountain girl and town tramp components, effectively critiquing gender conventions in country music as a genre, even as she has created her own elaborate, continually evolving models of gender performance.

Notes

1. Hardie, "Torque."
2. Williams, *Long Revolution*, 64.
3. Sanjek, Foreword.
4. See also Melissa Hardie's analysis of how Dollywood makes authenticity claims. Hardie, "Torque."
5. Parton discusses the history of Dollywood in her autobiography. Parton, *Dolly*, 269–273. See also the Dollywood.com website, and Miller, *Smart Blonde*, 223–231.
6. Severson, "Dollywood."
7. I hope we can eventually organize a subfield in country music studies—and perhaps call it "Dolly studies"—to debate these complex significations further, since Parton is such a key case study.
8. In other examples combining the two, Elizabeth Outka argues for a "commodified authentic" in late nineteenth- and early twentieth-century British literature and culture; authors sold nostalgic images of an idyllic, preindustrial past, separate from the mass market—but cheerfully turned them into commodities. She shows how high modernism banked on this contradiction of mass-produced authenticity, demonstrating how that dynamic is an important move in the history of modernity. Outka, *Consuming Traditions*.

Selected Bibliography

"1997: Dolly the Sheep Is Cloned." *BBC News*, 22 February 1997, http://news.bbc.co .uk/onthisday/hi/dates/stories/february/22/newsid_4245000/4245877.stm.

9 to 5: Sexist, Egotistical, Lying, Hypocritical Bigot Edition. 1981. DVD. 20th Century Fox, 2006.

Adorno, Theodor. "On Popular Music." In *Cultural Theory and Popular Culture: A Reader*, edited by John Storey, 2nd edition, 197–209. Athens: University of Georgia Press, 1998.

Allen, Robert C. *Horrible Prettiness: Burlesque and American Culture*. Chapel Hill: University of North Carolina Press, 1991.

Anderson, Benedict. *Imagined Communities: Reflections on the Origins and Spread of Nationalism*. 1983. London: Verso, 2006.

Andrejevic, Mark. *Reality TV: The Work of Being Watched*. Lanham, Md.: Rowman and Littlefield, 2003.

The Bachelorette. ABC, 28 May 2012.

Barbara Walters Special. ABC, 6 December 1977.

Barger, Lilian Calles. "Backlash: From *Nine to Five* to the *Devil Wears Prada*." *Women's Studies* 40, no. 3 (2011): 336–350.

Batchelor, Bob, ed. *Literary Cash: Writings Inspired by the Legendary Johnny Cash*. Dallas: Benbella Books: 2006.

Beebe, Roger, and Jason Middleton, eds. *Medium Cool: Music Videos from Soundies to Cell Phones*. Durham, N.C.: Duke University Press, 2007.

Ben-Amos, Dan. "Toward a Definition of Folklore in Context." In *Toward New Perspectives in Folklore*, edited by Américo Paredes and Richard Bauman, 3–15. Austin: University of Texas Press, 1972.

Berger, John. *Ways of Seeing*. 1972. New York: Penguin, 1990.

Bergman, David, ed. *Camp Grounds: Style and Homosexuality*. Amherst: University of Massachusetts Press, 1994.

Bertrand, Michael T. "I Don't Think Hank Done It That Way: Elvis, Country Music, and the Reconstruction of Southern Masculinity." In *A Boy Named Sue: Gender and Country Music*, edited by Kristine M. McCusker and Diane Pecknold, 59–85. Jackson: University Press of Mississippi, 2004.

———. *Race, Rock and Elvis*. Urbana: University of Illinois Press, 2000.

The Best Little Whorehouse in Texas. Directed by Colin Higgins. Performed by Dolly Parton and Burt Reynolds. 1982. DVD. Universal, 2010.

Blank, Trevor J., ed. *Folk Culture in the Digital Age: The Emergent Dynamics of Human Interaction*. Logan: Utah State University Press, 2012.

———, ed. *Folklore and the Internet: Vernacular Expressions in a Digital World*. Logan: Utah State University Press, 2009.

Bone, Martyn. *The Postsouthern Sense of Place in Contemporary Fiction*. Baton Rouge: Louisiana State University Press, 2005.

Bourdieu, Pierre. *Distinction: A Social Critique of the Judgment of Taste*. Translated by Richard Nice. Cambridge, Mass.: Harvard University Press, 1984.

Brackett, David. *Interpreting Popular Music*. 2nd ed. Berkeley: University of California Press, 2000.

Braidotti, Rosi. "Cyberfeminism with a Difference." In *The Feminism and Visual Culture Reader*, edited by Amelia Jones, 643–645. 2001. London: Routledge, 2003.

Buckley, John. "Country Music and American Values." *Popular Music and Society* 6, no. 4 (1978): 293–301.

Bufwack, Mary A., and Robert K. Oermann. *Finding Her Voice: Women in Country Music, 1800–2000*. Nashville: Country Music Foundation/Vanderbilt University Press, 2003.

Butler, Judith. *Gender Trouble: Feminism and the Subversion of Identity*. New York: Routledge, 1990.

Butterworth, Lisa. "All Dolled Up." *BUST*, June–July 2014, 42–49.

Caldwell, John. "Prime-Time Fiction Theorizes the Docu-Real." In *Reality Squared: Televisual Discourse on the Real*, edited by James Friedman, 259–292. New Brunswick, N.J.: Rutgers University Press, 2002.

Cardwell, Nancy. *The Words and Music of Dolly Parton: Getting to Know Country's "Iron Butterfly."* Santa Barbara, Calif.: Praeger, 2011.

Carrie Underwood: An All-Star Holiday Special. Fox, 7 December 2009.

The Carter Family: Will the Circle Be Unbroken. PBS, 2005.

Cash, Johnny. *Man in Black*. Grand Rapids, Mich.: Zondervan, 1975.

Cash, Johnny, with Patrick Carr. *Cash: The Autobiography*. New York: HarperCollins, 1997.

Cash, Wilber J. *The Mind of the South*. New York: Knopf, 1941.

Ching, Barbara. *Wrong's What I Do Best: Hard Country Music and Contemporary Culture*. New York: Oxford University Press, 2001.

Ching, Barbara, and Gerald W. Creeds, eds. *Knowing Your Place: Rural Identity and Cultural Hierarchy*. New York: Routledge, 1997.

Coates, Norma. "(R)evolution Now? Rock and the Political Potential of Gender." In *Sexing the Groove: Popular Music and Gender*, edited by Sheila Whiteley, 50–64. London: Routledge, 1997.

Cobb, James C. "Country Music and the 'Southernization' of America." In *All That Glitters: Country Music in America*, edited by George H. Lewis, 75–86. Bowling Green, Ohio: Bowling Green State University Popular Press, 1993.

Cohen, Ronald D. *Rainbow Quest: The Folk Music Revival and American Society, 1940–1970*. Amherst: University of Massachusetts Press, 2002.

Cole, Jennifer V. "Dolly Parton: The Southern Living Interview." *Southern Living*, 11 September 2014, http://thedailysouth.southernliving.com/2014/09/11/dolly -parton-the-southern-living-interview/.

Connell, R. W. *Masculinities*. 2nd ed. Berkeley: University of California Press, 2005.

Controversy: Johnny Cash vs. Music Row. Country Music Television, 16 July 2004.

Cusic, Don. *The Sound of Light: A History of Gospel Music*. Bowling Green, Ohio: Bowling Green State University Popular Press, 1990.

D'Acci, Julie. "Gender, Representation and Television." In *Television Studies*, edited by Toby Miller, 91–94. London: British Film Institute, 2002.

Davidson, Cathy N., and Jessamyn Hatcher, eds. *No More Separate Spheres!* Durham, N.C.: Duke University Press, 2002.

Dawidoff, Nicholas. *In the Country of Country: A Journey to the Roots of American Music*. New York: Vintage, 1998.

de Certeau, Michel. *The Practice of Everyday Life*. Berkeley: University of California Press, 1984.

deCordova, Richard. *Personalities: The Emergence of the Star System in America*. Urbana: University of Illinois Press, 1990.

Deloria, Vine, Jr. *Custer Died for Your Sins*. New York: Avon, 1969.

Dent, Alexander Sebastian. *River of Tears: Country Music, Memory, and Modernity in Brazil*. Durham, N.C.: Duke University Press, 2009.

Dickinson, Chris. "Hello Dolly: Parton Sparkles during Hall of Fame/CMT Appearance." CMT.com, 14 June 2001, http://www.cmt.com/news/1444509/hello-dolly -parton-sparkles-during-hall-of-famecmt-appearance/.

DiMaggio, Paul, Richard A. Peterson, and Jack Esco Jr. "Country Music: Ballad of the Silent Majority." In *The Sounds of Social Change: Studies in Popular Culture*, edited by R. Serge Denisoff and Richard A. Peterson., 38–55. Chicago: Rand McNally, 1972.

Dolly Parton. Biography Channel, 28 April 2006.

"Dolly Parton: Singer Disbanding Her Fan Club." Associated Press, 18 January 1997, https://news.google.com/newspapers?nid=1891&dat=19970118&id=-7ofAAAAIBAJ &sjid=QNgEAAAAIBAJ&pg=6046,2131533&hl=en.

Dolly Parton Productions. "Dolly Parton Life and Career." *Dolly Parton*, https://dolly parton.com/about-dolly-parton.

"Dolly Parton Releases New Single." *Country Standard Time*, 28 August 2007, http:// www.countrystandardtime.com/news/newsitem.asp?xid=867&t=Dolly_Parton _releases_new_single.

Doss, Erika. "Elvis Forever." In *Afterlife as Afterimage: Understanding Posthumous Fame*, edited by Steve Jones and Joli Jensen, 61–78. New York: Peter Lang, 2005.

Dovey, Jon. *Freakshow: First Person Media and Factual Television*. London: Pluto, 2000.

Dyer, Richard. "Four Films of Lana Turner." In *Star Texts: Image and Performance in Film and Television*, edited by Jeremy G. Butler, 214–239. Detroit: Wayne State University Press, 1991.

———. *Heavenly Bodies: Film Stars and Society*. London: British Film Institute, 1986.

———. *Stars*. 1979. London: British Film Institute, 1998.

Echard, William. *Neil Young and the Poetics of Energy*. Bloomington: Indiana University Press, 2005.

Edelman, Helen S. "Why Is Dolly Crying? An Analysis of Silicone Breast Implants in America as an Example of Medicalization." *Journal of Popular Culture* 28, no. 3 (Winter 1994): 19–32.

Edwards, Leigh H. "'Backwoods Barbie': Dolly Parton's Gender Performance." In *Country Boys and Redneck Women: New Essays in Gender and Country Music*, edited by Diane Pecknold and Kristine M. McCusker, 189–210. Jackson: University Press of Mississippi, 2016.

———. "*Big Smo*: Reality TV, Hick Hop, and Southern Stereotypes." In *Small Screen Souths: Interrogating the Televisual Archive*, edited by Lisa Hinrichsen, Gina Caison, and Stephanie Rountree. Baton Rouge, Louisiana State University Press, forthcoming.

———. "Contemporary Television Advertising: From Disney to the Kardashians." In *We Are What We Sell: How Advertising Shapes American Life*, edited by Bob Batchelor and Danielle Coombs, 172–183. Santa Barbara, CA: Praeger, 2013.

———. "Country Music and Class." In *The Oxford Handbook of Country Music*, edited by Travis Stimeling, 307–326. New York: Oxford University Press, 2017.

———. *Johnny Cash and the Paradox of American Identity*. Bloomington: Indiana University Press, 2009.

———. "Johnny Cash's 'Ain't No Grave' and Digital Folk Culture." *Journal of Popular Music Studies* 27, no. 4 (December 2015): 186–203.

———. "Mass Art: Digital Folk Culture and Country Music as Folk Mass Culture." In *Pop Culture Universe: Icons, Idols, Ideas*. Santa Barbara, Calif.: ABC-CLIO, 2013.

———. "Transmedia Storytelling, Corporate Synergy, and Audience Expression." *Global Media Journal* 12, no. 20 (Spring 2012), http://www.globalmediajournal.com/ArchiveGMJ/global-media-journal-archive.php?month=June&&year=2012&journal=gmj.

———. *The Triumph of Reality TV: The Revolution in American Television*. Santa Barbara, Calif.: Praeger, 2013.

———. "'What a Girl Wants': Gender Norming on Reality Game Shows." *Feminist Media Studies* 4, no. 2 (Summer 2004): 226–228.

Ellis, John. "Stars as a Cinematic Phenomenon." In *Star Texts: Image and Performance in Film and Television*, edited by Jeremy G. Butler, 300–315. Detroit: Wayne State University Press, 1991.

Ellison, Curtis W. *Country Music Culture: From Hard Times to Heaven.* Jackson: University Press of Mississippi, 1995.

Escott, Colin. *Lost Highway: The True Story of Country Music.* Washington, D.C.: Smithsonian Books, 2003.

Fetveit, Arild. "Reality TV in the Digital Era: A Paradox in Visual Culture?" *Media, Culture, and Society* 21, no. 6 (November 1999): 787–804.

Filene, Benjamin. *Romancing the Folk: Public Memory and American Roots Music.* Chapel Hill: University of North Carolina Press, 2000.

Fillingim, David. *Redneck Liberation: Country Music as Theology.* Macon, Ga.: Mercer University Press, 2003.

Flippo, Chet. "Dolly Parton." In *The Encyclopedia of Country Music*, edited by Paul Kingsbury, 406. New York: Oxford University Press, 1998.

———. *Your Cheatin' Heart: A Biography of Hank Williams.* New York: Simon and Schuster, 1981.

For the Love of Dolly. 2006. DVD. Wolf Video, 2007.

Fox, Aaron A. "'Alternative' to What? *O Brother*, September 11, and the Politics of Country Music." In *Country Music Goes to War*, edited by Charles K. Wolfe and James E. Akenson, 164–191. Lexington: University Press of Kentucky, 2005.

———. "The Jukebox of History: Narratives of Loss and Desire in the Discourse of Country Music." *Popular Music* 11 (1992): 53–72.

———. *Real Country: Music and Language in Working-Class Culture.* Durham, N.C.: Duke University Press, 2004.

Fox, Pamela. *Natural Acts: Gender, Race, and Rusticity in Country Music.* Ann Arbor: University of Michigan Press, 2009.

———. "Recycled Trash: Gender and Authenticity in Country Music Autobiography." *American Quarterly* 50, no. 2 (June 1998): 234–266.

Frith, Simon. *Performing Rites: On the Value of Popular Music.* Cambridge, Mass.: Harvard University Press, 1996.

Gamson, Joshua. *Claims to Fame: Celebrity in Contemporary America.* Berkeley: University of California Press, 1994.

Gardner, Abigail. "Grit, Glitter and Glamour: Tracing Authenticity in the Aging Artifice of Dolly Parton." In *Aging Femininities: Troubling Representations*, edited by Josephine Dolan and Estella Tincknell, 183–194. Newcastle-upon-Tyne: Cambridge Scholars Press, 2012.

Garman, Bryan K. *Race of Singers: Whitman's Working Class Hero from Guthrie to Springsteen.* Chapel Hill: University of North Carolina Press, 2000.

Garofalo, Reebee, ed. *Rockin' the Boat: Mass Music and Mass Movements.* Cambridge, Mass.: South End Press, 1992.

Geertz, Clifford. *The Interpretation of Cultures.* New York: Basic Books, 1973.

Gillan, Jennifer. *Television and New Media: Must-Click TV.* New York: Routledge, 2011.

Gordon, Duane. "Frequently Asked Questions." *Dollymania*, http://www.dollymania.net/faq.html#025.

Gramsci, Antonio. *Selections from Prison Notebooks.* Edited and translated by Quintin Hoare and Geoffrey Nowell-Smith. London: Lawrence and Wishart, 1971.

Greeson, Jennifer. *Our South: Geographic Fantasy and the Rise of National Literature.* Cambridge, Mass.: Harvard University Press, 2010.

Grosz, Elizabeth. *Volatile Bodies: Toward a Corporeal Feminism.* Bloomington: Indiana University Press, 1994.

Gundersen, Edna. "A 'Trio' in Tune with One Another." *USA Today,* 12 March 1999, 12E.

Gussow, Adam. "Playing Chicken with the Train: Cowboy Troy's Hick-Hop and the Transracial Country West." In *Hidden in the Mix: The African American Presence in Country Music,* edited by Diane Pecknold, 234–262. Durham, N.C.: Duke University Press, 2013.

Halberstam, J. Jack. *Gaga Feminism: Sex, Gender, and the End of Normal.* Boston: Beacon Press, 2013.

Hall, Christine, and Susan Jones. "Making Sense in the City: Dolly Parton, Early Reading and Educational Policy-Making." *Literacy* 50, no. 1 (January 2016): 40–48.

Hall, Stuart. "Notes on Deconstructing 'the Popular.'" In *Cultural Theory and Popular Culture: A Reader,* edited by John Storey, 2nd ed., 442–453. Athens: University of Georgia Press, 1998.

———. *Stuart Hall: Cultural Dialogues in Cultural Studies.* Edited by David Morley and Kuan-Hsing Chen. London: Routledge, 1996.

Hall, Stuart, and Paddy Whannel. *The Popular Arts.* London: Hutchinson, 1964.

Hardie, Melissa Jane. "Torque: Dollywood, Pigeon Forge, and Authentic Feeling in the Smoky Mountains." In *The Themed Space: Locating Culture, Nations, and Self,* edited by Scott A. Lukas, 23–37. Lanham: Lexington Books, 2007.

Harkins, Anthony. *Hillbilly: A Cultural History of an American Icon.* New York: Oxford University Press, 2004.

Haun, Harry. "Dolly Does Broadway." Playbill for *9 to 5: The Musical* (2009), 6–7.

Heidemann, Kate. "Remarkable Women and Ordinary Gals: Performance of Identity in Songs by Loretta Lynn and Dolly Parton." In *Country Boys and Redneck Women: New Essays in Gender and Country Music,* edited by Diane Pecknold and Kristine M. McCusker, 166–188. Jackson: University Press of Mississippi, 2016.

Hight, Jewly. "Female Country Stars Kacey Musgraves, Cam, Maren Morris and More on Industry Sexism." *Billboard,* 28 July 2016, http://www.billboard.com /articles/news/magazine-feature/7453638/kacey-musgraves-cam-maren-morris -female-country-artists-industry-sexism.

Hill, Annette. *Reality TV: Factual Entertainment and Television Audiences.* London: Routledge, 2005.

———. *Restyling Factual TV: Audiences and News, Documentary and Reality Genres.* London: Routledge, 2007.

Holmes, Su. "'All You've Got to Worry about Is the Task, Having a Cup of Tea, and Doing a Bit of Sunbathing': Approaching Celebrity in *Big Brother.*" In *Understanding Reality Television,* edited by Su Holmes and Deborah Jermyn, 111–133. London: Routledge, 2004.

Holmlund, Chris. *Impossible Bodies: Femininity and Masculinity at the Movies.* London: Routledge, 2002.

Hubbs, Nadine. "'Jolene,' Genre, and the Everyday Homoerotics of Country Music." *Women and Music* 19 (August 2015): 71–76.

———. *Rednecks, Queers, and Country Music*. Berkeley: University of California Press, 2014.

———. "'Redneck Woman' and the Gendered Poetics of Class Rebellion." *Southern Cultures* 17, no. 4 (Winter 2011): 44–70.

Huber, Patrick. *Linthead Stomp: The Creation of Country Music in the Piedmont South*. Chapel Hill: University of North Carolina Press, 2008.

Huyssen, Andreas. *After the Great Divide: Modernism, Mass Culture, Postmodernism*. Bloomington: Indiana University Press, 1986.

"An Interview with Porter Wagoner." *Country Song Roundup*, February 1969, 15.

Jenkins, Henry. *Convergence Culture: Where Old and New Media Collide*. New York: New York University Press, 2006.

Jenkins, Henry, Sam Ford, and Joshua Green. *Spreadable Media: Creating Value and Meaning in a Networked Culture*. New York: New York University Press, 2013.

Jensen, Joli. *The Nashville Sound: Authenticity, Commercialization, and Country Music*. Nashville: Country Music Foundation/Vanderbilt University Press, 1998.

———. "Patsy Cline's Crossovers." In *A Boy Named Sue: Gender and Country Music*, edited by Kristine M. McCusker and Diane Pecknold, 107–131. Jackson: University Press of Mississippi, 2004.

Jhally, Sut. "Image-Based Culture: Advertising and Popular Culture." In *Gender, Race, and Class in Media: A Text-Reader*, edited by Gail Dines and Jean M. Humez, 2nd ed., 249–257. Thousand Oaks, Calif.: Sage, 2003.

Kaplan, E. Ann. *Rocking around the Clock: Music Television, Postmodernism, and Consumer Culture*. New York: Routledge, 1987.

Keel, Beverly. "Tomato-Gate Galvanizes Women in Country Music." *The Tennessean*, 22 June 2015, http://www.tennessean.com/story/entertainment/music/2015/06/18/tomato-gate-galvanizes-women-country/28936501/.

Kenny and Dolly: Real Love. RCA Musicvision. VHS. 1985.

Kimmel, Michael. *The Gendered Society*. New York: Oxford University Press, 2000.

———. *Manhood in America: A Cultural History*. 2nd ed. New York: Oxford University Press, 2006.

Kumari, Ashanka. "'You and I': Identity and the Performance of Self in Lady Gaga and Beyoncé." *Journal of Popular Culture* 49, no. 2 (2016): 403–416

Kun, Josh. *Audiotopia: Music, Race, and America*. Berkeley: University of California Press, 2005.

Larry King Live. CNN, 3 July 2003.

Larry King Live. CNN, 27 July 2011.

Larry King Now. Hulu, 24 August 2016.

Leppert, Richard, and George Lipsitz. "Age, the Boy and Experience in the Music of Hank Williams." In *All That Glitters: Country Music in America*, edited by George H. Lewis, 22–37. Bowling Green, Ohio: Bowling Green State University Press, 1993.

Lewis, George H. "Lap Dancer or Hillbilly Deluxe? The Cultural Constructions of Modern Country Music." *Journal of Popular Culture* 31, no. 3 (Winter 1997): 163–173.

———. "Tension, Conflict and Contradiction in Country Music." In *All That Glitters: Country Music in America*, edited by George H. Lewis, 208–220. Bowling Green, Ohio: Bowling Green State University Popular Press, 1993.

Lewis, Lisa. *Gender Politics and MTV: Voicing the Difference*. Philadelphia: Temple University Press, 1990.

Lipsitz, George. *Dangerous Crossroads: Popular Music, Postmodernism, and the Poetics of Place*. New York: Verso, 1994.

———. *Time Passages: Collective Memory and American Popular Culture*. Minneapolis: University of Minnesota Press, 1990.

Liss, Sarah. "Blond Ambition: Country Treasure Dolly Parton Comes Alive." *CBC News*, 9 November 2009, http://www.cbc.ca/arts/music/story/2009/11/09/f-dolly-parton-live-in-london.html.

Literat, Ioana. "The Work of Art in the Age of Mediated Participation: Crowdsourced Art and Collective Creativity." *International Journal of Communication* 6 (2012): 2962–2984.

Lost Highway: The Story of Country Music. Part 1. Country Music Television, 22 February 2003.

Lost Highway: The Story of Country Music. Part 3. Country Music Television, 8 March 2003.

Lund, Jens. "Country Music Goes to War: Song for the Red-Blooded American." *Popular Music and Society* 1 (1972): 221–223.

———. "Fundamentalism, Racism, and Political Reaction in Country Music." In *The Sounds of Social Change*, edited by R. Serge Denisoff and Richard A. Peterson, 79–91. Chicago: Rand McNally, 1972.

Mackay, Jock. "Populist Ideology and Country Music." In *All That Glitters: Country Music in America*, edited by George H. Lewis, 285–304. Bowling Green, Ohio: Bowling Green State University Popular Press, 1993.

Maglio, Tony. "Dolly Parton's 'Coat of Many Colors' Lands Largest Ever Delayed-Viewing Gain for a Broadcast Movie." *The Wrap*, 17 December 2015, http://www.thewrap.com/dolly-parton-coat-of-many-colors-nbc-tv-ratings-delayed-viewing/.

Malone, Bill C. *Country Music U.S.A.: A Fifty-Year History*. Austin: University of Texas Press, 1968.

———. *Don't Get above Your Raisin': Country Music and the Southern Working Class*. Urbana: University of Illinois Press, 2002.

———. *Singing Cowboys and Musical Mountaineers: Southern Culture and the Roots of Country Music*. 2nd ed. Athens: University of Georgia Press, 2003.

Malone, Bill C., and Jocelyn R. Neal. *Country Music U.S.A.* 3rd revised ed. Austin: University of Texas Press, 2010.

Mansfield, Brian. "Dolly Parton Returns to the Ryman." *USA Today*, 2 August 2015, http://www.usatoday.com/story/life/music/2015/08/02/dolly-parton-ryman-auditorium-nashville/31012507/.

Marshall, P. David. *Celebrity and Power*. Minneapolis: University of Minnesota Press, 1997.

May, Elaine Tyler. *Homeward Bound: American Families in the Cold War Era*. New York: Basic Books, 1988.

McCusker, Kristine M. *Lonesome Cowgirls and Honky-Tonk Angels: The Women of Barn Dance Radio*. Urbana: University of Illinois Press, 2008.

McCusker, Kristine M., and Diane Pecknold, eds. *A Boy Named Sue: Gender and Country Music*. Jackson: University of Mississippi Press, 2004.

McPherson, Tara. *Reconstructing Dixie: Race, Gender, and Nostalgia in the Imagined South*. Durham, N.C.: Duke University Press, 2003.

McRobbie, Angela. "Post-Feminism and Popular Culture." *Feminist Media Studies* 4, no. 3 (2004): 255–264.

———. *Postmodernism and Popular Culture*. London: Routledge, 1994.

———. *The Uses of Cultural Studies*. London: Sage, 2005.

Meehan, Eileen R. *Why TV Is Not Our Fault: Television Programming, Viewers, and Who's Really in Control*. Lanham, Md.: Rowman and Littlefield, 2005.

"Melissa Etheridge and Dolly Parton." *CMT Crossroads*, CMT, 8 November 2003.

Meyer, Moe, ed. *The Politics and Poetics of Camp*. New York: Routledge, 1993.

Miller, Bill, ed. *Cash: An American Man*. New York: CMT and Pocket Books, 2004.

Miller, Kiri. "Grove Street Grimm: Grand Theft Auto and Digital Folklore." *Journal of American Folklore* 121, no. 481 (2008): 255–285.

Miller, Stephen. *Smart Blonde: Dolly Parton*. London: Omnibus Press, 2008.

Modleski, Tania. *Feminism without Women: Culture and Criticism in a "Postfeminist" Age*. New York: Routledge, 1991.

Morris, Mitchell. *The Persistence of Sentiment: Display and Feeling in Popular Music of the 1970s*. Berkeley: University of California Press, 2013.

Moynihan, Maura, and Andy Warhol. "Dolly Parton." *Interview*, July 1994, 36.

Mulvey, Laura. "Visual Pleasure and Narrative Cinema." *Screen* 16, no. 3 (1974): 6–18.

"Music: On the Rock Road with Dolly Parton." *Time*, 18 April 1977, http://www.time.com/time/magazine/article/0,9171,914918-1,00.html.

Naby, Robin L., et al. "Reality Based Television Programming and the Psychology of Its Appeal." *Media Psychology* 5 (2003): 303–330.

Nash, Alanna. *Dolly: The Biography*. 1994. Lanham, Md.: Rowman and Littlefield, 2002.

"Nashville." *Drunk History*. Comedy Central, 20 August 2013.

"Nashville Memories." *Dolly*. ABC, episode 18, 9 April 1988.

Neal, Jocelyn. *Country Music: A Cultural and Stylistic History*. New York: Oxford University Press, 2013.

———. *The Songs of Jimmie Rodgers: A Legacy in Country Music*. Bloomington: Indiana University Press, 2009.

Newitz, Annalee, and Matt Wray, eds. *White Trash: Race and Class in America*. New York: Routledge, 1996.

Newton, Esther. *Mother Camp: Female Impersonators in America*. 1972. Chicago: University of Chicago Press, 1979.

Nightline. ABC, 26 November 2012.

Oermann, Robert K. *Behind the Grand Ole Opry Curtain: Tales of Romance and Tragedy*. New York: Center Street, 2008.

Ouellette, Laurie, and James Hay. *Better Living through Reality TV: Television and Post-Welfare Citizenship*. New York: Wiley-Blackwell, 2008.

Outka, Elizabeth. *Consuming Traditions: Modernity, Modernism, and the Commodified Authentic*. New York: Oxford University Press, 2008.

Parton, Dolly. *Dolly: My Life and Other Unfinished Business*. New York: Harper-Collins, 1994.

——. *Dream More: Celebrate the Dreamer in You*. New York: Putnam, 2012.

"Parton Stuns Fans by Rapping." *Toronto Sun*, 25 July 2011, http://www.torontosun .com/2011/07/25/parton-stuns-fans-by-rapping.

Pecknold, Diane. *Hidden in the Mix: The African American Presence in Country Music*. Durham, N.C.: Duke University Press, 2013.

——. "'I Wanna Play House': Configurations of Masculinity in the Nashville Sound Era." In *A Boy Named Sue: Gender and Country Music*, edited by Kristine M. McCusker and Diane Pecknold, 86–106. Jackson: University of Mississippi Press, 2004.

——. "Negotiating Gender, Race, and Class in Post–Civil Rights Country Music: How Linda Martell and Jeannie C. Riley Stormed the Plantation." In *Country Boys and Redneck Women: Essays in Gender and Country Music*, edited by Diane Pecknold and Kristine A. McCusker, 146–165. Jackson: University of Mississippi Press, 2016.

——. *The Selling Sound: The Rise of the Country Music Industry*. Durham, N.C.: Duke University Press, 2007.

Pecknold, Diane, and Kristine M. McCusker, eds. *Country Boys and Redneck Women: New Essays in Gender and Country Music*. Jackson: University Press of Mississippi, 2016.

Peoples, Glenn. "Are Women Finally Getting a Fair Shake on Country Radio? A *Billboard* Analysis." *Billboard*, 5 February 2016, http://www.billboard.com/articles /business/6867108/women-country-radio-billboard-analysis.

Peterson, Richard. *Creating Country Music: Fabricating Authenticity*. Chicago: University of Chicago Press, 1997.

Price, Deborah Evans. "Dolly Parton Q&A: The Country Legend on Nashville and Why She Supports Her Gay Fans." *Billboard*, 1 November 2014, http://www .billboard.com/articles/columns/the-615/6296620/dolly-parton-talks-50-years-in -nashville-and-supporting-gay-fans.

Robertson, Pamela. *Guilty Pleasures: Feminist Camp from Mae West to Madonna*. Durham, N.C.: Duke University Press, 1996.

Roediger, David. *The Wages of Whiteness: Race and the Making of the American Working Class*. New York: Verso, 1991.

Rogers, Jimmie N. *The Country Music Message: Revisited*. Fayetteville: University of Arkansas Press, 1989.

Rogers, Jimmie N., and Stephen A. Smith. "Country Music and Organized Religion." In *All That Glitters: Country Music in America*, edited by George H. Lewis, 270–284. Bowling Green, Ohio: Bowling Green State University Popular Press, 1993.

Rogers, Kenny. *Luck or Something Like It*. New York: William Morrow, 2012.

Romine, Scott. *The Real South: Southern Narrative in the Age of Cultural Reproduction*. Baton Rouge: Louisiana State University Press, 2008.

Ross, Andrew. *No Respect: Intellectuals and Popular Culture*. New York: Routledge, 1989.

Rowe, Kathleen. *The Unruly Woman: Gender and the Genres of Laughter*. Austin: University of Texas Press, 2011.

Samuels, David W. *Putting a Song on Top of It: Expression and Identity on the San Carlos Apache Reservation*. Tucson: University of Arizona Press, 2004.

Sanjek, David. Foreword to *A Boy Named Sue: Gender and Country Music*, edited by Kristine M. McCusker and Diane Pecknold, vii–xv. Jackson: University Press of Mississippi, 2004.

Savage, Mark. "Dolly Parton Draws Huge Crowd to Glastonbury Pyramid Stage." BBC, 29 June 2014, http://www.bbc.com/news/entertainment-arts-28080039.

Scarborough, Dorothy. *A Songcatcher in the Southern Mountains*. New York: Columbia University Press, 1937.

Severson, Kim. "Dollywood: A Little Bit Country, a Little Bit Gay." *New York Times*, 22 August 2014, http://www.nytimes.com/2014/08/24/travel/dollywood-a-little-bit-country-a-little-bit-gay.html?_r=0.

Shank, Barry. *Dissonant Identities: The Rock 'n' Roll Scene in Austin, Texas*. Hanover, N.H.: Wesleyan University Press, 1994.

———. "'That Wild Mercury Sound': Bob Dylan and the Illusion of American Culture." *boundary 2* 29, no. 1 (2002): 97–123.

Shugart, Helene A., and Catherine Egley Waggoner. "A Bit Much: Spectacle as Discursive Resistance." *Feminist Media Studies* 5 (March 2005): 65–81.

Smith, Jon. *Finding Purple America: The South and the Future of American Cultural Studies*. Athens: University of Georgia Press, 2013.

Smith, Stephen A., and Jimmie N. Rogers. "Political Culture and the Rhetoric of Country Music: A Revisionist Interpretation." In *Politics in Familiar Contexts: Projecting Politics through Popular Media*, edited by Robert L. Savage and Dan Nimmo, 185–198. Norwood, N.J.: Ablex, 1990.

Sontag, Susan. "Notes on 'Camp.'" In *Against Interpretation*, 275–292. 1964. New York: Farrar Straus Giroux, 1966.

Stallybrass, Peter, and Allon White. *The Politics and Poetics of Transgression*. Ithaca, N.Y.: Cornell University Press, 1986.

Steinem, Gloria. "Dolly Parton." *Ms.*, January 1987, 66, 94.

Sterdan, Darryl. "Dolly Parton a Quote Machine." *Toronto Sun*, 4 July 2011, http://www.torontosun.com/2011/07/04/dolly-parton-a-quote-machine.

Stimeling, Travis. *Cosmic Cowboys and New Hicks: The Countercultural Sounds of Austin's Progressive Country Music Scene*. New York: Oxford University Press, 2011.

———. "Narrative, Vocal Staging, and Masculinity in the 'Outlaw' Country Music of Waylon Jennings." *Popular Music* 32, no. 3 (2013): 343–358.

Storey, John. *Inventing Popular Culture*. Oxford: Blackwell, 2003.

Streissguth, Michael. *Johnny Cash: The Biography*. New York: Da Capo Press, 2006.

The Summer Adventures of Travelin' Dolly. YouTube, 22 November 2010, https://www
.youtube.com/watch?v=bGq4zwNXK8U.

Szalai, Georg. "Glastonbury Music Festival: Dolly Parton Draws Biggest BBC TV
Audience." *The Hollywood Reporter,* 30 June 2014, http://www.hollywoodreporter
.com/news/glastonbury-music-festival-dolly-parton-715689.

Terranova, T. "Free Labor: Producing for the Digital Economy." *Social Text* 18, no. 2
(2000): 33–58.

Thompson, Stephen I. "Forbidden Fruit: Interracial Love Affairs in Country Music."
Popular Music and Society 13, no. 2 (Summer 1989): 23–37.

Tichi, Cecelia. "Consider the Alternative." *Women's Review of Books* 18, no. 3 (December 2000): 14.

———. *High Lonesome: The American Culture of Country Music.* Chapel Hill: University of North Carolina Press, 1994.

———, ed. *Reading Country Music: Steel Guitars, Opry Stars, and Honky-Tonk Bars.*
Durham, N.C.: Duke University Press, 1998.

The Tonight Show Starring Jimmy Fallon. NBC, 14 May 2014.

The Tonight Show Starring Jimmy Fallon. NBC, 24 August 2016.

The Tonight Show Starring Johnny Carson. NBC, 19 January 1977.

The Tonight Show Starring Johnny Carson. NBC, 17 February 1977.

The Tonight Show with Jay Leno. NBC, 9 October 2003.

Tucker, Stephen. "Pentecostalism and Popular Culture in the South: A Study of
Four Musicians." *Journal of Popular Culture* 16, no. 3 (1982): 68–80.

Tyler, Carole-Anne. "Boys Will Be Girls: The Politics of Gay Drag." In *Inside/Out:
Lesbian Theories, Gay Theories,* edited by Diana Fuss, 32–70. New York: Routledge, 1991.

Unspoiled Country. The Nashville Network, 1998.

Wald, Gayle F. *Shout, Sister, Shout! The Untold Story of Rock-and-Roll Trailblazer
Sister Rosetta Tharpe.* Boston: Beacon Press, 2007.

Watch What Happens Live. Bravo, 17 May 2016.

Weisbard, Eric. *Top 40 Democracy: The Rival Mainstreams of American Music.* Chicago: University of Chicago Press, 2014.

Weller, Jack E. *Yesterday's People: Life in Contemporary Appalachia.* Lexington: University Press of Kentucky, 1965.

Whitaker, Sterling. "Dolly Parton Earns Huge Ratings with Christmas of Many Colors Movie." *Taste of Country,* 3 December 2016, http://tasteofcountry.com/dolly
-parton-christmas-of-many-colors-circle-of-love-ratings/.

Whiteley, Sheila, ed. *Sexing the Groove: Popular Music and Gender.* London: Routledge, 1997.

———. *Women and Popular Music: Sexuality, Identity and Subjectivity.* London:
Routledge, 2000.

Williams, Raymond. *The Long Revolution.* Harmondsworth, U.K.: Penguin, 1965.

Willman, Chris. *Rednecks and Bluenecks: The Politics of Country Music.* New York:
New Press, 2005.

Wilson, Pamela. "Mountains of Contradictions: Gender, Class, and Region in the
Star Image of Dolly Parton." In *Reading Country Music: Steel Guitars, Opry*

Stars, and Honky-Tonk Bars, edited by Cecelia Tichi, 98–120. Durham, N.C.: Duke University Press, 1998.

Wolfe, Charles K. "Postlude." In *A Boy Named Sue: Gender and Country Music,* edited by Kristine M. McCusker and Diane Pecknold, 196–198. Jackson: University Press of Mississippi, 2004.

Wolfe, Charles K., and James E. Akenson. *The Women of Country Music: A Reader.* Lexington: University Press of Kentucky, 2003.

Zwonitzer, Mark, with Charles Hirshberg. *Will You Miss Me When I'm Gone? The Carter Family and Their Legacy in American Music.* New York: Simon and Schuster, 2002.

Index

LEIGH H. EDWARDS is Associate Professor of English at Florida State University. She is the author of *Johnny Cash and the Paradox of American Identity* and *The Triumph of Reality TV: The Revolution in American Television.*

MAY - - 2018

Liv

CPSIA information can be obtained
at www.ICGtesting.com
Printed in the USA
BVOW03s0149301117
501597BV00001B/2/P